**TEST ITEM FILE
WITH ACHIEVEMENT TEST**

SIXTH EDITION

COLLEGE ACCOUNTING

A Practical Approach

CHAPTERS 1 - 15

Production manager: Lisa Friedrichs
Acquisitions editor: Annie Todd
Associate editor: Natacha St. Hill
Manufacturing buyer: Ken Clinton

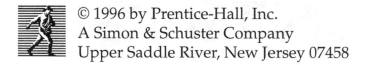 © 1996 by Prentice-Hall, Inc.
A Simon & Schuster Company
Upper Saddle River, New Jersey 07458

Printed in the United States of America

10 9 8 7 6 5 4 3 2 1

ISBN 0-13-364051-5

Prentice-Hall International (UK) Limited, *London*
Prentice-Hall of Australia Pty. Limited, *Sydney*
Prentice-Hall Canada Inc., *Toronto*
Prentice-Hall Hispanoamericana, S.A., *Mexico*
Prentice-Hall of India Private Limited, *New Delhi*
Prentice-Hall of Japan, Inc., *Tokyo*
Simon & Schuster Asia Pte. Ltd., *Singapore*
Editora Prentice-Hall do Brasil, Ltda., *Rio de Janeiro*

CONTENTS

Achievement Tests with Solutions

- Achievement Tests 1A-9A
- Solutions 1A-9A
- Achievement Tests 1B-9B
- Solutions 1B-9B

1. Introduction to Accounting Concepts and Procedures

1.1: The purpose of the accounting process is to provide information to:
   a) individuals.   b) small businesses.
   c) large corporations.   d) All of the above.

Answer: (d)
   MC   Easy

1.2: Accounting provides information to:
   a) customers.
   b) decision makers inside the firm.
   c) decision makers outside the firm.
   d) All of the above.

Answer: (d)
   MC   Easy

1.3: Which of the following is not the role of a public accountant?
   a) Tax specialist
   b) Auditor
   c) Consultant
   d) Recording day to day transactions

Answer: (d)
   MC   Easy

1.4: Bookkeeping is primarily:
   a) preparing financial reports.
   b) analyzing the company's financial position.
   c) record-keeping.
   d) preparing tax reports.

Answer: (c)
   MC   Easy

1.5: The advantage of a sole proprietorship includes:

   a) limited personal risk.
   b) can continue indefinitely.
   c) owner makes all the decisions.
   d) All the above.

Answer: (c)
   MC   Moderate

1.6: Which of the following forms of business organization can exist indefinitely?

    a) Corporation.   b) Partnership.
    c) Sole proprietorship.   d) None of the above.

Answer: (a)
MC Moderate

1.7: Items owned by the business such as land, supplies, and equipment are its:
    a) assets.   b) liabilities.
    c) owner's equity.   d) revenue.

Answer: (a)
MC Easy

1.8: All of the following are business assets except:
    a) cash.   b) supplies.
    c) owner's capital.   d) buildings.

Answer: (c)
MC Easy

1.9: The rights or claims of owners against assets are:
    a) entities.   b) valuations.
    c) liabilities.   d) owner's equity.

Answer: (d)
MC Easy

1.10: An obligation that is payable to creditors is:
    a) an asset.   b) a liability.
    c) the owner's equity. d) an expense.

Answer: (b)
MC Easy

1.11: The claims of creditors against the assets are:
    a) expenses.   b) revenues.
    c) liabilities.   d) assets.

Answer: (c)
MC Easy

1.12: A sample of a liability account is:
    a) Supplies.   b) Fees Earned.
    c) Accounts Receivable. d) Accounts Payable.

Answer: (d)
MC Moderate

1.13: Owner's equity is equal to:
a) assets + liabilities.   b) liabilities - assets.
c) assets - liabilities.   d) None of the above.

Answer: (c)
MC   Easy

1.14: Assets are equal to:
a) Liabilities + owner's equity.
b) Liability - owner's equity.
c) Liabilities - revenues.
d) Revenues - expenses.

Answer: (a)
MC   Easy

1.15: The basic accounting equation is:
a) assets = revenues - expenses.
b) assets = liabilities - owner's equity.
c) assets = owner's equity - liabilities.
d) assets = liabilities + owner's equity.

Answer: (d)
MC   Easy

1.16: Which of the following is an acceptable variation of the accounting equation?
a) Assets - Liabilities = Owner's Equity
b) Assets + Owner's Equity = Liabilities
c) Assets = Liabilities - Owner's Equity
d) All of the above

Answer: (a)
MC   Moderate

1.17: If total assets are $10,000 and total liabilities are $3,500, then owner's equity must be:
a) $8,000.   b) $5,000.   c) $6,500.   d) $13,500.

Answer: (c)
MC   Easy

1.18: If total liabilities are $8,000 and owner's equity is $10,000, the total assets must be:
a) $20,000.   b) $18,000.   c) $14,000.   d) $2,000.

Answer: (b)
MC   Easy

1.19: Alice Cann's cash investment in her new business will:
   a) increase an asset and increase a liability.
   b) decrease an asset and increase a liability.
   c) increase an asset and increase an owner's equity.
   d) increase an asset and decrease an owner's equity.

Answer: (c)
   MC   Moderate

1.20: R.J. Richie's investment of cash and equipment in her existing business will:
   a) decrease assets and increase a liability.
   b) increase assets and a liability.
   c) decrease assets and increase an owner's equity.
   d) increase assets and owner's equity.

Answer: (d)
   MC   Moderate

1.21: Downtown Hardware has total assets of $75,000. What are the total assets if new baking equipment is purchased for $10,000 cash?
   a) $85,000   b) $65,000   c) $10,000   d) $75,000

Answer: (d)
   MC   Moderate

1.22: Tiger Town, Inc. has total assets of $25,000. If $4,000 cash is used to purchase a new computer, the total assets would be:
   a) $25,000.   b) $29,000.   c) $7,000.   d) $3,000.

Answer: (a)
   MC   Moderate

1.23: GreenLawn Landscaping, with total assets of $84,000, borrows $15,000 from the bank. Which of the following is a true statement upon borrowing the money?
   a) Total assets are still $84,000
   b) Total assets are now $99,000
   c) Total assets are now $69,000
   d) Owner's equity is $15,000 more

Answer: (b)
   MC   Moderate

1.24: Toy Soldiers Hobby Shop borrows $10,000 from a finance company. Which of the following is a true statement?
a) Owner's equity is unchanged
b) Total assets are unchanged
c) Total liabilities decrease by $10,000
d) Net income is $10,000 less

Answer: (a)
MC   Moderate

1.25: J.J. Roberts Law Firm purchases $1,000 worth of office equipment on account. This causes:
a) Cash and Roberts, Capital to decrease by $1,000.
b) Office Equipment and Accounts Payable to increase by $1,000.
c) Office Equipment to decrease and Accounts Payable to increase by $1,000.
d) Accounts Payable to increase and Roberts, Capital to decrease by $1,000.

Answer: (b)
MC   Moderate

1.26: M. Casey Company purchases a new computer for $3,000 on account. This causes:
a) Cash and M. Casey, Capital to increase by $3,000.
b) Equipment and Accounts Payable to increase by $3,000.
c) Equipment to decrease and Accounts Payable to increase by $3,000.
d) Accounts Payable to increase and M. Casey, Capital to increase by $3,000.

Answer: (b)
MC   Moderate

1.27: Paul Haig purchases a new $12,000 delivery van for his company. He pays $2,000 cash and promises to pay the balance over 24 months. The transaction will:
a) decrease Cash $2,000, increase Delivery Van $10,000, increase Paul Haig, Capital $12,000.
b) decrease Cash $2,000, increase Delivery Van $8,000, increase Accounts Payable $10,000.
c) decrease Cash $12,000 and increase Delivery Van $12,000.
d) decrease Cash $2,000, increase Delivery Van $12,000, increase Accounts Payable $10,000.

Answer: (d)
MC   Difficult

1.28: Van Nguyen purchased new equipment for his construction company. He pays $5,000 cash and agrees to pay the $15,000 remainder by the end of the year. The effect on the basic accounting equation will be:
a) decrease Cash $5,000 and increase Equipment $5,000.
b) decrease Cash $5,000, increase Equipment $20,000, and increase Accounts Payable $15,000.
c) decrease Cash $5,000, increase Equipment $15,000, and increase Accounts Payable $10,000.
d) decrease Cash $20,000 and increase Equipment $20,000.

Answer: (b)
MC Difficult

1.29: Kay's Klothes collects $3,500 of its accounts receivables. The expanded accounting equation changes include:
a) Cash and Kay's Klothes, Capital increase, $3,500.
b) Cash and Revenue increase $3,500.
c) Cash increases and Accounts Receivable decreases $3,500.
d) Accounts Receivable decreases and Kay's Klothes, Capital increases $3,500.

Answer: (c)
MC Difficult

1.30: If Vegas Service collects $5,200 from customers on account:
a) total assets are unchanged.
b) owner's equity decreases.
c) owner's equity increases.
d) liabilities increase.

Answer: (a)
MC Moderate

1.31: If Reno Enterprises pays $7,000 of its accounts payable:
a) owner's equity increases.
b) total assets decrease.
c) owner's equity decreases.
d) total assets increase.

Answer: (b)
MC Moderate

1.32: If Miami Visuals pays $2,000 of its accounts payable:
a) total assets and owner's equity decrease $2,000.
b) liabilities decrease and owner's equity increases $2,000.
c) assets decrease and liabilities decrease $2,000.
d) assets increase and liabilities decrease $2,000.

Answer: (c)
MC Moderate

1.33: What three elements make up a balance sheet?
  a) Liabilities, expenses, and owner's equity
  b) Assets, liabilities, and revenues
  c) Debts, assets, and cash
  d) Assets, liabilities, and owner's equity

Answer: (d)
  MC   Easy

1.34: Which of the following items is not in a balance sheet?
  a) Accounts Payable   b) Holmes, Capital
  c) Commissions Earned   d) Equipment

Answer: (c)
  MC   Moderate

1.35: An accounting report that shows business results in terms of revenue and expenses is:
  a) an income statement.
  b) a balance sheet.
  c) a statement of owner's equity.
  d) the owner's financial report.

Answer: (a)
  MC   Moderate

1.36: All of the following may be on an income statement except:
  a) Accounts Receivable.   b) Salaries Expense.
  c) Legal Fees.   d) Rent Expense.

Answer: (a)
  MC   Moderate

1.37: An accounting report that shows the changes in capital during the accounting period is:
  a) a balance sheet.
  b) an income statement.
  c) a statement of owner's equity.
  d) All of the above.

Answer: (c)
  MC   Easy

1.38: Which of the following items are on both an income statement and the statement of owner's equity?
  a) Owner's equity
  b) Net loss
  c) Additional owner's investments
  d) Owner's withdrawals

Answer: (b)
  MC   Moderate

1.39: Revenue and expenses are part of:
    a) assets.   b) liabilities.
    c) owner's equity.   d) All of the above.

Answer: (c)
    MC Easy

1.40: A decrease in owner's equity that results from the business operations is:
    a) an expense.   b) revenue.
    c) a liability.   d) an asset.

Answer: (a)
    MC Easy

1.41: A decrease in owner's equity resulting from the owner's use of cash or assets for personal use is:
    a) an expense.   b) a liability.
    c) an asset.   d) a withdrawal.

Answer: (d)
    MC Easy

1.42: Which of the following statements is true?
    a) Owner withdrawals decrease net income
    b) Net income causes liabilities to decrease
    c) Net losses cause liabilities to increase
    d) Owner's withdrawals decrease owner's equity

Answer: (d)
    MC Moderate

1.43: If Chang Company revenues are greater than its expenses during the accounting period:
    a) assets will increase more than liabilities.
    b) owner's equity will increase more than assets.
    c) the cash account will increase.
    d) the business will earn a net income.

Answer: (d)
    MC Moderate

1.44: If Des Moines Services Company expenses were greater than its revenues during the accounting period:
    a) assets will decrease more than liabilities.
    b) owner's equity will decrease more than assets.
    c) the business incurred a net loss.
    d) the cash account will decrease.

Answer: (c)
    MC Moderate

1.45: On September 1, 19xx, Georgia Peach provided $1,500 in accounting services on account for several clients. This transaction:
  a) is recorded only when the cash is received.
  b) is recorded as a $1,500 increase in accounts receivable and revenues.
  c) is recorded as a $1,500 increase in cash and revenues.
  d) None of the above.

Answer: (b)
    MC   Moderate

1.46: Sandy Beaches billed her legal clients for $2,000 for legal work completed during the month. This transaction will:
  a) cause a $2,000 increase in revenues and owner's equity.
  b) cause a $2,000 increase in revenues and a decrease in liabilities.
  c) cause a $2,000 increase in assets and revenues.
  d) not be recorded until the cash is collected.

Answer: (c)
    MC   Moderate

1.47: Jacque's Beauty Services paid $4,000 in salaries and wages for February. This transaction will:
  a) increase expenses and decrease revenue.
  b) increase expenses and increase liabilities.
  c) decrease cash and increase expenses.
  d) decrease cash and expenses.

Answer: (c)
    MC   Moderate

1.48: Orlando Company received a utility bill for $550 for the month of November to be paid by December 10. This affects the basic accounting equation:
  a) as a $550 decrease in cash and a $550 increase in utility expense.
  b) as a $550 increase in liabilities and a $550 increase in utility expense.
  c) but would not be shown until the bill was paid.
  d) as an increase in expenses and a decrease in capital.

Answer: (b)
    MC   Difficult

1.49: Increasing a company's revenues and decreasing its expenses will:
  a) decrease net income.
  b) increase net income.
  c) decrease assets.
  d) not affect owner's equity.

Answer: (b)
    MC   Moderate

1.50: An increase in expenses results in:
   a) an increase in owner's equity.
   b) a decrease in owner's equity.
   c) an increase in assets.
   d) no effect on owner's equity.

Answer: (b)
   MC   Moderate

1.51: Equities are the rights of creditors and the owners to the assets of a business.

Answer: True
   TF   Moderate

1.52: The left side of the accounting equation must always equal the right side of the equation.

Answer: True
   TF   Moderate

1.53: Withdrawals are considered a liability of doing business.

Answer: False
   TF   Moderate

1.54: Revenues generate an inflow of assets.

Answer: True
   TF   Moderate

1.55: The time period covered in a balance sheet is of a specific date.

Answer: True
   TF   Moderate

1.56: The income statement is for a particular date.

Answer: False
   TF   Easy

1.57: A transaction can occur that affects only the assets side of the accounting equation.

Answer: True
   TF   Moderate

1.58: In a shift of assets, the composition of the assets changes but total assets do not.

Answer: True
TF Moderate

1.59: Expenses generate an inflow of assets.

Answer: False
TF Moderate

1.60: The four parts of owner's equity can include: capital, withdrawals, revenue, and expenses.

Answer: True
TF Moderate

1.61: A withdrawal is a business expense that decreases owner's equity.

Answer: False
TF Moderate

1.62: The ending capital figure on the statement of owner's equity will be used on the balance sheet.

Answer: True
TF Moderate

1.63: The income statement is prepared first so the information can be used to prepare the statement of owner's equity.

Answer: True
TF Moderate

1.64: The accounting functions involve: analyzing, recording, classifying, summarizing, and reporting information.

Answer: True
TF Moderate

1.65: Supplies are assets that have a longer life than equipment.

Answer: False
TF Easy

1.66: The owner's personal finances are not considered to be separate from the business finances.

Answer: False
TF Moderate

1.67: Creditors' claims against assets are called owner's equity.

Answer: False
TF   Moderate

1.68: The purpose of accounting is to provide decision makers with useful information.

Answer: True
TF   Easy

1.69: The accounting equation states that total assets must always equal total liabilities plus owner's equity.

Answer: True
TF   Moderate

1.70: The balance sheet shows assets as well as revenue and expenses.

Answer: False
TF   Moderate

1.71: Capital and cash will always be the same amount.

Answer: False
TF   Easy

1.72: Total assets are included in the statement of owner's equity.

Answer: False
TF   Moderate

1.73: Withdrawals are business expenses that are included on the income statement.

Answer: False
TF   Moderate

1.74: The statement of owner's equity is the link between the income statement and balance sheet.

Answer: True
TF   Moderate

1.75: If assets are $5,000 and liabilities are $3,000, owner's equity will be $2,000.

Answer: True
TF   Moderate

1.76: It does not matter in what order financial statements are prepared.

Answer: False
TF   Moderate

1.77: If expenses are more than revenue, a net loss is incurred.

Answer: True
TF   Moderate

1.78: If revenue is less than expenses, a net income is incurred.

Answer: False
TF   Moderate

1.79: If an expense is less than a revenue, a net income is incurred.

Answer: True
TF   Easy

1.80: The first financial statement prepared is the income statement.

Answer: True
TF   Easy

1.81: Record the following transactions in the basic accounting equation:
a. Saul Schmitt invests $2,000 cash to begin a lawn mowing service.
b. The company buys mower equipment for cash, $900.
c. The company buys additional equipment on account, $600.
d. The company makes a payment on the mower equipment, $300.

Saul Schmitt Mowing Service

ASSETS		=	LIABILITIES	+	OWNER'S EQUITY
Cash	+ Mowing Equipment	=	Accounts Payable	+	Saul Schmitt Capital
a.					
b.					
c.					
d.					
Totals					

Answer:

Saul Schmitt Mowing Service

ASSETS		=	LIABILITIES	+	OWNER'S EQUITY
Cash +	Mowing Equipment	=	Accounts Payable	+	Saul Schmitt Capital
a.+$2,000		=			+$2,000
b. -900	+$900				
c.	+ 600	=	+$600		
d. -300		=	-300		
T +$ 800	+$1,500		+$300		+$2,000
ES Easy					

14

1.82: Frances Change Company completes the following transactions:
a. Ms. Change invests $3,500 cash in her company.
b. The company purchases equipment on account, $800.
c. The company purchases additional equipment for cash, $300.
d. The company makes a payment on account for the equipment, $500.

Required: Record the above transactions in the basic accounting equation.

Frances Change Company

ASSETS		=	LIABILITIES	+	OWNER'S EQUITY
Cash + Equipment		=	Accounts Payable	+	F. Change, Cap.
a.					
b.					
c.					
d.					
Totals					

Answer:

Frances Change Company

ASSETS		=	LIABILITIES	+	OWNER'S EQUITY
Cash +	Equipment=		Accounts Payable	+	F. Change, Cap.
a. +$3,500		=			+$3,500
b.	+$800	=	+$800		
c. -300	+300				
d. -500		=	-500		
T +$2,700	+$1,100		+$300		+$3,500

ES   Easy

15

1.83: Prepare a balance sheet in proper form for New York Cleaners for the period ended December 31, 19xx. Use the following information:

Accounts Payable	$2,500
Accounts Receivable	800
Cash	2,200
Equipment	4,000
K. Carson, Capital	?

Answer:

NEW YORK CLEANERS
BALANCE SHEET
December 31, 19xx

Assets		Liabilities and Owner's Equity	
		Liabilities	
Cash	$2,200	Accounts Payable	$2,500
Accounts Receivable	800		
Equipment	4,000	Owner's Equity	
		K. Carson, Cap.	4,500
Total Assets	$7,000	Total Liab. & Owner's Equity	$7,000
	======		======

ES Moderate

1.84: Use the following information to prepare a balance sheet for Blume's Clothing for the period ended November 30, 19xx.

B. Blume, Capital	$8,000
Office Equipment	3,000
Accounts Payable	2,000
Cash	?
Supplies on Hand	6,000

Answer:

BLUME'S CLOTHING
BALANCE SHEET
November 30, 19xx

Assets		Liabilities and Owner's Equity	
Cash	$ 1,000	Liabilities	
Supplies on Hand	6,000	Accounts Payable	$ 2,000
Office Equipment	3,000		
		Owner's Equity	
		B. Blume, Capital	8,000
Total Assets	$10,000	Total Liab. & Owner's Equity	$10,000
	=======		=======

ES Moderate

1.85: Record the following transactions into the expanded
accounting equation for the Jose Perez Company. Note all
titles have beginning balances. (You will need to determine
the beginning capital balance.)

a. Rendered services for cash, $40
b. Billed customers for services rendered, $200
c. Received the monthly utility bill to be paid later, $30
d. Collected $60 on account from customers
e. Paid the utility bill recorded in c.
f. Withdrew $30 cash for personal use

Jose Perez Company

	ASSETS		= LIABILITIES +	OWNER'S EQUITY			
	Cash +	Accts. Rec.	= Accts. Pay.	+ J.Perez Capital	+ Rev.	- Exp.	- J.Perez With
B	+$800 +	$ 50	= +$200	+ ?	+ $700	-$400	-$200
a.							
b.							
c.							
d.							
e.							
f.							
Totals							

Answer: **Jose Perez Company**

	ASSETS		= LIABILITIES +	OWNER'S EQUITY			
	Cash +	Accts. Rec.	= Accts. Pay. +	J.Perez Capital	+ Rev.	- Exp.	- J.Perez With
B	$800 +	$ 50	= +$200	+ $550	+$700	-$400	-$200
a.	+40		=		+40		
b.		+200	=		+200		
c.			+30			+30	
d.	+60	-60					
e.	-30		= -30				
f.	-30		=				-30
T	+$840	+$190	= +$200	+$550	+$940	-$430	-$230

ES   Moderate

17

1.86: Hans Hauser Tax Service completed the following transactions:

    a. Billed clients for service, $250.
    b. Completed tax work for cash clients, $950.
    c. Received a bill for computer rental to be paid later, $40.
    d. Collected cash on account from clients, $100.
    e. Paid the amount due for computer rental.
    f. Withdrew $50 cash for personal use.

Required: Record the above transactions in the expanded accounting equation. Note that the items have beginning balances.

Hans Hauser Tax Service

	ASSETS	= LIABILITIES	+	OWNER'S EQUITY			
	Cash + Accts. Rec.	= Accts. Pay.	+	H.Hauser Capital	+ Rev.	- Exp.	- Hauser With
	+$800 + $85	= +$300	+	?	+$900	-$400	- $150
a.							
b.							
c.							
d.							
e.							
f.							
Totals							

Answer:

Hans Hauser Tax Service

	ASSETS	= LIABILITIES	+	OWNER'S EQUITY			
	Cash + Accts. Rec.	= Accts. Pay.	+	H. Hauser Capital	+ Rev.	- Exp.	- Hauser With
	+$800 + $85	= $300	+	$235	+ $900	-$400	-$150
a.	+250	=			+250		
b.	+950	=			+950		
c.		+40				+40	
d.	+100 -100	=					
e.	-40	-40					
f.	-50	=					+50
T	+$1760 +$235	= +$300		+$235	+$2100	-$440	-$200

ES Moderate

1.87: Use the following information to prepare 1) an income statement and 2) a statement of owner's equity for the month ended March 31, 19xx for Dallas Company.

J. White, Capital	$1,350
Revenue	800
Expenses	300
Withdrawals	150

Answer:

DALLAS COMPANY
INCOME STATEMENT
For the month ended March 31, 19xx

Revenue	$800
Expenses	300
Net Income	$500
	====

DALLAS COMPANY
STATEMENT OF OWNER'S EQUITY
For the month ended March 31, 19xx

J. White, Capital, March 1		$1,350
Net Income	$500	
Less Withdrawals	150	
Increase in Capital		350
J. White, Capital, March 31		$1,700
		======

ES Moderate

19

1.88: Discuss the advantages and disadvantages of sole proprietorship, partnerships, and corporations.

Answer: Sole proprietorship is a business that has one owner. The advantage of a sole proprietorship is that the owner makes all of the decisions for the business. Another advantage is ease of formation. A disadvantage is that if the business cannot pay its obligations, the business owner must pay them. The business ends with the death of owner or closing of the business.

Partnership is a business owned by more than one person. Its advantage is ease of formation. The disadvantages are partners could lose personal assets to meet obligations of partnership and it ends with death of a partner or exit of a partner.

Corporation is business owned by stockholders. The advantages are stockholders have limited personal risk-limited to their investment in the company. The disadvantage is it is more difficult to form.
ES Moderate

1.89: Explain the purpose of the following:
    a. Income Statement
    b. Statement of Owner's Equity
    c. Balance Sheet

Answer: a. The income statement in an accounting report that shows business results in terms of revenue and expenses. If revenue is greater than expenses, the result is net income. If expenses are greater than revenue, the result is a net loss. An income statement can cover any period of time up to one year.

b. The statement of owner's equity shows for a certain time period the changes that occurred in the owner's equity. Increases are due to owner investments and net income, while decreases are due to owner withdrawals and net loss.

c. The balance sheet, or statement of financial position, presents information from the ending balances of the company's assets, liabilities and owner's equity. It summarizes the business' financial position on a given date.

ES Moderate

2. Debits and Credits

2.1: What device is used to record the increases and decreases caused by business transactions to individual assets, liabilities, and owner's equity?
   a) Chart of accounts   b) Account
   c) Trial Balance   d) Footings

Answer: (b)
   MC   Easy

2.2: A chart of accounts:
   a) is set up in alphabetical order.
   b) includes account balances.
   c) is a listing of all the accounts used by a company.
   d) All of the above.

Answer: (c)
   MC   Easy

2.3: A list of all the accounts and account numbers used by a business is the:
   a) chart of accounts.   b) account.
   c) ledger.   d) footings.

Answer: (a)
   MC   Easy

2.4: A formal account that has columns for date, explanation, post reference, debit, and credit is called the:
   a) T account.   b) standard account.
   c) ledger.   d) chart of accounts.

Answer: (b)
   MC   Easy

2.5: A simple form used to analyze a transaction that has a left and right side is called a:
   a) ledger.   b) footings.
   c) chart of accounts.   d) T account.

Answer: (d)
   MC   Easy

2.6: The left side of any account is the:
   a) debit side.   b) credit side.
   c) ending balance.   d) footings.

Answer: (a)
   MC   Easy

2.7: The right side of any account is the:
- a) debit side.
- b) credit side.
- c) ending balance.
- d) footings.

Answer: (b)
MC   Easy

2.8: When an amount is placed on the left side of an account, it is said to be:
- a) increased.
- b) decreased.
- c) debited.
- d) credited.

Answer: (c)
MC   Easy

2.9: The Office Supplies account is:
- a) a revenue, and it has a normal debit balance.
- b) an expense, and it has a normal credit balance.
- c) an asset, and it has a normal debit balance.
- d) an asset, and it has a normal credit balance.

Answer: (c)
MC   Moderate

2.10: An account that would be increased by a credit is:
- a) Supplies.
- b) Fees Earned.
- c) Salary Expense.
- d) J. Smith, Withdrawals.

Answer: (b)
MC   Moderate

2.11: The increase side of an account is the account's:
- a) debit.
- b) credit.
- c) stated amount.
- d) normal balance.

Answer: (d)
MC   Easy

2.12: A system used to list the accounts by account title and account number is:
- a) chart of accounts.
- b) accounts.
- c) ledger.
- d) footings.

Answer: (a)
MC   Easy

2.13: Every transaction affects at least _____ T account(s).
- a) one
- b) two
- c) three
- d) unlimited

Answer: (b)
MC   Easy

2.14: A transaction that has more than one debit or credit is called a:
a) chart of accounts.   b) compound entry.
c) ledger.   d) credit entry.

Answer: (b)
MC Easy

2.15: The first step in analyzing a transaction is:
a) to decide if the accounts are increasing or decreasing.
b) to decide to which categories the accounts belong.
c) to decide where the amounts belong.
d) to decide which accounts are affected.

Answer: (d)
MC Moderate

2.16: When recording transactions in two or more accounts and the totals of the debits and credits are equal, it is called:
a) debiting.
b) crediting.
c) posting.
d) double entry bookkeeping.

Answer: (d)
MC Easy

2.17: Which account category increases on the debit side, and decreases on the credit side?
a) Revenue   b) Assets
c) Capital   d) Liabilities

Answer: (b)
MC Easy

2.18: Which of the following is not a financial statement?
a) Balance Sheet
b) Income Statement
c) Statement of Owner's Equity
d) Trial Balance

Answer: (d)
MC Easy

2.19: A listing of all the accounts from the ledger with their ending balances is called a:
a) normal balance.   b) trial balance.
c) chart of accounts.   d) footing.

Answer: (b)
MC Easy

2.20: The left column of a financial report is often used to:
   a) show debits.   b) show credits.
   c) subtotal numbers.   d) show totals.

Answer: (c)
   MC   Easy

2.21: Which type of account would not be reported on the income statement?
   a) Revenue   b) Expenses
   c) Withdrawals   d) None of the above

Answer: (c)
   MC   Easy

2.22: Accounts Receivable would appear on which financial report?
   a) Balance sheet   b) Income statement
   c) Owner's equity statement   d) None of the above

Answer: (a)
   MC   Easy

2.23: On which financial report would Dental Fees Earned be shown?
   a) Balance sheet   b) Income statement
   c) Owner's equity statement   d) None of the above

Answer: (b)
   MC   Easy

2.24: Salaries Payable would be reported on the:
   a) balance sheet.
   b) income statement.
   c) owner's equity statement.
   d) None of the above.

Answer: (a)
   MC   Easy

2.25: The beginning capital account would appear on which financial report?
   a) Statement of Owner's Equity
   b) Balance Sheet
   c) Income Statement
   d) None of the above

Answer: (a)
   MC   Easy

2.26: Net income appears on which of the following financial reports?
  a) Balance sheet   b) Income statement
  c) Trial balance   d) All of the above

Answer: (b)
      MC   Easy

2.27: Expenses are found on which financial report?
  a) Income statement
  b) Balance sheet
  c) Statement of owner's equity
  d) Does not appear on a financial report

Answer: (a)
      MC   Easy

2.28: Which of the following is prepared first?
  a) Balance Sheet
  b) Income Statement
  c) Statement of Owner's Equity
  d) Trial Balance

Answer: (d)
      MC   Easy

2.29: Which of the following is prepared last?
  a) Balance Sheet
  b) Income Statement
  c) Statement of Owner's Equity
  d) Trial Balance

Answer: (a)
      MC   Moderate

2.30: Net income for a period is calculated by the following formula:
  a) total revenues - total withdrawals.
  b) total revenues - total expenses - total withdrawals.
  c) total revenues - total expenses.
  d) total revenues - total expenses + capital.

Answer: (c)
      MC   Easy

2.31: What is the effect when the owner withdraws cash for personal use?
  a) A decrease in Cash and increase in Withdrawals
  b) A decrease in Cash and decrease in Withdrawals
  c) An increase in Cash and increase in Withdrawals
  d) An increase in Cash and decrease in Withdrawals

Answer: (a)
      MC   Moderate

2.32: What is the effect when cash is received at the time legal fees are earned?
  a) Accounts Receivable increases and Legal Fees increase
  b) Cash decreases and Legal Fees increase
  c) Cash increases and Legal Fees increase
  d) Cash increases and Legal Fees decrease

Answer: (c)
  MC   Moderate

2.33: When a computer is bought on account the result is:
  a) an increase in the asset Computer and an increase in the liability Accounts Payable.
  b) an increase in the asset Computer and a decrease in the liability Accounts Payable.
  c) a decrease in the asset Computer and an increase in the liability Accounts Payable.
  d) a decrease in the asset Computer and a decrease in the liability Accounts Payable.

Answer: (a)
  MC   Moderate

2.34: A lawyer performs $1,000 of services for a client and receives $1,000 cash. The entry would be:
  a) debit to Cash and credit to Attorney Fees.
  b) debit to Cash and credit to Accounts Receivable.
  c) debit to Cash and debit to Attorney Fees.
  d) debit to Cash and credit to Accounts Payable.

Answer: (a)
  MC   Moderate

2.35: The correct entry to record the owner's additional investment of $500 cash in the business would include:
  a) debit Withdrawals, credit Accounts Payable.
  b) credit Capital, debit Accounts Payable.
  c) credit Capital, debit Cash.
  d) credit Service Fees, debit Cash.

Answer: (c)
  MC   Moderate

2.36: Jason Lynn, owner of Jason's Sport Club, withdrew $500 in cash from the business. Record the transaction by a:
  a) debit Jason Lynn, Capital, $500; credit Cash, $500.
  b) debit Accounts Receivable, $500; credit Cash, $500.
  c) debit Jason Lynn, Withdrawals, $500; credit Cash, $500.
  d) debit Jason Lynn, Withdrawals, $500; credit Jason Lynn, Capital, $500.

Answer: (c)
  MC   Moderate

2.37: The entry to record the Molly Company payment of $300 for repairs to computer equipment it owns would include:
a) debit Repair Expense, $300; credit Accounts Payable, $300.
b) debit Accounts Payable, $300; credit Cash, $300.
c) debit Repair Expense, $300; credit Cash, $300.
d) debit Cash, $300; credit Repair Expense, $300.

Answer: (c)
MC   Moderate

2.38: JD Motors bought alignment equipment on account for $6,500. The entry would include:
a) debit to Supplies Expense, $6,500; credit to Cash, $6,500.
b) debit to Equipment, $6,500; credit to Accounts Payable, $6,500.
c) debit to Equipment, $6,500; credit to Cash, $6,500.
d) debit to Supplies Expense, $6,500; credit to Accounts Payable, $6,500.

Answer: (b)
MC   Moderate

2.39: Chuck, the owner of Computer Sales, paid his personal VISA bill using a company check. The correct entry to record the transaction is:
a) credit Cash, debit Withdrawals.
b) credit Cash, debit Supplies Expense.
c) credit Cash, debit Capital.
d) credit Cash, debit Accounts Receivable.

Answer: (a)
MC   Moderate

2.40: Jeremy Lynn Company purchased on account a $400 airplane ticket to Boston. The entry to record the transaction is:
a) debit Accounts Payable, $400; credit Travel Expense, $400.
b) debit Travel Expense, $400; credit Accounts Payable, $400.
c) debit Capital, $400; credit Accounts Payable, $400.
d) debit Travel Expense, $400; credit Cash, $400.

Answer: (b)
MC   Moderate

2.41: The Accounts Receivable account has total debit postings of $2,300 and credit postings of $1,800. The balance of the account is:
a) $4,100 debit.   b) $500 debit.
c) $500 credit.   d) $4,100 credit.

Answer: (b)
MC   Moderate

2.42: The Accounts Payable account has total debit postings of $600 and credit postings of $900. The balance is:
a) $1,500 debit.
b) $1,500 credit.
c) $300 credit.
d) $300 debit.

Answer: (c)
MC   Moderate

2.43: Accounts Payable had a normal starting balance of $600. There were debit postings of $350 and credit postings of $200 during the month. The ending balance is:
a) $750 credit.
b) $750 debit.
c) $450 debit.
d) $450 credit.

Answer: (d)
MC   Difficult

2.44: Accounts Receivable had a normal starting balance of $300. There were debit postings of $500 and credit postings of $600 during the month. The ending balance is:
a) $200 debit.
b) $200 credit.
c) $400 debit.
d) $400 credit.

Answer: (a)
MC   Difficult

2.45: Accounts Receivable has a normal balance of $300. After collecting $200, the balance in the account is:
a) debit $500.
b) debit $100.
c) credit $500.
d) credit $100.

Answer: (b)
MC   Moderate

2.46: The beginning balance in Cash was $400. Additional cash of $800 was received. Checks were written for $700. The Cash balance is:
a) $900.
b) $500.
c) $700.
d) $800.

Answer: (b)
MC   Moderate

2.47: The Tiger Company's books show total Service Fees of $12,000, total expenses of $7,000, and cash received from customers total of $2,000. The company's net income was:
a) $6,000.
b) $2,000.
c) $5,000.
d) $12,000.

Answer: (c)
MC   Difficult

2.48: What is the James Long Company's net income or net loss if it had revenue of $1,200, salary expense of $300, utility expense of $500, and withdrawals of $500 during May?
    a) $400   b) ($100)   c) $100   d) $900

Answer: (a)
    MC   Difficult

2.49: Given the following list of accounts with normal balances, what are the trial balance totals of the debits and credits?
        Cash $500
        Accounts Receivable   100
        Capital   200
        Withdrawals   100
        Service Fees   700
        Rent Expense   200
    a) $800 debit, $1,000 credit
    b) $800 debit, $800 credit
    c) $1,000 debit, $1,000 credit
    d) $900 debit, $900 credit

Answer: (d)
    MC   Difficult

2.50: Given the following list of accounts with normal balances, what are the trial balance totals of the debits and credits?
        Cash $500
        Equipment   900
        Accounts Payable   100
        Capital   800
        Service Fees   700
        Salaries Expense   200
    a) $1,600 debit, $1,600 credit
    b) $1,400 debit, $1,400 credit
    c) $1,000 debit, $1,000 credit
    d) $900 debit, $900 credit

Answer: (a)
    MC   Difficult

2.51: Each part of a business transaction is recorded in the accounting equation under a specific account.

Answer: True
    TF   Moderate

2.52: A ledger is a listing of all debits and credits.

Answer: False
    TF   Easy

2.53: The debit side of all accounts is the increase side and the credit side is the decrease side.

Answer: False
TF   Easy

2.54: The debit side is always the right side of the account.

Answer: False
TF   Easy

2.55: The total of each side of a T account is called the footing.

Answer: True
TF   Easy

2.56: A chart of accounts is a listing of the accounts and their ending balances.

Answer: False
TF   Easy

2.57: The increase side of an account is always the normal balance side.

Answer: True
TF   Easy

2.58: Double-entry accounting requires transactions to affect two or more accounts and the total of the debits and credits must equal.

Answer: True
TF   Moderate

2.59: A trial balance is a listing of all the accounts in the ledger and their ending balances.

Answer: True
TF   Easy

2.60: When preparing a trial balance, it is not necessary to use dollar signs.

Answer: True
TF   Easy

2.61: A trial balance is a formal report prepared after the balance sheet.

Answer: False
TF   Easy

2.62: Debit and credit columns are not used on the financial reports.

Answer: True
TF   Easy

2.63: Liabilities increase on the debit side of the account, and decrease on the credit side.

Answer: False
TF   Easy

2.64: At least two T accounts are affected in every transaction.

Answer: True
TF   Easy

2.65: Withdrawals increase on the debit side of the account, and decrease on the credit side.

Answer: True
TF   Moderate

2.66: Revenue has a normal credit balance, and increases are recorded on the credit side.

Answer: True
TF   Easy

2.67: After deciding which accounts are affected, the next step in analyzing a transaction is to decide to which categories the accounts belong.

Answer: True
TF   Moderate

2.68: Office Equipment has a normal balance of a credit.

Answer: False
TF   Easy

2.69: A compound entry is when more than one transaction occurs.

Answer: False
TF   Moderate

2.70: When cash is increased, the Cash account is debited.

Answer: True
      TF Easy

2.71: Legal Fees is a liability account and is normally credited.

Answer: False
      TF Moderate

2.72: Accounts Receivable indicates amounts owed to us by our clients or customers.

Answer: True
      TF Moderate

2.73: Accounts Receivable is an asset account.

Answer: True
      TF Easy

2.74: Advertising Expense is a liability account.

Answer: False
      TF Easy

2.75: Withdrawals and expenses are reported on the income statement.

Answer: False
      TF Moderate

2.76: Accounts Payable is an asset account that is increased on the credit side.

Answer: False
      TF Moderate

2.77: Accounts Payable appears on the income statement.

Answer: False
      TF Easy

2.78: Increases to assets are recorded on the debit side of the account, while increases to liabilities are recorded on the credit side.

Answer: True
      TF Easy

2.79: Rent Expense appears on the balance sheet.

Answer: False
       TF   Easy

2.80: A credit means the right-hand side of an account and a
      decrease for all accounts.

Answer: False
       TF   Moderate

2.81: Identify the normal balance for each of the following
      accounts by using a Dr. (debit) or a Cr. (credit).
      _____   1. Salaries Expense
      _____   2. R. Johns, Withdrawals
      _____   3. R. Johns, Capital
      _____   4. Accounting Fees
      _____   5. Cash
      _____   6. Accounts Receivable
      _____   7. Accounts Payable
      _____   8. Rent Expense
      _____   9. Equipment
      _____   10. Advertising Expense

Answer: 1. Dr.
          2. Dr.
          3. Cr.
          4. Cr.
          5. Dr.
          6. Dr.
          7. Cr.
          8. Dr.
          9. Dr.
         10. Dr.
          ES Easy

2.82: Identify whether a debit or credit would be correct for each of the following account changes. Use a Dr. (debit) or Cr. (credit).

Dr.	0.	Increase Cash
_____	1.	Increase Equipment
_____	2.	Decrease Accounts Receivable
_____	3.	Decrease in Accounts Payable
_____	4.	Increase in Salaries Expense
_____	5.	Increase in Service Fees
_____	6.	Decrease in Cash
_____	7.	Increase J. Russell, Capital
_____	8.	Increase J. Russell, Withdrawals
_____	9.	Increase Rent Expense
_____	10.	Decrease Equipment

Answer: 1. Dr.
         2. Cr.
         3. Dr.
         4. Dr.
         5. Cr.
         6. Cr.
         7. Cr.
         8. Dr.
         9. Dr.
        10. Cr.
         ES Moderate

2.83: Below is a chart of accounts. Following is a series of transactions. Indicate for each transaction the accounts that should be debited and credited by inserting the proper account number in the space provided.

111	Cash	312	M. Martin, Withdrawals
112	Accounts Receivable	411	Legal Fees
121	Computer Equipment	511	Salaries Expense
211	Accounts Payable	512	Rent Expense
311	M. Martin, Capital	513	Advertising Expense

Debit   **Credit**   **Transaction**

_____   _____   1. Purchased computer equipment on account.

_____   _____   2. Paid salaries for the week.

_____   _____   3. Invested additional cash in the business.

_____   _____   4. Received cash for services performed.

_____   _____   5. Billed a client on account for services performed.

_____   _____   6. Paid accounts payable.

_____   _____   7. Collected accounts receivable.

_____   _____   8. Withdrew cash for personal use.

_____   _____   9. Paid advertising expense.

_____   _____   10. Paid rent expense for the month.

Answer: 1.   121   211
          2.   511   111
          3.   111   311
          4.   111   411
          5.   112   411
          6.   211   111
          7.   111   112
          8.   312   111
          9.   513   111
         10.   512   111

ES   Moderate

2.86: Jeremy's Photography began business on July 1.
   a. Jeremy invested $5,000 in his business from his personal savings account.
   b. Bought photographic equipment on account, $1,000.
   c. Performed services for a customer on account, $800.
   d. Utilities expense due but unpaid, $80.
   e. Collected $100 from customer in transaction c.
   f. Jeremy withdrew $70 for personal use.

Required:
1. Record transactions in the T accounts. (Place the letter of the transaction next to the entry.)
2. Foot the T accounts where appropriate.

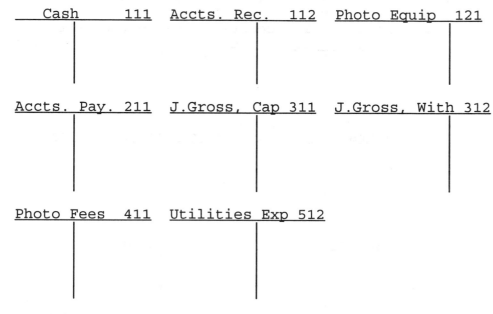

```
        Cash        111    Accts. Rec.   112    Photo Equip   121



    Accts. Pay. 211    J.Gross, Cap 311    J.Gross, With 312



    Photo Fees   411    Utilities Exp 512



```

Answer:

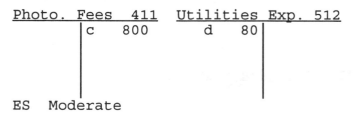
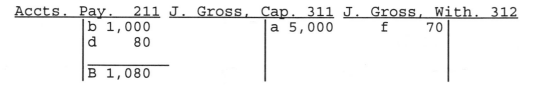

```
         Cash       111    Accts. Rec.    112    Photo. Equip. 121
    a 5,000 | f   70      c  800 | e  100        b 1,000 |
    e   100 |                    |_____
    _____ |               B   700 |
    B 5,030 |                       |

    Accts. Pay.   211   J. Gross, Cap. 311   J. Gross, With. 312
            | b 1,000            | a 5,000         f   70 |
            | d    80
            |_____
            | B 1,080

    Photo. Fees   411   Utilities Exp. 512
            | c  800      d   80 |



```

ES   Moderate

2.87: The following is a list of accounts and their balances for Morris Company for the month ended May 31. Prepare a trial balance in good form.

Cash	$1,000	L.Morris, Withdrawals	$ 100
Accounts Payable	500	Accounts Receivable	700
Office Equipment	2,000	Service Fees	1,000
L.Morris, Capital	2,500	Rent Expense	200

Answer:

Morris Company
Trial Balance
May 31, 19xx

	Debit	Credit
Cash	1,000	
Accounts Receivable	700	
Office Equipment	2,000	
Accounts Payable		500
L.Morris, Capital		2,500
L.Morris, Withdrawals	100	
Service Fees		1,000
Rent Expense	200	
Totals	4,000	4,000

ES   Moderate

2.88: The following is a list of accounts and their balances for Ronald Company for the month ended June 30. Prepare a trial balance in good form.

Cash	$1,200	K.Ronald, Withdrawals	$ 300
Accounts Payable	600	Accounts Receivable	700
Office Equipment	1,000	Service Fees	1,500
K.Ronald, Capital	1,500	Salaries Expense	400

Answer:

Ronald Company
Trial Balance
June 30, 19xx

	Debit	Credit
Cash	1,200	
Accounts Receivable	700	
Office Equipment	1,000	
Accounts Payable		600
K. Ronald, Capital		1,500
K.Ronald, Withdrawals	300	
Service Fees		1,500
Salaries Expense	400	
Totals	3,600	3,600

ES   Moderate

2.89: Explain the difference between expenses and withdrawals.

Answer: Withdrawals is a subdivision of owner's equity. It is used for recording the owner's withdrawal of company assets for personal use, and not related to the business. Expenses are costs the company incurs in carrying on operations in its effort to create revenue. Expenses are also a subdivision of owner's equity.
ES   Moderate

2.90: Following are the five steps in analyzing business transactions. Apply the five steps in analyzing the following transaction:

Paid the monthly telephone expense, $100.

1.   Which accounts are affected?

2.   To which categories do the accounts belong?

3.   Are the accounts increasing or decreasing? How much?

4.   What are the debit and credit rules?

5.   On what side of the accounts do the amounts belong?

Answer: 1.   Telephone Expense and Cash
        2.   Telephone Expense is a subcategory of owner's equity. Cash is an asset.
        3.   Telephone Expense is increasing $100. Cash is decreasing $100.
        4.   Debit Telephone Expense, credit Cash
        5.   Telephone Expense, left side; Cash, right side
        ES   Easy

3. Beginning the Accounting Cycle

3.1: The process that begins with recording business transactions into a journal and ends with completion of a post-closing trial balance is:
   a) calendar year.
   b) natural business years.
   c) fiscal year.
   d) accounting cycle.

Answer: (d)
MC   Moderate

3.2: The twelve-month period a business chooses for its accounting period is a(n):
   a) calendar year.
   b) accounting period.
   c) fiscal year.
   d) accounting cycle.

Answer: (c)
MC   Easy

3.3: The time period for which an income statement is prepared is a (an):
   a) calendar year.
   b) accounting period.
   c) fiscal period.
   d) accounting cycle.

Answer: (b)
MC   Easy

3.4: Financial reports that are prepared for a month or a quarter during the fiscal year are called:
   a) accounting period reports.
   b) fiscal year reports.
   c) interim reports.
   d) journal reports.

Answer: (c)
MC   Easy

3.5: The first step of the accounting cycle is:
   a) recording journal entries.
   b) posting to the ledger.
   c) preparing a trial balance.
   d) analyzing business transactions.

Answer: (d)
MC   Easy

3.6: A journal entry affecting more than two accounts is called a:
   a) multi-level entry.
   b) multi-step entry.
   c) compound entry.
   d) simple entry.

Answer: (c)
MC   Easy

3.7: Business transactions are first recorded in the:
   a) ledger.   b) journal.
   c) trial balance.   d) balance sheet.

Answer: (b)
   MC   Easy

3.8: The simplest form of a journal is a(n):
   a) special journal.   b) interim journal.
   c) accounting journal.   d) general journal.

Answer: (d)
   MC   Easy

3.9: Where are business transactions listed in chronological order?
   a) Ledger   b) Trial balance
   c) Journal   d) Balance sheet

Answer: (c)
   MC   Easy

3.10: Which of the following would be considered a book of original entry?
   a) Ledger   b) Journal
   c) Trial balance   d) Work sheet

Answer: (b)
   MC   Easy

3.11: Which of the following would be considered the book of final entry?
   a) Ledger   b) Journal
   c) Trial balance   d) Work sheet

Answer: (a)
   MC   Easy

3.12: The process of recording transactions in a journal is:
   a) posting.   b) footing.
   c) summarizing.   d) journalizing.

Answer: (d)
   MC   Easy

3.13: The specific titles to be used in the journal are provided in the:
   a) chart of accounts.   b) trial balance.
   c) journal.   d) balance sheet.

Answer: (a)
   MC   Easy

3.14: Which account in a transaction is first recorded in the journal?
   a) Debit   b) Credit   c) Increase   d) Decrease

Answer: (a)
   MC   Easy

3.15: In a journal entry, how are credits distinguished from debits?
   a) A line separation   b) A different color
   c) Indenting   d) No distinction

Answer: (c)
   MC   Easy

3.16: When a journal entry has more than two accounts, it is called a(n):
   a) extra journal entry.   b) compound journal entry.
   c) vital journal entry.   d) final journal entry.

Answer: (b)
   MC   Easy

3.17: _____ is the process of transferring information from the journal to ledger:
   a) Journalizing
   b) Preparing a trial balance
   c) Transposition
   d) Posting

Answer: (d)
   MC   Easy

3.18: Prepaid Rent is a(n):
   a) asset that decreases on the debit side.
   b) asset that increases on the debit side.
   c) expense that decreases on the debit side.
   d) expense that increases on the debit side.

Answer: (b)
   MC   Easy

3.19: The entry to record the payment of office salaries would be:
   a) a debit to an asset account and a credit to an asset account.
   b) a debit to an asset account and a credit to an expense account.
   c) a debit to an asset account and a credit to a liability account.
   d) a debit to an expense account and a credit to an asset account.

Answer: (d)
   MC   Moderate

43

3.20: When the telephone bill is paid:
a) Telephone Expense is debited and Cash is credited.
b) Telephone Expense is credited and Cash is debited.
c) Telephone Expense is debited and Accounts Payable is credited.
d) Accounts Payable is credited and Telephone Expense is debited.

Answer: (a)
MC Moderate

3.21: When the owner withdraws cash for personal use, the entry is:
a) Cash debit, Withdrawals credit.
b) Withdrawals debit, Cash credit.
c) Accounts Receivable debit, Cash credit.
d) Accounts Receivable credit, Cash debit.

Answer: (b)
MC Moderate

3.22: Transferring information from the journal to the ledger is called:
a) journalizing.   b) ledgering.
c) footing.   d) posting.

Answer: (d)
MC Easy

3.23: The post reference column in the ledger is used to:
a) record the journal and page the reference.
b) record the ledger number.
c) record the date.
d) not used.

Answer: (a)
MC Easy

3.24: The form used to list each ledger account with its balance is the:
a) worksheet.   b) trial balance.
c) balance sheet.   d) income statement.

Answer: (b)
MC Easy

3.25: An error that results from adding or deleting zeros in recording numbers is called:
a) transposition.   b) committed entry.
c) a slide.   d) None of the above.

Answer: (c)
MC Easy

3.26: When a number is recorded as 576 instead of 756, a _____
error was made.
a) slide   b) rearrangement
c) transposition   d) composition

Answer: (c)
MC   Easy

3.27: If a trial balance does not equal, you should first:
a) recompute the ledger balances.
b) trace all postings.
c) re-add the trial balance and calculate the difference.
d) hit your head against a wall.

Answer: (c)
MC   Moderate

3.28: A trial balance difference divisible by 9 could indicate:
a) a slide or transposition.
b) a slide only.
c) a transposition only.
d) a journal entry error.

Answer: (a)
MC   Easy

3.29: If an error is detected before posting, the error should be
corrected:
a) in the journal.
b) in the journal and ledger.
c) in the ledger.
d) by complaining.

Answer: (a)
MC   Easy

3.30: If an error in the journal entry is detected after posting,
you should:
a) erase the incorrect entry.
b) initial where the error was made.
c) make a correcting entry.
d) do nothing in hopes it will go away.

Answer: (c)
MC   Moderate

3.38: A transaction completed by Sunshine Company caused a $12,000 increase in both the total assets and the total liabilities. This transaction could have been:
a) purchase of office equipment for $32,000, paying $20,000 cash and the rest on account.
b) investment by the owner of an additional $12,000.
c) purchase of office equipment, paying $3,000 cash, and $10,000 on account.
d) None of the above.

Answer: (a)
MC   Moderate

3.39: Brown Company's total assets and total liabilities increased $800. The transaction could have been:
a) purchase of supplies for cash, $800.
b) purchase of supplies for $1,000 with a down payment of $200.
c) paid the rent for the month, $800.
d) None of the above.

Answer: (b)
MC   Moderate

3.40: The entry to record Roman Company's payment of $300 for repairs to equipment it owns would include:
a) debit Cash, $300; credit Repairs Expense, $300.
b) debit Cash, $300; credit Accounts Payable, $300.
c) debit Repair Expense, $300; credit Cash, $300.
d) debit Repairs Expense, $300; credit Accounts Payable, $300.

Answer: (c)
MC   Moderate

3.41: D. Sharp, CPA, collected fees of $650 not previously billed or recorded. The journal entry to record the collection would include:
a) debit Cash, $650; credit Accounting Fees, $650.
b) debit Cash, $650; credit D. Sharp, Capital, $650.
c) debit Accounts Receivable, $650; credit Accounting Fees, $650.
d) debit Accounting Fees, $650; credit Accounting Fees, $650.

Answer: (a)
MC   Moderate

3.42: The journal entry to record Tom Starr's withdrawal of $500 from his company for personal use would be:
a) debit T. Starr, Capital, $500; credit Cash, $500.
b) debit T. Starr, Withdrawals, $500; credit Cash, $500.
c) debit Accounts Receivable, $500; credit Cash, $500.
d) debit Accounts Payable, $500; credit Cash, $500.

Answer: (b)
MC Moderate

3.43: Which of the following errors would cause the trial balance to be out of balance?
a) The payment of utilities expense was recorded as a debit to Rent Expense for $200 and a credit to Cash for $200.
b) The payment of an accounts payable for $200 was recorded as a debit to Cash, $200, and a credit to Accounts Payable, $200.
c) The collection of an account was not recorded.
d) The payment of an accounts payable for $200 was recorded as a debit to Accounts Payable $100 and a credit to Cash for $200.

Answer: (d)
MC Difficult

3.44: Which of the following transactions would cause the trial balance to be out of balance?
a) A debit to Cash and a debit to Equipment for $400.
b) A credit to Cash and a debit to Supplies for the same amount.
c) A debit to Accounts Receivable and a credit to Accounting Fees for $300.
d) All of the above.

Answer: (a)
MC Moderate

3.45: Jenny journalized and posted the payment of a telephone expense as a rent expense. The proper journal entry to correct the error is:
a) Telephone Expense   b) Rent Expense
    Rent Expense   Telephone Expense
c) Telephone Expense   d) Rent Expense
    Cash   Cash

Answer: (a)
MC Moderate

3.46: Sam journalized and posted the receipt of payment from a customer as a debit to Cash and a credit to Accounts Payable. The proper journal entry to correct this entry is:
   a) Accounts Payable
         Cash
   b) Accounts Receivable
         Accounts Payable
   c) Accounts Payable
         Accounts Receivable
   d) No correction is necessary.

Answer: (c)
   MC   Moderate

3.47: Shawn journalized and posted an entry for $2,000 debit to Cash; and $2,000 credit to Service Fees. The correct amount on the billing was $200. The entry to correct this error is:
   a) debit Cash, $1,800; credit Service Fees, $1,800.
   b) debit Service Fees, $1,800; credit Cash, $1,800.
   c) debit Service Fees, $2,800; credit Cash, $2,000.
   d) debit Service Fees, $200; credit Cash, $200.

Answer: (b)
   MC   Moderate

3.48: A $600 check written for supplies was journalized as $60. The entry to correct this error is:
   a) debit Supplies, $540; credit Cash, $540.
   b) debit Cash, $540; credit Supplies, $540.
   c) debit Supplies, $60; credit Cash, $60.
   d) debit Cash, $60; credit Cash, $60.

Answer: (a)
   MC   Moderate

3.49: An example of a transposition is:
   a) debit to Accounts Receivable for $2,000 instead of $200.
   b) debit to Rent Expense instead of a debit to Prepaid Rent for $200.
   c) debit to Telephone Expense for $250 instead of $520.
   d) debit to Equipment for $1,200 instead of $1,000.

Answer: (c)
   MC   Moderate

3.50: In preparing the trial balance of the Computer Store, the withdrawal account was listed as a credit for $150. What will be the difference between the debit and credit side of the trial balance?
   a) $150   b) $200   c) $300   d) $600

Answer: (c)
   MC   Difficult

3.51: A fiscal period is any twelve-month period that a business chooses for its accounting year.

Answer: True
TF Easy

3.52: Interim reports are usually prepared once a year.

Answer: False
TF Easy

3.53: An accounting cycle includes the normal accounting procedures performed over a period of time.

Answer: True
TF Easy

3.54: A calendar year is any twelve-month period.

Answer: False
TF Easy

3.55: The same information is contained in the journal and the ledger but in a different form.

Answer: True
TF Easy

3.56: The chart of accounts contains the same information as the journal.

Answer: False
TF Easy

3.57: The journal and ledger are recorded in the same book.

Answer: False
TF Easy

3.58: A journal is considered to be a book of final entry.

Answer: False
TF Easy

3.59: A book of original entry is the book that contains the first information about business transactions.

Answer: True
TF Easy

3.60: Journalizing is the process whereby transactions are recorded in the journal.

Answer: True
TF   Easy

3.61: The ledger is sometimes referred to as a book of final entry.

Answer: True
TF   Easy

3.62: The general journal is the simplest form of a journal.

Answer: True
TF   Easy

3.63: A chart of accounts is a list of the accounts and their balances.

Answer: False
TF   Easy

3.64: A running balance is maintained in the ledger after each transaction is posted.

Answer: True
TF   Easy

3.65: Liabilities increase on the credit side of the account and decrease on the debit side.

Answer: True
TF   Easy

3.66: To record rent paid in advance, Prepaid Rent would be debited.

Answer: True
TF   Moderate

3.67: The credit part of the transaction is first recorded in the journal.

Answer: False
TF   Easy

3.68: The debit is indented in a journal entry.

Answer: False
TF   Easy

3.69: An expense is recorded when the asset Prepaid Rent expires.

Answer: True
TF Moderate

3.70: A compound journal entry affects more than two accounts in the transaction.

Answer: True
TF Moderate

3.71: The first step of completing the journal is to fill in the post reference column.

Answer: False
TF Easy

3.72: An expense is recorded when it is incurred, not when it is paid.

Answer: True
TF Easy

3.73: Withdrawals increase owner's equity.

Answer: False
TF Easy

3.74: Revenue is recorded when earned.

Answer: True
TF Moderate

3.75: When journalizing, the month and year are repeated for each transaction.

Answer: False
TF Easy

3.76: Posting is the transferring of information from the ledger to the chart of accounts.

Answer: False
TF Moderate

3.77: A slide is an error that results when zeros have been added or deleted when writing a number. Example: 20,000 becomes 2,000.

Answer: True
TF Moderate

3.78: Posting is the first step of recording transactions.

Answer: False
    TF Easy

3.79: When the total debits equal the total credits on the trial balance, this is proof that all transactions have been recorded properly.

Answer: False
    TF Moderate

3.80: An addition error could cause the total debit and total credit columns on the trial balance to show a difference of 10,100.

Answer: True
    TF Moderate

3.81: Prepare journal entries for the following transactions that occurred during May. Omit explanations.

    May 2   Purchased supplies on account, $600.
          10   Paid May salaries, $500.
          15   Paid for supplies purchased on May 2.
          21   Received telephone bill, to be paid later, $50.

Answer: May 2   Supplies   600
                   Accounts Payable   600

          10   Salaries Expense   500
                   Cash   500

          15   Accounts Payable   600
                   Cash   600

          21   Telephone Expense   50
                   Accounts Payable   50
    ES Easy

3.82: Journalize the following transactions that occurred during September. Omit explanations.

Sep. 5 S. Richman invested $4,000 cash and $100 of equipment into his new business.
10 Paid three months' rent in advance, $1,500.
23 Purchased equipment on account, $2,000.
24 Billed client for services rendered, $1,000.

Answer: Sep. 5 Cash   4,000
                 Equipment   100
                     S. Richman, Capital   4,100

           10 Prepaid Rent   1,500
                 Cash   1,500

           23 Equipment   2,000
                 Accounts Payable   2,000

           24 Accts. Receivable   1,000
                 Fees Earned   1,000
       ES Easy

3.83: Starr Company began business in June. Following are the transactions during that period. Prepare the journal entries for June. Omit explanations.

Jun. 2 J. Starr invested $2,000 cash and $1,000 equipment into her new business.
12 Billed customer for services performed, $500.
16 Purchased supplies on account, $200.
20 Received one-half amount due from June 12.
25 J. Starr withdrew cash for personal use, $100.

Answer: Jun. 2 Cash   2,000
                 Equipment   1,000
                     J. Starr, Capital   3,000

           12 Accts. Receivable   500
                 Service Fees   500

           16 Supplies   200
                 Accounts Payable   200

           20 Cash   250
                 Accts. Receivable   250

           25 J. Starr, With.   100
                 Cash   100
       ES Moderate

3.84: J.J. Company began business in July. Following are the transactions during that period. Journalize the transactions below. Omit explanations.

Jul.   2   J. J. Step invested $8,000 cash and $1,000 equipment into her new business.
       10   Paid salaries expense, $800.
       12   Billed customer for services performed, $500.
       16   Purchased equipment on account, $200.
       20   Received one-half amount due from July 12.
       25   Paid a $100 personal telephone bill.

Answer: Jul.   2   Cash   8,000
                   Equipment   1,000
                       J. J. Step, Capital   9,000

              10   Salaries Expense   800
                       Cash   800

              12   Accts. Receivable   500
                       Services Fees   500

              16   Equipment   200
                       Accounts Payable   200

              20   Cash   250
                       Accts. Receivable   250

              25   J.J. Step, With.   100
                       Cash   100
       ES   Moderate

56

3.85: You have been hired to correct the following trial balance that was improperly recorded. All the accounts have normal balances. Prepare a corrected trial balance in good form.

Kassie Korn Company
Trial Balance
April 30, 19xx

	Debit	Credit
Cash	1,200	
Accounts Receivable		600
Equipment	2,000	
Accounts Payable	700	
B. Kassie, Capital		3,000
B. Kassie, Withdrawals		100
Service Fees	1,000	
Rent Expense	200	
Salaries Expense	600	
Totals	5,700	3,700
	=====	=====

Answer:

Kassie Korn Company
Trial Balance
April 30, 19xx

	Debit	Credit
Cash	1,200	
Accounts Receivable	600	
Equipment	2,000	
Accounts Payable		700
B. Kassie, Capital		3,000
B. Kassie, Withdrawals	100	
Service Fees		1,000
Rent Expense	200	
Salaries Expense	600	
Totals	4,700	4,700
	=====	=====

ES   Moderate

57

3.86: The following trial balance has been improperly recorded.
All the accounts have normal balances. Prepare a corrected
trial balance in good form.

Home Town Cleaning Company
Trial Balance
March 31, 19xx

	Debit	Credit
Cash		500
Salaries Expense		600
Rent Expense		200
Accounts Receivable	600	
Equipment	2,000	
K. Carlsen, Capital	2,300	
K. Carlsen, Withdrawals		100
Service Fees	1,000	
Accounts Payable		700
Totals	5,900	2,100

Answer:

Home Town Cleaning Company
Trial Balance
March 31, 19xx

	Debit	Credit
Cash	500	
Accounts Receivable	600	
Equipment	2,000	
Accounts Payable		700
K. Carlsen, Capital		2,300
K. Carlsen, Withdrawals	100	
Service Fees		1,000
Rent Expense	200	
Salaries Expense	600	
Totals	4,000	4,000

ES Difficult

3.87: Discuss the concept of cross-referencing. Include in your
discussion the benefits provided by cross-referencing.

Answer: Cross-referencing is the recording in the post reference
column of the journal the account number of the ledger
account that was updated from the journal entry.
Cross-referencing can tell which transactions have or have
not been posted and also to which accounts they were posted.
In the ledger the posting reference leads us back to the
journal page number of the original transaction, so that we
may see why the debit or credit was recorded and all other
accounts affected.
ES Moderate

3.88: Karen Brown, a student in your class, is not sure the effect of the following unrelated situations would have on the accuracy of the financial statements. Identify the account(s) that are affected and if the trial balance would balance.
   a. Equipment was purchased for $1,500 cash. The debit was recorded properly, but the credit was omitted.
   b. A debit to cash for $69 was posted as $96; the credit was posted correctly.
   c. A purchase of supplies on account for $300 was posted as a debit to equipment and a credit to cash.

Answer: a. Cash is overstated by $1,500; the debit side is $1,500 greater than the credit side on the trial balance. The trial balance would not balance.
   b. Cash is overstated by $27; the debit side is $27 greater than the credit side on the trial balance.
   c. Equipment is overstated and Supplies is understated by $300; Accounts Payable is understated and Cash is understated by $300. Trial balance is in balance.
   ES Moderate

4. The Accounting Cycle Continued

4.1: A form used to organize and check data before preparing
financial reports is known as a(n):
    a) trial balance.   b) income statement.
    c) balance sheet.   d) worksheet.

Answer: (d)
    MC   Easy

4.2: Bringing accounts up to date before preparing financial
reports is called:
    a) posting.   b) adjusting.
    c) journalizing.   d) analyzing.

Answer: (b)
    MC   Easy

4.3: An adjustment for supplies would indicate:
    a) the amount bought.
    b) the amount used up.
    c) the amount on hand.
    d) the amount of the trial balance.

Answer: (b)
    MC   Easy

4.4: If you had $500 of supplies available and at the end of the
month you had $300 on hand, the adjustment for Supplies
would be:
    a) $300.   b) $500.   c) $200.   d) $100.

Answer: (c)
    MC   Moderate

4.5: The adjustment on the worksheet for supplies used during the
period would be:
    a) debit Supplies, credit Supplies Expense.
    b) debit Supplies Expense, credit Cash.
    c) debit Supplies Expense, credit Supplies.
    d) debit Supplies, credit Cash.

Answer: (c)
    MC   Easy

4.6: A contra asset is:
    a) in reality a liability.
    b) an asset with a debit balance.
    c) an account with an opposite balance of an asset.
    d) an account that increases the asset.

Answer: (c)
    MC   Easy

4.7: If the adjustment for Office Supplies used during the period was not made:
a) expenses would be too low.
b) asset Office Supplies would be too low.
c) expenses would be too high.
d) None of the above.

Answer: (a)
MC   Moderate

4.8: A mixed account is an account that is:
a) partly a balance sheet amount and partly an income statement amount on the trial balance.
b) partially an expense and partially a revenue.
c) partially an owner's equity account and partially a balance sheet account.
d) None of the above.

Answer: (a)
MC   Easy

4.9: Rent paid in advance is considered to be a(n):
a) liability.   b) asset.
c) contra asset.   d) revenue.

Answer: (b)
MC   Easy

4.10: As prepaid rent expires, the asset becomes a(n):
a) liability.   b) expense.
c) contra asset.   d) revenue.

Answer: (b)
MC   Easy

4.11: If Prepaid Rent for the period is not adjusted:
a) assets will be overstated and expenses will be overstated.
b) assets will be overstated and expenses will be understated.
c) assets will be understated and expenses will be overstated.
d) assets will be understated and expenses will be understated.

Answer: (b)
MC   Difficult

4.12: If Supplies account is not adjusted:
a) assets will be overstated and expenses will be understated.
b) assets will be overstated and expenses will be overstated.
c) assets will be understated and expenses will be overstated.
d) assets will be understated and expenses will be understated.

Answer: (a)
MC Difficult

4.13: When historical cost is used to record equipment, it would appear as the:
a) original cost on the balance sheet.
b) residual value on the income statement.
c) residual value on the balance sheet.
d) original cost on the income statement.

Answer: (a)
MC Moderate

4.14: When historical cost is used in the accounting records, the book value of the asset is:
a) the original cost.
b) the market value.
c) original cost less accumulated depreciation.
d) closed out.

Answer: (c)
MC Moderate

4.15: Residual value is the:
a) value of the asset when it is purchased.
b) value of the asset at the end of its useful life.
c) cost of the asset.
d) allocation of the cost.

Answer: (b)
MC Easy

4.16: After the adjustment for depreciation has been made, the original cost of the equipment:
a) increases with a credit.   b) decreases with a debit.
c) remains the same.   d) None of the above.

Answer: (c)
MC Moderate

4.17: An adjustment that is made to allocate the cost of a building over its expected life is called:
   a) depreciation.
   b) residual value.
   c) accumulated depreciation.
   d) None of the above.

Answer: (a)
   MC   Easy

4.18: If a truck cost $13,000, has a residual value of $1,000, and has a useful life of 10 years, the depreciation for a month would be:
   a) $1,200.   b) $108.33.   c) $1,300.   d) $100.

Answer: (d)
   MC   Moderate

4.19: Which of the following would be an example of a contra asset?
   a) Depreciation expense   b) Residual value
   c) Accumulated depreciation d) Supplies

Answer: (c)
   MC   Easy

4.20: The cost of an asset less accumulated depreciation equals:
   a) residual value.   b) book value.
   c) depreciation expense.   d) None of the above.

Answer: (b)
   MC   Easy

4.21: The estimated value of an item at the end of its useful life is:
   a) depreciation expense.
   b) residual value.
   c) accumulated depreciation.
   d) None of the above.

Answer: (b)
   MC   Easy

4.22: Accumulated Depreciation is found on which of the following financial statements?
   a) Balance sheet   b) Income statement
   c) Owner's equity statement d) All of the above.

Answer: (a)
   MC   Easy

4.23: Depreciation Expense would be found on which of the following financial statements?
a) Balance sheet   b) Income statement
c) Owner's equity statement   d) Depreciation report

Answer: (b)
MC   Easy

4.24: As depreciation is recorded, the book value:
a) increases.   b) decreases.
c) remains the same.   d) is closed out.

Answer: (b)
MC   Moderate

4.25: Which of the following are unpaid and unrecorded expenses that are accumulating but payment is not due?
a) Rent expense   b) Depreciation expense
c) Accrued salaries   d) None of the above.

Answer: (c)
MC   Moderate

4.26: What type of account is Salaries Payable?
a) Asset   b) Expense
c) Liability   d) Owner's equity

Answer: (c)
MC   Easy

4.27: What types of accounts appear in the income statement section of the worksheet?
a) Revenue and expenses   b) Assets and liabilities
c) Only contra accounts   d) Assets and revenues

Answer: (a)
MC   Easy

4.28: In this chapter, financial statements are prepared from the:
a) trial balance.
b) worksheet income and balance sheet columns.
c) adjusted trial balance.
d) ledger.

Answer: (b)
MC   Easy

4.29: The ending figure for capital is:
   a) extended to the balance sheet columns.
   b) revealed by the net income.
   c) indicated in the trial balance.
   d) not on the worksheet.

Answer: (d)
   MC Moderate

4.30: The two columns for figures on financial statements are used for:
   a) indicating debits and credits.
   b) balancing accounts.
   c) subtotaling and totaling.
   d) None of the above.

Answer: (c)
   MC Easy

4.31: Sam's Shoe Store showed store supplies available, $400. A count of the supplies left on hand as of May 31 is $150. The adjusting entry for Store Supplies would include:
   a) a debit to Store Supplies Expense for $250.
   b) a credit to Store Supplies Expense for $250.
   c) a debit to Store Supplies for $150.
   d) a credit to Store Supplies Expense for $150.

Answer: (a)
   MC Moderate

4.32: Boston Harbor Company showed store supplies available, $100. If at the end of the month supplies on hand are $10, the adjusting entry would include a:
   a) debit to Supplies Expense for $10.
   b) debit to Supplies Expense for $90.
   c) credit to Supplies Expense for $10.
   d) credit to Supplies Expense for $90.

Answer: (b)
   MC Moderate

4.33: Peabody Company's estimated depreciation for office equipment is $100. The adjusting entry would include:
   a) a credit to Accumulated Depreciation for $100.
   b) a credit to Depreciation Expense for $100.
   c) a debit to Accumulated Depreciation for $100.
   d) a credit to Office Equipment for $100.

Answer: (a)
   MC Moderate

4.34: Beverly's Apparel estimated depreciation on buildings at $7,000. The adjusting entry for depreciation of the buildings would include:
a) a debit to Accumulated Depreciation for $7,000.
b) a credit to Depreciation Expense for $7,000.
c) a credit to Buildings for $7,000.
d) a credit to Accumulated Depreciation for $7,000.

Answer: (d)
MC   Moderate

4.35: Russell Company purchased a one-year insurance policy for $2,400. The adjusting entry for one month would include a:
a) debit to Insurance Expense, $200.
b) credit to Cash, $200.
c) debit to Prepaid Insurance, $200.
d) None of the above.

Answer: (a)
MC   Moderate

4.36: The Salem Repair trial balance indicated Prepaid Insurance, $100. If $20 had expired, what would be the adjusting entry?
a) Debit Prepaid Insurance, $20; credit Insurance Expense, $20
b) Debit Insurance Expense, $20; credit Prepaid Insurance, $20
c) Debit Insurance Expense, $80; credit Prepaid Insurance, $80
d) Debit Prepaid Insurance, $80; credit Insurance Expense, $80

Answer: (b)
MC   Moderate

4.37: Gerald Company's accrued wages are $300. Which of the following is the required adjusting entry?
a) Debit Salaries Expense, $300; debit Salaries Payable, $300
b) Debit Salaries Expense, $300; credit Salaries Payable, $300
c) Debit Salaries Payable, $300; credit Salaries Expense, $300
d) Debit Salaries Payable, $300; credit Cash, $300

Answer: (b)
MC   Moderate

4.38: Employees work a five-day week and the total wages per week are $500. Wages for the last three working days in the month will not be paid to employees until the next month. The adjusting entry would include which of the following?
a) Debit Wages Expense, $500; credit Wages Payable, $500
b) Debit Wages Expense, $200; credit Wages Payable, $200
c) Debit Wages Expense, $300; credit Wages Payable, $300
d) Debit Wages Expense, $300; credit Cash, $300

Answer: (c)
MC   Difficult

4.39: The adjusted trial balance on the worksheet shows Prepaid Rent, $3,000, and Rent Expense, $2,500. What was the balance in the Prepaid Rent account before the adjustment?
a) $3,000   b) $2,500   c) $5,500   d) $2,000

Answer: (c)
MC   Easy

4.40: On March 1, Ronald Company paid in advance $7,000 for seven months' rent. The March 31 adjusting entry for rent expense should include:
a) debit Rent Expense, $2,500.
b) credit Prepaid Rent, $3,500.
c) debit Rent Expense, $2,000.
d) debit Rent Expense, $1,000.

Answer: (d)
MC   Moderate

4.41: Dorothy's Maids purchased $3,000 of office furniture at the beginning of the month. Depreciation Expense at the end of the month is $100. What is the balance of the Office Furniture account at the end of the year?
a) $2,900   b) $3,000   c) $3,100   d) $2,800

Answer: (b)
MC   Moderate

4.42: Spectator Sports bought $8,000 of equipment at the beginning of the month. Depreciation Expense at the end of the month is $120. What is the balance of the Accumulated Depreciation, Equipment at the end of the first month?
a) $120   b) $7,800   c) $0   d) $100

Answer: (a)
MC   Moderate

4.43: Deer and Fishing Company owns $6,000 of office furniture. Accumulated Depreciation had a balance of $3,000 before recording this year's depreciation. Depreciation Expense for the current year is $1,000. What is the book value at the end of the year?

a) $3,000   b) $6,000   c) $2,000   d) $1,000

Answer: (c)
MC   Moderate

4.44: Equipment with a cost of $20,000 has an accumulated depreciation of $2,000. What is the book value of the equipment?

a) $30,000   b) $20,000   c) $22,000   d) $18,000

Answer: (d)
MC   Moderate

4.45: On a worksheet, the Income Statement debit column totals $8,100 and the credit column totals $7,100. Which of the following statements is correct?

a) The company had a net income of $1,000.
b) The company had a loss of $1,000.
c) The company's revenues were greater than expenses.
d) None of the above.

Answer: (b)
MC   Moderate

4.46: On a worksheet, the Balance Sheet debit column total is $12,000 and the credit column total is $15,000. Which of the following statements is correct?

a) The company had a net income of $3,000.
b) The company had a loss of $3,000.
c) The company's expenses were greater than revenues.
d) None of the above are correct statements.

Answer: (b)
MC   Difficult

4.47: Clarion Newspaper received its electric bill for December on December 31 but did not pay or record it. This resulted in:

a) understated assets.
b) overstated net income.
c) overstated liabilities.
d) understated owner's equity.

Answer: (b)
MC   Difficult

4.48: A coffee shop received its telephone bill for May at the end
of May. What adjustment is needed to recognize the bill?
a) Debit Telephone Expense, credit Telephone Payable
b) Debit Telephone Payable, credit Telephone Expense
c) Debit Telephone Expense, credit Cash
d) Debit Telephone Payable, credit Cash

Answer: (a)
MC Moderate

4.49: Which of the following is most likely to result in an
adjusting entry at the end of the period?

a) Payment of two months'insurance in advance
b) Payment of one month's rent
c) Owner's withdrawals
d) Payment for routine maintenance on the company van

Answer: (a)
MC Difficult

4.50: Which of the following is most likely to result in an
adjusting entry at the end of the period?
a) Salaries accrued
b) Use of supplies during the period
c) Payment of one year's rent in advance
d) All of the above

Answer: (d)
MC Moderate

4.51: The worksheet is a tool used in preparing the financial
statements for a business.

Answer: True
TF Easy

4.52: The worksheet is a formal report.

Answer: False
TF Easy

4.53: Dollar signs are not used when preparing a worksheet.

Answer: True
TF Easy

4.54: The worksheet contains a debit and credit column for making
adjustments to accounts that need updating.

Answer: True
TF Moderate

4.55: An important function of the worksheet is for the accountant to find and correct errors before the financial statements are prepared.

Answer: True
TF Moderate

4.56: The trial balance is a list of accounts and their balances.

Answer: True
TF Easy

4.57: Adjusting is the process of bringing accounts up to date at the end of the accounting period.

Answer: True
TF Easy

4.58: Adjustments are the result of outside transactions.

Answer: False
TF Easy

4.59: The amount of supplies used during the period would be shown in the adjustments column of the worksheet.

Answer: True
TF Moderate

4.60: Supplies and prepaid rent are assumed to have a longer life than equipment.

Answer: False
TF Easy

4.61: The adjustment for supplies used during the period is called depreciation.

Answer: False
TF Easy

4.62: When an asset expires or is used up, it becomes an expense.

Answer: True
TF Easy

4.63: If an adjustment to supplies is not made, the asset Office Supplies will be too low.

Answer: False
TF Moderate

4.64: A mixed account is an account that is partly a balance sheet amount and partly an income statement amount.

Answer: True
TF Moderate

4.65: On the income statement, Office Supplies Expense would indicate the amount of supplies on hand.

Answer: False
TF Easy

4.66: The income statement is the only statement affected when an adjustment is made.

Answer: False
TF Easy

4.67: Rent expired at the end of an accounting period requires an adjustment.

Answer: True
TF Moderate

4.68: The original cost of equipment is adjusted for any depreciation expense recorded during the period.

Answer: False
TF Moderate

4.69: The spreading or allocating of the cost of an asset is called depreciation.

Answer: True
TF Easy

4.70: The book value of an asset equals the cost of the asset minus the accumulated depreciation.

Answer: True
TF Easy

4.71: Each time depreciation expense is recorded, the corresponding asset account decreases.

Answer: False
TF Moderate

4.72: Depreciation expense decreases net income and therefore results in a tax savings.

Answer: True
TF Moderate

4.73: The worksheet is not a formal report.

Answer: True
TF Easy

4.74: Depreciation Expense is debited when recording the depreciation for the period.

Answer: True
TF Easy

4.75: The use of straight-line depreciation results in equal amounts of depreciation being taken over a period of time.

Answer: True
TF Easy

4.76: Office Supplies Expense increases on the credit side.

Answer: False
TF Easy

4.77: To compute net income or net loss, the debit and credit columns of the income statement section of the worksheet are totaled and the difference is placed on the smaller side.

Answer: True
TF Moderate

4.78: On the formal income statement, the left column is the debit column and the right column is the credit column.

Answer: False
TF Moderate

4.79: Revenue is recorded when earned and expenses are only recorded when paid.

Answer: False
TF Moderate

4.80: The Balance Sheet is the first financial statement prepared.

Answer: False
TF Easy

4.81: Complete the following table by indicating the category, normal balance, and type of financial statement.

ACCOUNT	CATEGORY	NORMAL BALANCE	FINANCIAL REPORT
0. Cash	Asset	Dr.	Balance Sheet
a. P. Gray, Capital			
b. Salaries Payable			
c. Prepaid Insurance			
d. Rent Expense			
e. Accumulated Depr.			
f. Equipment			
g. P. Gray, Withdrawals			
h. Accounts Receivable			

Answer:

	CATEGORY	NORMAL BALANCE	FINANCIAL REPORT
a.	Owner's Equity	Cr.	Balance Sheet/Stat of OE
b.	Liability	Cr.	Balance Sheet
c.	Asset	Dr.	Balance Sheet
d.	Expense	Dr.	Income Statement
e.	Contra Asset	Cr.	Balance Sheet
f.	Asset	Dr.	Balance Sheet
g.	Owner's Equity	Dr.	Stat. of Owner's Equity
h.	Asset	Dr.	Balance Sheet

ES Easy

4.82: Complete the following table by indicating the category, normal balance, and type of financial statement.

ACCOUNT	CATEGORY	NORMAL BALANCE	FINANCIAL REPORT
0. Cash	Asset	Dr.	Balance Sheet
a. Depreciation Exp.			
b. Accounts Payable			
c. Supplies			
d. Advertising Exp.			
e. Accumulated Depr.			
f. Computer Equip.			
g. G. Yawn, Withd.			
h. Accounts Receivable			

Answer:

	CATEGORY	NORMAL BALANCE	FINANCIAL REPORT
a.	Expense	Dr.	Income Statement
b.	Liability	Cr.	Balance Sheet
c.	Asset	Dr.	Balance Sheet
d.	Expense	Dr.	Income Statement
e.	Contra Asset	Cr.	Balance Sheet
f.	Asset	Dr.	Balance Sheet
g.	Owner's Equity	Dr.	Stat. of Owner's Equity
h.	Asset	Dr.	Balance Sheet

ES Easy

4.83: From the following data, prepare the adjustments for the month and record the appropriate debits and credits in T accounts.
   a. Office furniture costing $3,000 with no residual value has a life expectancy of 60 months.
   b. Supplies available $800, supplies on hand $500.
   c. Prepaid Insurance balance $500, one-fifth has expired.

Answer: a.

Depreciation Expense		Accumulated Depreciation	
50			50

b.

Supplies Expense		Supplies	
300			300

c.

Insurance Expense		Prepaid Insurance	
100			100

ES Moderate

4.84: From the following data, journalize the adjusting entries in proper form for the month.
   a. Equipment costing $2,120 with a residual value of $200 has an expected life of 48 months.
   b. Accrued salaries of $100.
   c. Supplies ledger balance $700, supplies on hand $200.

Answer: a. Depreciation Expense   40
              Accumulated Depreciation   40

         b. Salaries Expense   100
                 Salaries Payable   100

         c. Supplies Expense   500
                 Supplies on Hand   500
         ES Moderate

4.85: Provide the adjusting entries to account for the differences between the trial balance amounts and the adjusted trial balance amounts for the accounts shown. Only a partial trial balance is provided. Use T accounts to show the adjustments.

	Trial Balance		Adjusted Trial Balance	
	Debit	Credit	Debit	Credit
Supplies	325		175	
Prepaid Insurance	800		500	
Equipment	8,000		8,000	
Accum. Depr.		700		1,200
Service Fees		1,200		1,200
Depreciation Exp.			500	
Telephone Exp.	100		100	
Salaries Exp.	375		375	
Insurance Expense			300	

Answer:

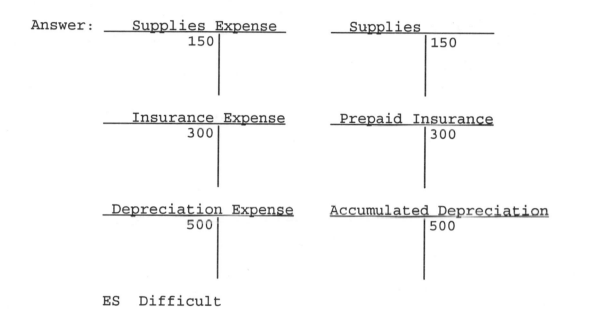

ES   Difficult

4.86: Provide the adjusting entries to account for the differences between the trial balance amounts and the adjusted trial balance amounts for the accounts shown. Only a partial trial balance is provided. Use T accounts to show the adjustments.

	Trial Balance Debit	Trial Balance Credit	Adjusted Trial Balance Debit	Adjusted Trial Balance Credit
Supplies	325		175	
Prepaid Insurance	800		500	
Equipment	8,000		8,000	
Accum. Depr.		700		1,200
Service Fees		1,200		1,200
Depreciation Exp.			500	
Telephone Exp.	100		100	
Salaries Exp.	375		375	
Insurance Expense			300	

Answer:

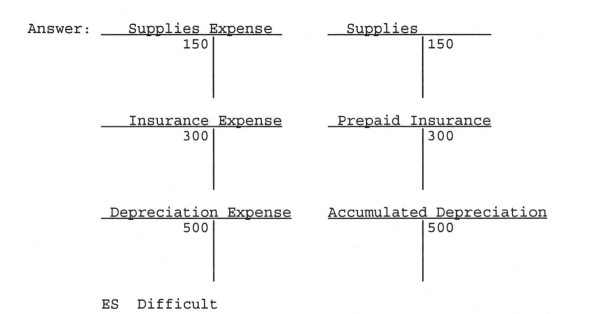

ES   Difficult

4.87: Provide the adjusting entries to account for the differences
between the trial balance amounts and the adjusted trial
balance amounts for the accounts shown. Only a partial
trial balance is provided. Use T accounts to show the
adjustments.

	Trial Balance		Adjusted Trial Balance	
	Debit	Credit	Debit	Credit
Supplies	325		175	
Prepaid Insurance	800		500	
Equipment	8,000		8,000	
Accum. Depr.		700		1,200
Service Fees		1,200		1,200
Depreciation Exp.			500	
Telephone Exp.	100		100	
Salaries Exp.	375		375	
Insurance Expense			300	

Answer:

Supplies Expense		Supplies	
150			150

Insurance Expense		Prepaid Insurance	
300			300

Depreciation Expense		Accumulated Depreciation	
500			500

ES   Moderate

4.88: Journalize the adjusting entries for the differences between the trial balance amounts and the adjusted trial balance amounts for the accounts shown. Only a partial trial balance is provided.

	Trial Balance Debit	Trial Balance Credit	Adjusted Trial Balance Debit	Adjusted Trial Balance Credit
Accounts Rec.	1,000		1,000	
Supplies	400		200	
Prepaid Rent	600		200	
Office Equipment	3,500		3,500	
Accumulated Depr.		250		450
Salaries Payable				550
Rental Fees		2,200		2,200
Depreciation Exp.			200	
Supplies Expense			200	
Advertising Exp.	100		100	
Salaries Exp.	350		900	
Rent Expense			400	

Answer:

Supplies Expense	200	
Supplies		200
Rent Expense	400	
Prepaid Rent		400
Depreciation Expense	200	
Accumulated Depr.		200
Salaries Expense	550	
Salaries Payable		550

ES Difficult

4.89: Journalize the adjusting entries for the differences between the trial balance amounts and the adjusted trial balance amounts for the accounts shown. Only a partial trial balance is provided.

	Trial Balance Debit	Trial Balance Credit	Adjusted Trial Balance Debit	Adjusted Trial Balance Credit
Accounts Rec.	1,000		1,000	
Supplies	400		200	
Prepaid Rent	600		200	
Office Equipment	3,500		3,500	
Accumulated Depr.		250		450
Salaries Payable				550
Rental Fees		2,200		2,200
Depreciation Exp.			200	
Supplies Expense			200	
Advertising Exp.	100		100	
Salaries Exp.	350		900	
Rent Expense			400	

Answer:

	Debit	Credit
Supplies Expense	200	
Supplies		200
Rent Expense	400	
Prepaid Rent		400
Depreciation Expense	200	
Accumulated Depr.		200
Salaries Expense	550	
Salaries Payable		550

ES Moderate

79

4.90: Given the Income Statement columns and the Balance Sheet columns of the worksheet, prepare an income statement for the month of July 31, 19xx for Billy's Company.

| | Income Statement | | Balance Sheet | |
	Debit	Credit	Debit	Credit
Cash			10,000	
Accounts Rec.			2,300	
Office Supplies			200	
T. Billy, Capital				11,000
T. Billy, With.			500	
Repair Fees		3,300		
Salaries Expense	900			
Rent Expense	500			
Office Sup. Exp.	100			
Salaries Payable				200
	1,500	3,300	13,000	11,200
Net Income	1,800			1,800
	3,300	3,300	13,000	13,000

Answer:

Billy's Company
Income Statement
For the month ended July 31, 19xx

Revenue
  Repair Fees $3,300

Operating Expenses:
  Salaries Expense $900
  Rent Expense   500
  Office Supplies Expense   100

  Total Operating Expense   1,500

Net Income $1,800

ES Moderate

4.91: Given the Income Statement columns and the Balance Sheet columns of the worksheet, prepare a balance sheet statement for the month of August 31, 19xx, for Billy's Company.

	Income Statement Debit	Income Statement Credit	Balance Sheet Debit	Balance Sheet Credit
Cash			4,000	
Accounts Rec.			1,300	
Prepaid Ins.			200	
Equipment			2,000	
Accum. Deprec.				800
T. Billy, Capital				6,000
T. Billy, With.			600	
Attorney Fees		3,500		
Salaries Expense	1,100			
Insurance Exp.	500			
Depreciation Exp.	800			
Salaries Payable				200
	2,400	3,500	8,100	7,000
Net Income	1,100			1,100
	3,500	3,500	8,100	8,100
	=====	=====	=====	=====

Answer:

Billy's Company
Balance Sheet
August 31, 19xx

Assets

Cash		$4,000
Accounts Receivable		1,300
Prepaid Insurance		200
Equipment	$2,000	
Less Acc. Dep.	800	1,200
Total Assets		$6,700
		======

Liabilities and Owner's Equity

Liabilities
Salaries Payable	$ 200

Owner's Equity
T. Billy, Capital	6,500 (6000 + 1100 - 600)

Total Liab. and Owner's
Equity $6,700
                      ======

ES Moderate

81

4.92: Discuss the benefits of the worksheet. Explain how the financial reports are prepared from the worksheet.

Answer: An accountant uses a worksheet like a scratch pad in order to organize and check data before preparing the financial reports. Its most important function is to allow the accountant to find and correct errors before the financial statements are prepared. Data in the income statement and balance sheet columns can be used to prepare the financial statements without returning to the ledger.
ES   Moderate

4.93: What is the purpose of adjusting entries? Discuss the effect of not preparing adjusting entries on various accounts.

Answer: The purpose of adjusting entries is to adjust the balances in the various accounts to better match revenues and expenses and update the balances of the assets and liabilities. If adjustments were not prepared, assets might be overstated, and expenses understated, or liabilities and expenses might be understated. For example, if an adjustment was not made for accrued salaries, Salaries Expense and Salaries Payable would be understated.
ES   Moderate

5. The Accounting Cycle Completed

5.1: Adjusting journal entries:
   a) close the ledger.
   b) bring accounts up to date.
   c) are recorded in the ledger.
   d) are recorded before finishing the worksheet.

Answer: (b)
   MC   Easy

5.2: Adjusting journal entries are prepared from:
   a) source documents.
   b) the balance sheet.
   c) the income statement.
   d) the adjustments column of the worksheet.

Answer: (d)
   MC   Moderate

5.3: These entries are prepared and posted to the ledger in order to update the ledger accounts before the next accounting period:
   a) trial balance.   b) adjusting entries.
   c) journalizing.   d) None of the above.

Answer: (b)
   MC   Easy

5.4: The adjusting entries are journalized:
   a) before preparing financial reports.
   b) after preparing financial reports.
   c) at the beginning of the accounting period.
   d) whenever time permits.

Answer: (b)
   MC   Moderate

5.5: The adjusting entry to record depreciation for office equipment would be:
   a) debit Accumulated Depreciation, Office Equipment; credit Depreciation Expense, Office Equipment.
   b) debit Accumulated Depreciation, Office Equipment; credit Office Equipment.
   c) debit Depreciation Expense, Office Equipment; credit Office Equipment.
   d) debit Depreciation Expense, Office Equipment; credit Accumulated Depreciation, Office Equipment.

Answer: (d)
   MC   Moderate

5.28: A nominal account is the same as:
    a) a real account.   b) a temporary account.
    c) an unusual account.   d) a permanent account.

Answer: (b)
    MC   Easy

5.29: Adjusting journal entries are:
    a) entered directly from the worksheet to the ledger.
    b) prepared before the completion of the worksheet.
    c) not needed if a worksheet has been completed.
    d) None of the above.

Answer: (d)
    MC   Moderate

5.30: Adjusting journal entries are:
    a) prepared before beginning the worksheet.
    b) prepared from the completed worksheet.
    c) prepared before the preparation of the financial
    statements.
    d) prepared after the posting of closing entries.

Answer: (b)
    MC   Moderate

5.31: Q. Tea Company depreciation for the month is $150. The
adjusting journal entry is:
    a) Depreciation Expense   150
       Accumulated Depreciation   150
    b) Depreciation Expense   150
       Depreciation Payable   150
    c) Depreciation Expense   150
       Equipment   150
    d) Accumulated Depreciation   150
       Depreciation Expense   150

Answer: (a)
    MC   Moderate

5.32: G. Quin service purchased a printer for $1,500. It has an
expected life of 40 months and no residual value. The
adjusting journal entry for the month is:
    a) Depreciation Expense   37.50
       Accumulated Depreciation   37.50
    b) Depreciation Expense   375
       Accumulated Depreciation   375
    c) Accumulated Depreciation   37.50
       Depreciation Expense   37.50
    d) Accumulated Depreciation   375
       Equipment   375

Answer: (a)
    MC   Moderate

5.33: W. Word Company showed office supplies available, $300. A count of the supplies left on hand as of June 30 was $250. The adjusting journal entry is:

    a) Office Supplies   250
         Office Supplies Expense   250
    b) Office Supplies Expense   50
         Office Supplies   50
    c) Office Supplies   50
         Office Supplies Expense   50
    d) Office Supplies Expense 250
         Office Supplies   250

Answer: (b)
    MC   Moderate

5.34: B. Bee Honey showed store supplies available, $150. After counting the inventory of supplies, it was determined $100 of supplies were used. The adjusting journal entry is:

    a) Store Supplies   50
         Store Supplies Expense   50
    b) Store Supplies   100
         Store Supplies Expense   100
    c) Store Supplies Expense   100
         Cash   100
    d) Store Supplies Expense   100
         Store Supplies   100

Answer: (d)
    MC   Moderate

5.35: Linda's Flowers purchased a two-year insurance policy for $2,400. The adjusting journal entry for one month is:

    a) Insurance Expense   100
         Prepaid Insurance   100
    b) Prepaid Insurance   100
         Insurance Expense   100
    c) Insurance Expense   200
         Prepaid Insurance   200
    d) Prepaid Insurance   200
         Insurance Expense   200

Answer: (a)
    MC   Moderate

5.36: Ruel Records', weekly payroll of $500 is paid on Fridays. Assume that the last day of the month falls on Tuesday. Which of the following adjusting journal entries is needed?
a) Salaries Payable   500
     Cash   500
b) Salaries Expense   300
     Cash   300
c) Salaries Expense   200
     Salaries Payable   200
d) Salaries Payable   100
     Salaries Expense   100

Answer: (c)
    MC   Moderate

5.37: Prepaid Advertising appeared as $1,200 on the trial balance and as $1,000 on the adjusted trial balance. The proper adjusting journal entry to reflect the change is:
a) Prepaid Advertising   200
     Cash   200
b) Cash   200
     Prepaid Advertising   200
c) Advertising Expense   200
     Cash   200
d) Advertising Expense   200
     Prepaid Advertising   200

Answer: (d)
    MC   Moderate

5.38: Prepaid Rent appeared as $1,500 on the trial balance and as $500 on the adjusted trial balance. The proper adjusting journal entry to reflect the change is:
a) Rent Expense   500
     Prepaid Rent   500
b) Rent Payable   1,000
     Prepaid Rent   1,000
c) Rent Expense   1,000
     Prepaid Rent   1,000
d) Rent Expense   500
     Rent Payable   500

Answer: (c)
    MC   Moderate

5.39: On Frazier's Investment Company's worksheet the Investment Fees account has a normal balance of $5,500. The entry to close the account would include:
a) debit to Investment Fees for $5,500.
b) credit to Investment Fees for $5,500.
c) debit to Income Summary for $5,500.
d) debit to J. Frazier, Capital for $5,500.

Answer: (a)
    MC   Moderate

90

5.40: The Rent Expense account has a normal balance of $600. The entry to close the account would include:
   a) debit to Rent Expense, $600.
   b) debit to Income Summary, $600.
   c) debit to Rent Payable, $600.
   d) credit to Income Summary, $600.

Answer: (b)
   MC   Moderate

5.41: S. View showed a net income of $50,000. The entry to close the Income Summary account would include:
   a) debit to Income Summary, $50,000.
   b) credit to S. View, Withdrawals, $50,000.
   c) debit to S. View, Capital, $50,000.
   d) None of the above.

Answer: (a)
   MC   Moderate

5.42: A company showed a net loss of $500. The entry to close the Income Summary account would include:
   a) debit to Income Summary, $500.
   b) debit to Capital, $500.
   c) credit to Capital, $500.
   d) credit to Cash, $500.

Answer: (b)
   MC   Moderate

5.43: The balance in the A. Graydon, Withdrawals account was $6,600. The entry to close the account would include:
   a) debit to Income Summary, $6,600.
   b) credit to Income Summary, $6,600.
   c) credit to A. Graydon, Capital, $6,600.
   d) credit to A. Graydon, Withdrawals, $6,600.

Answer: (d)
   MC   Moderate

5.44: The balance in the Insurance Expense account of the worksheet was $355. The journal entry to close the Insurance Expense account is:
   a) Insurance Expense   355
         Prepaid Insurance   355
   b) Insurance Expense   355
         Income Summary   355
   c) Insurance Expense   355
         Capital   355
   d) Income Summary   355
         Insurance Expense   355

Answer: (d)
   MC   Moderate

5.45: J. Anken Company's worksheet showed Ship Rental Fees, $950. The journal entry to close the account is:

a) Ship Rental Fees   950
    J. Anken, Capital   950
b) J. Anken, Capital   950
    Ship Rental Fees   950
c) Ship Rental Fees   950
    Income Summary   950
d) Income Summary   950
    Ship Rental Fees   950

Answer: (c)
MC Moderate

5.46: The Income Summary account shows debits of $20,000 and credits of $18,000. This is a result of:

a) net income of $2,000.   b) net loss of $2,000.
c) net income of $38,000.   d) net loss of $38,000.

Answer: (b)
MC Difficult

5.47: After closing the revenue and expense accounts, Income Summary showed a credit balance of $6,000. Which of the following statements is true?

a) The company had a net income of $6,000.
b) The company had a net loss of $6,000.
c) The company's cash increased $6,000.
d) None of the above.

Answer: (a)
MC Difficult

5.48: After closing the revenue, expense, and withdrawals accounts, the capital increased by $2,000. Which of the following situations could cause this to happen?

a) The company had a net income of $5,000.
b) The owner invested an additional amount.
c) The owner made withdrawals.
d) All of the above.

Answer: (d)
MC Difficult

5.49: The Income Statement debit column of the worksheet showed the following expenses:

Supplies Expense $400
Depreciation Expense 300
Salaries Expense 200

The journal entry to close the expense accounts is:

a) Income Summary 900
    Supplies Expense 400
    Depreciation Expense 300
    Salaries Expense 200
b) Income Summary 900
    Expenses 900
c) Supplies Expense 400
   Depreciation Expense 300
   Salaries Expense 200
    Income Summary 900
d) None of the above.

Answer: (a)
MC   Moderate

5.50: The Income Statement credit column of the worksheet showed the following revenues:

Catering Fees $900
Cleaning Fees 850

The journal entry to close the revenue accounts is:

a) Income Summary 1,750
    Catering Fees 900
    Cleaning Fees 850
b) Catering Fees 900
   Cleaning Fees 850
    Income Summary 1,750
c) All Revenues 1,750
    Income Summary 1,750
d) None of the above.

Answer: (b)
MC   Moderate

5.51: After formal financial reports have been prepared, journal entries and posting must be performed before the ledger is updated.

Answer: True
TF   Easy

5.52: It is not necessary to journalize the adjusting entries from the work sheet because the financial statements have already been prepared.

Answer: False
TF   Moderate

93

5.53: Adjusting entries bring the ledger up to date.

Answer: True
TF Easy

5.54: After the closing process is completed, all nominal accounts will have a zero balance.

Answer: True
TF Easy

5.55: When the post-closing trial balance is prepared, the adjusting entries have not been made.

Answer: False
TF Moderate

5.56: When posting adjusting entries, the word "adjusting" can be written in the explanation column in the ledger.

Answer: True
TF Moderate

5.57: Adjusting entries are prepared (not journalized) before financial reports are prepared.

Answer: True
TF Moderate

5.58: Real accounts are those accounts with balances that are brought forward to the next accounting period.

Answer: True
TF Moderate

5.59: Nominal accounts are called temporary accounts because their balances are not carried forward to the next accounting period.

Answer: True
TF Moderate

5.60: Revenue and expenses are closed to the Income Summary account.

Answer: True
TF Moderate

5.61: The Withdrawal account is closed to Income Summary.

Answer: False
    TF Moderate

5.62: Closing entries are normally prepared after the post-closing trial balance is prepared.

Answer: False
    TF Moderate

5.63: Closing entries are found in the adjustments column of the worksheet.

Answer: False
    TF Moderate

5.64: The balance in the Accumulated Depreciation account will be larger each period, while the debit to Depreciation Expense remains the same.

Answer: True
    TF Difficult

5.65: The income statement and balance sheet sections of the worksheet provide the information needed to prepare the closing entries.

Answer: True
    TF Difficult

5.66: When closing Income Summary, the balance is transferred to the Capital account.

Answer: True
    TF Moderate

5.67: Each individual expense account is debited when closing, and the total of all the expense accounts is transferred to Income Summary.

Answer: False
    TF Moderate

5.68: The Income Summary account is used during closing to summarize all revenue and expense accounts.

Answer: True
    TF Moderate

5.69: A nominal account is the same as a permanent account.

Answer: False
    TF   Moderate

5.70: A real account is the same as a permanent account.

Answer: True
    TF   Moderate

5.71: After posting adjusting entries, the temporary accounts will
      be set back to zero.

Answer: False
    TF   Moderate

5.72: After closing entries, the accounting equation will be
      reduced to Assets = Liabilities + Ending Capital.

Answer: True
    TF   Moderate

5.73: All revenue, expenses, and withdrawals will have zero
      balances before closing.

Answer: False
    TF   Moderate

5.74: Closing entries will update the capital account to the same
      figure that is on the balance sheet for that date.

Answer: True
    TF   Moderate

5.75: Income Summary is a permanent account.

Answer: False
    TF   Easy

5.76: Income Summary does not have a normal balance.

Answer: True
    TF   Moderate

5.77: The goal of closing is to clear all temporary accounts and
      update capital.

Answer: True
    TF   Moderate

5.78: The post-closing trial balance is used to determine if the ledger is in balance after closing.

Answer: True
TF   Moderate

5.79: The post-closing trial balance lists all the nominal accounts in the ledger and their balances after adjusting and closing entries are posted.

Answer: False
TF   Moderate

5.80: The post-closing trial balance comes before the closing entries are posted.

Answer: False
TF   Moderate

5.81: In the first space below, indicate whether each account is a real or nominal account using (R) Real Account and (N) Nominal Account. In the second space below, indicate by an (X) if the account should be closed.

N	X		
___	___	0.	Advertising Expense
___	___	1.	Accounts Receivable
___	___	2.	Rental Fees
___	___	3.	Depreciation Expense
___	___	4.	Accumulated Depreciation
___	___	5.	Salaries Payable
___	___	6.	Prepaid Rent
___	___	7.	Income Summary
___	___	8.	Insurance Expense

Answer: 1.   R
        2.   N   X
        3.   N   X
        4.   R
        5.   R
        6.   R
        7.   N   X
        8.   N   X
        ES   Easy

5.82: In the first space below, indicate whether each account is a real or nominal account using (R) Real Account and (N) Nominal Account. In the second space below, indicate by an (X) if the account should be closed.

N	X	0.	Advertising Expense
___	___	1.	Cash
___	___	2.	Attorney Fees
___	___	3.	Accounts Payable
___	___	4.	Accumulated Depreciation
___	___	5.	Withdrawals
___	___	6.	Prepaid Rent
___	___	7.	Income Summary
___	___	8.	Salaries Expense

Answer: 1. R
        2. N   X
        3. R
        4. R
        5. N   X
        6. R
        7. N   X
        8. N   X
        ES Easy

5.83: From the following accounts, prepare in proper form a post-closing trial balance for Adams Company on December 31, 19xx. Note: These balances are before closing.

J. Adams, Capital	$5,500
Cash	1,000
Accumulated Depreciation	2,000
Equipment	6,000
Accounts Payable	500
J. Adams, Withdrawals	700
Wages Expense	5,000
Supplies Expense	300
Accounts Receivable	2,000
Janitor Fees	7,000

Answer:

Adams Company
Post-Closing Trial Balance
December 31, 19xx

	Debit	Credit
Cash	1,000	
Accounts Receivable	2,000	
Equipment	6,000	
Accumulated Depreciation		2,000
Accounts Payable		500
J. Adams, Capital		6,500
Totals	9,000	9,000
	=====	=====

ES Difficult

5.84: From the following accounts, prepare in proper form a post-closing trial balance for Brown Company on December 31, 19xx.

Accounts Receivable	$2,200
Accounts Payable	2,000
Cash	1,000
Salaries Payable	1,200
Supplies	300
Prepaid Insurance	2,000
R. Brown, Capital	2,300

Answer:

Brown Company
Post-Closing Trial Balance
December 31, 19xx

	Debit	Credit
Cash	1,000	
Accounts Receivable	2,200	
Supplies	300	
Prepaid Insurance	2,000	
Accounts Payable		2,000
Salaries Payable		1,200
R. Brown, Capital		2,300
Totals	5,500	5,500
	=====	=====

ES   Moderate

5.88: Prepare the journal entries reflecting the following adjustments:

Adjustment data:
a. Increase in Accumulated Depreciation, $500
b. Decrease in Prepaid Insurance, $200
c. Increase in Salaries Expense, $500
d. Supplies used, $1,000.

Answer:
a. Depreciation Expense   500
       Accumulated Depr.   500

b. Insurance Expense   200
       Prepaid Insurance   200

c. Salaries Expense   500
       Salaries Payable   500

d. Supplies Expense   1,000
       Supplies   1,000

ES   Moderate

5.89: Name the steps in the accounting cycle.

Answer:
a. Source documents; example, a check
b. Analyze and record business transactions into a journal
c. Post from journal to ledger
d. Prepare a trial balance
e. Prepare financial statements
f. Journalize and post adjusting entries
g. Journalize and post closing entries
h. Prepare a post-closing trial balance
ES   Moderate

5.90: What are the major goals of the closing process?

Answer: Closing is a mechanical process that aids the accountant in recording transactions for the next period. Closing entries are usually done only at year end. Interim reports can be prepared from work sheets which are prepared monthly, quarterly, etc. When the closing journal entries are prepared, they reduce or clear all temporary accounts to a zero balance, and update capital to a new balance.
ES   Moderate

6. Banking Procedures and Control of Cash

6.1: Internal control over a company's assets should include the following policy:
a) responsibilities and duties of employees will be divided.
b) all cash receipts will be deposited into the bank the same day they arrive.
c) all cash payments will be made by check (except petty cash).
d) All of the above.

Answer: (d)
MC   Moderate

6.2: Company policy for internal control should include all of the following except:
a) employees will be rotated.
b) all checks are signed by the owner (or responsible employee) after receiving authorization to pay from the departments concerned.
c) at time of payment, all supporting invoices or documents will be stamped "paid."
d) one employee should have the total responsibility for approving purchases, authorizing payments, and signing checks.

Answer: (d)
MC   Moderate

6.3: Bank statements show all the following except:
a) deposits received and checks paid.
b) the beginning and ending balances shown on the bank's records.
c) the beginning and ending balances shown on the depositor's general ledger.
d) items debited and credited to the checking account.

Answer: (c)
MC   Moderate

6.4: The bank statement shows:
a) the beginning bank balance of the cash at the start of the month.
b) the checks the bank has paid and any deposits received.
c) any other charges or additions to the bank balance.
d) All of the above.

Answer: (d)
MC   Easy

6.5: When a deposit is made, the bank will:
   a) credit the depositor's account.
   b) debit the depositor's account.
   c) hold the deposit until checks are cleared.
   d) None of the above.

Answer: (a)
   MC   Easy

6.6: When a check is presented for payment, the bank will:
   a) credit the depositor's account.
   b) debit the depositor's account.
   c) hold the check until deposits are cleared.
   d) None of the above.

Answer: (b)
   MC   Moderate

6.7: Signing one's name on the back left-hand side of the check
   is called:
   a) payment.   b) endorsement.
   c) cancellation.   d) signaturing.

Answer: (b)
   MC   Easy

6.8: Endorsing a check:
   a) guarantees payment.
   b) transfers the right to cash or deposit the check to the
   bank, which can collect the money from the person or
   company that issued the check.
   c) cancels the transaction.
   d) All of the above.

Answer: (b)
   MC   Easy

6.9: A blank endorsement on a check:
   a) can be further endorsed by someone else.
   b) cannot be further endorsed by someone else.
   c) is the safest type of endorsement.
   d) only permits the original endorser to get the money.

Answer: (a)
   MC   Easy

6.10: A restrictive endorsement on a check:
   a) can be further endorsed by someone else.
   b) is the safest endorsement for businesses.
   c) permits the bank to use its best judgment.
   d) None of the above.

Answer: (b)
   MC   Moderate

6.11: The check is a written order signed by the:
   a) drawer.   b) drawee.   c) payee.   d) payer.

Answer: (a)
   MC   Easy

6.12: The one to whom the check is payable is the:
   a) drawee.   b) drawer.   c) payee.   d) payer.

Answer: (c)
   MC   Easy

6.13: Key points in working with a checkbook should include:
   a) the number of the check is preprinted on the check.
   b) the stub is filled out first and will be used in
   recording transactions and future reference.
   c) the amount written in words should start on the far
   left.
   d) All of the above.

Answer: (d)
   MC   Moderate

6.14: If the written amount in words on a check does not match the
   amount expressed in figures, the bank may:
   a) pay the amount written in words.
   b) do nothing, because of the confusion.
   c) call the drawer and verify the amount expressed in
   figures.
   d) either a or c above.

Answer: (a)
   MC   Moderate

6.15: Checks that have been processed by the bank and are no
   longer negotiable are:
   a) outstanding checks.   b) cancelled checks.
   c) checks in process.   d) blank checks.

Answer: (b)
   MC   Moderate

6.16: Deposits not yet added into the bank balance are called:
a) deposits in transit.   b) late deposits.
c) deposits on hold.   d) outstanding deposits.

Answer: (a)
MC   Easy

6.17: Outstanding checks:
a) have been subtracted on the bank records but not the
checkbook records.
b) have not been presented to the bank for payment and have
not been subtracted from the checkbook.
c) have not been presented to the bank for payment but have
been subtracted on the checkbook.
d) have been returned to the business for nonpayment.

Answer: (c)
MC   Easy

6.18: If a business deposits a customer's check and later learns
that it is an insufficient funds check, the:
a) bank will try to collect the amount.
b) the checkbook balance will be less than the bank
balance.
c) the business will receive a credit memorandum from the
bank.
d) the business will receive a debit memorandum from the
bank.

Answer: (d)
MC   Moderate

6.19: When the bank issues a debit memorandum to the depositor,
the bank is:
a) adding to the depositor's account.
b) subtracting from the depositor's account.
c) stating that a collection was made.
d) showing a "forged" check occurred.

Answer: (b)
MC   Moderate

6.20: The bank would issue a credit memorandum to Rocking Horse
Toy Company when the bank:
a) collects a note receivable from a Rocking Horse Toy
Company customer.
b) posted the monthly service charges.
c) discovered a check previously deposited by the Rocking
Horse Toy Company is an insufficient funds check.
d) None of the above.

Answer: (a)
MC   Moderate

6.21: How would outstanding checks be handled when reconciling the ending cash balance per the bank statement to the correct adjusted cash balance?
  a) Added to the balance of the bank statement
  b) Subtracted from the balance of the bank statement
  c) Added to the balance per books
  d) Outstanding checks would be ignored

Answer: (b)
  MC Moderate

6.22: When reconciling the ending cash balance per the company records to the correct adjusted cash balance, outstanding checks are:
  a) subtracted from the company's records balance.
  b) added to the company's records balance.
  c) added to the bank statement balance.
  d) subtracted from the bank statement balance.

Answer: (d)
  MC Easy

6.23: What type of an account is the petty cash fund?
  a) Revenue   b) Expense   c) Asset   d) Liability

Answer: (c)
  MC Easy

6.24: The original amount of the petty cash fund should equal:
  a) the sum of the petty cash on hand and the paid petty cash vouchers.
  b) cash on hand at the end of the day.
  c) the cash received plus the cash in the petty cash box.
  d) the total payments made during the day.

Answer: (a)
  MC Moderate

6.25: Petty cash disbursements for expenses should be reported daily in the:
  a) journal.   b) ledger.
  c) auxiliary record.   d) not recorded.

Answer: (c)
  MC Moderate

6.26: When a petty cash fund is in use:
   a) custodians are obligated to make up any shortages and keep any overages to keep the fund balanced.
   b) daily posting will be made to the general journal.
   c) the Petty Cash account in the general ledger will have numerous transactions posted to it during the accounting period.
   d) None of the above.

Answer: (d)
   MC   Moderate

6.27: A fund that is placed in the cash register drawer and used to make change for customers who pay cash is called:
   a) petty cash fund.
   b) change fund.
   c) cash short/over fund.
   d) electronic funds transfer.

Answer: (b)
   MC   Easy

6.28: Determine the correct adjusted ending cash balance for the Candy Kite Company from the following information:
   Bank statement ending cash balance $1,500
   General ledger cash balance ending   1,750
   Bank monthly service charge   25
   Deposit in transit   400
   Outstanding checks   265
   NSF check returned with bank statement   90
   a) $1,500   b) $1,750   c) $1,635   d) $1,725

Answer: (c)
   MC   Moderate

6.29: Calculate from the following information accumulated by Linda Green the adjusted cash balance at the end of August, 19xx.

   Bank statement ending cash balance $2,500
   General ledger cash balance ending   2,750
   Bank monthly service charge   20
   Deposits in transit   1,400
   Outstanding checks   1,235
   NSF check returned with bank statement   65
   a) $2,665   b) $2,500   c) $2,750   d) $2,435

Answer: (a)
   MC   Moderate

6.30: Determine the adjusted cash balance for Candy Kite Company on March 31, 19xx, from the following information:

Cash balance on the bank statement	$2,700
Customer's check returned-NSF	300
Customer's note collected by the bank	500
Deposits in transit, March 31	1,750
Outstanding checks, March 31	2,200

a) $3,200   b) $2,900   c) $2,700   d) $2,250

Answer: (d)
MC   Moderate

6.31: Calculate the adjusted cash balance for Rocking Horse Toy Company on June 30, 19xx, from the following information:

Cash balance on the bank statement	$1,500
Customer's check returned-NSF	200
Customer's note collected by the bank	300
Deposits in transit, June 30	2,300
Outstanding checks, June 30	900

a) $1,500   b) $1,600   c) $2,900   d) $3,000

Answer: (c)
MC   Moderate

6.32: Information to calculate the adjusted cash balance for Don's Foods is as follows:

Cash balance per general ledger (unadjusted)	$1,900
Customer's check returned-NSF	60
Bank service charges	15
Deposits in transit	700
Outstanding checks	600
Customer's note collected by bank	410

a) $2,325   b) $1,900   c) $1,835   d) $2,235

Answer: (d)
MC   Moderate

6.33: Calculate the adjusted cash balance for Stacy's Sew and Sew from the following information:

Cash balance per general ledger (unadjusted)	$2,100
Customer's check returned-NSF	80
Bank service charges	20
Deposits in transit	800
Outstanding checks	500
Customer's note collected by bank	600

a) $2,600   b) $2,100   c) $2,180   d) $2,400

Answer: (a)
MC   Moderate

6.34: Compute the adjusted cash balance on May 31, 19xx, from the following information:

Checkbook balance on May 31	$7,200
Outstanding checks	500
NSF check returned	100
Deposits in transit	250
Service charges	10
Note collected by bank	250

a) $7,200   b) $7,340   c) $6,615   d) $7,560

Answer: (b)
    MC Difficult

6.35: From the following information, calculate the adjusted cash balance on August 31, 19xx:

Checkbook balance on August 31	$6,000
Outstanding checks	400
NSF check returned	150
Deposits in transit	550
Service charges	15

a) $5,835   b) $6,000   c) $5,985   d) $6,015

Answer: (a)
    MC Difficult

6.36: A check for $89 is incorrectly recorded on the checkbook stub as $98. The $9 error should be shown on the bank reconciliation as:
    a) added to the balance per books.
    b) deducted from the balance per books.
    c) added to the balance per bank statement.
    d) deducted from the balance per bank statement.

Answer: (a)
    MC Moderate

6.37: A check for $97 is incorrectly recorded on the checkbook stub as $79. The $18 error should be shown on the bank reconciliation as:
    a) added to the balance per books.
    b) deducted from the balance per books.
    c) added to the balance per bank statement.
    d) deducted from the balance per bank statement.

Answer: (b)
    MC Moderate

6.38: Bank interest earned on a checking account cash balance
would be shown on a bank reconciliation as:
   a) added to the balance per books.
   b) deducted from the balance per books.
   c) added to the balance per bank statement.
   d) deducted from the balance per bank statement.

Answer: (a)
   MC   Moderate

6.39: Bank service charges on a checking account would be shown on
a bank reconciliation as:
   a) added to the balance per books.
   b) deducted from the balance per books.
   c) added to the balance per bank statement.
   d) deducted from the balance per bank statement.

Answer: (b)
   MC   Moderate

6.40: Which of the following bank reconciliation items would <u>not</u>
be reflected in a journal entry?
   a) Bank service charges
   b) Collection of a note by the bank
   c) Outstanding checks
   d) NSF customer check

Answer: (c)
   MC   Moderate

6.41: Which of the following bank reconciliation items would be
reflected in a general entry?
   a) Outstanding checks
   b) Deposits in transit
   c) The bank incorrectly charges another company's check to
   your account
   d) The bank service charges for the period

Answer: (d)
   MC   Moderate

6.42: Information on the Boise Mining Company bank reconciliation included the following items:

Bank service charges	$ 20
Deposits in transit	700
Outstanding checks	600

The journal entry to record the above items would include a:
a) credit to the Cash account for $20.
b) debit to the Cash account for $20.
c) debit to the Cash account for $720.
d) credit to the Cash account for $600.

Answer: (a)
MC Difficult

6.43: The journal entry to adjust the records from Candy Cane Confectionary's bank reconciliation would include:
a) the total of outstanding checks.
b) deposits in transit.
c) correction of any errors on the bank statement.
d) correction of any errors or omissions in the company cash account.

Answer: (d)
MC Moderate

6.44: In what way should Tina Tenant show a check she issued for rent expense which has not been cancelled by the bank on her bank reconciliation?
a) Add the amount back to the balance per books.
b) Deduct the amount from the balance per books.
c) Add the amount to the balance per bank statement.
d) Deduct the amount from the balance per bank statement.

Answer: (d)
MC Moderate

6.45: A $100 petty cash fund has cash of $40 and valid receipts for $60. The entry to replenish the fund would include a:
a) debit to Cash for $60.
b) credit to Cash for $60.
c) debit to Petty Cash for $60.
d) credit to Petty Cash for $60.

Answer: (b)
MC Easy

6.46: The entry to replenish a $50 petty cash fund which has cash
      of $10 and valid receipts for $38 would include:
      a) a credit to Cash for $38.
      b) a debit to Cash for $38.
      c) a credit to Cash for $40.
      d) a credit to Petty Cash for $40.

Answer: (c)
      MC Moderate

6.47: The entry establishing a $75 petty cash fund would include
      a:
      a) debit to Cash for $75.
      b) debit to Petty Cash for $75.
      c) credit to Petty Cash for $75.
      d) debit to Miscellaneous Expense for $75.

Answer: (b)
      MC Easy

6.48: Southern Cooking Restaurant's journal entry to establish a
      $100 petty cash fund for the office would include a:
      a) credit to Cash for $100.
      b) credit to Petty Cash for $100.
      c) debit to Cash for $100.
      d) debit to Office Expense for $100.

Answer: (a)
      MC Easy

6.49: Roadside Motel's $200 Petty Cash fund has a shortage
      of $8. The facts are: $160 in valid receipts for expenses;
      $32 in coins and currency. The journal entry to replenish
      the petty cash fund would include a:
      a) credit to Cash for $160.
      b) credit to Petty Cash for $168.
      c) debit to Cash Short and Over for $8.
      d) credit to Cash Short and Over for $8.

Answer: (c)
      MC Moderate

6.50: Hometown Food Market's cash register tapes do not agree with cash receipts. The facts are: total cash register tapes $600; total coins and currency $605.
The summary journal entry to record the day's transactions would include a:
   a) $600 debit to Cash, $5 debit to Cash Short and Over, and $605 credit to Sales.
   b) $605 debit to Cash, $5 credit to Cash Short and Over, and $600 credit to Sales.
   c) $605 debit to Cash and $605 credit to Sales.
   d) $600 debit to Cash and $600 credit to Sales.

Answer: (b)
   MC Difficult

6.51: External control includes control over the assets as well as ways of monitoring the company's operations.

Answer: False
   TF Moderate

6.52: Using correct cash handling procedures, deposits should be made by the end of the week.

Answer: False
   TF Moderate

6.53: A signature card is kept in the bank files so that possible forgeries could be spotted.

Answer: True
   TF Easy

6.54: When a bank credits your account, it is increasing the balance.

Answer: True
   TF Difficult

6.55: A restrictive endorsement limits further use of a check.

Answer: True
   TF Moderate

6.56: A blank endorsement is safer than a full endorsement.

Answer: False
   TF Moderate

6.57: The drawer writes the check.

Answer: True
       TF Moderate

6.58: The drawee of the check is the person receiving the money.

Answer: False
       TF Moderate

6.59: The drawee of a check is normally the bank.

Answer: True
       TF Moderate

6.60: When the word "and" is written in the amount column for a
      check, it designates the decimal point location.

Answer: True
       TF Moderate

6.61: A bank statement reports the beginning balance, deposits in
      transit, cancelled checks, and outstanding checks for the
      month.

Answer: False
       TF Moderate

6.62: Cancelled checks are negotiable at the bank for the face
      value.

Answer: False
       TF Moderate

6.63: Deposits that have been added to the bank balance but not
      the checkbook balance are called deposits in transit.

Answer: False
       TF Difficult

6.64: Deposits in transit result because of a timing difference
      between the bank records and checkbook records.

Answer: True
       TF Moderate

6.65: When a company receives a debit memorandum from the bank for NSF checks, the business should subtract this amount from the checkbook balance.

Answer: True
TF Moderate

6.66: The bank would send the depositor a credit memorandum to show an increase in the balance of the depositor's account.

Answer: True
TF Difficult

6.67: When adjustments are made to the checkbook balance in preparing a bank reconciliation, a journal entry is needed to bring the ledger up to date.

Answer: True
TF Moderate

6.68: Transferring money without paper checks is called electronic funds transfer.

Answer: True
TF Moderate

6.69: Check truncation is the process of reconciling a bank account.

Answer: False
TF Easy

6.70: Petty Cash is a Contra Asset shown on the Balance Sheet.

Answer: False
TF Moderate

6.71: A credit to petty cash is made to replenish the fund.

Answer: False
TF Easy

6.72: Petty cash is used to write checks for small items such as postage stamps and supplies.

Answer: False
TF Difficult

6.73: The auxiliary petty cash record is not a special journal.

Answer: True
TF   Moderate

6.74: The petty cash fund is the same thing as a change fund.

Answer: False
TF   Moderate

6.75: The auxiliary petty cash record is used to post to the ledger.

Answer: False
TF   Moderate

6.76: The form used when money is taken out of petty cash is called a petty cash voucher.

Answer: True
TF   Moderate

6.77: A shift in assets occurs when a petty cash account is established.

Answer: True
TF   Moderate

6.78: If the petty cash fund is too large, the Petty Cash Fund account should be increased.

Answer: False
TF   Easy

6.79: If the ending balance in the Cash Short and Over account is an overage, it is reported on the income statement as miscellaneous income.

Answer: True
TF   Difficult

6.80: Construct a bank reconciliation for Candy Land Confectionary
as of July 31, 19xx, from the following information:

Ending checkbook balance	$420
Ending bank statement balance	320
Deposits in transit	220
Outstanding checks	155
Bank service charge (debit memo)	35

Answer:

CANDY LAND CONFECTIONARY
BANK RECONCILIATION AS OF JULY 31, 19XX

Checkbook Balance			Balance per Bank		
Ending Checkbook Bal.	$420		Ending Bank Bal. Stat.	$320	
			Add:		
			Deposits in Transit	220	
					$540
Deduct:			Deduct:		
Service Charge	35		Outstanding checks	155	
Reconciled Balance	$385		Reconciled Balance	$385	
	====			====	

ES   Easy

6.81: From the following information, prepare a bank
reconciliation for Rocking Horse Toy Company as of November
30, 19xx:

Ending checkbook balance	$400
Ending bank statement balance	280
Deposits in transit	180
Outstanding checks	75
Bank service charge	15

Answer:

ROCKING HORSE TOY COMPANY
BANK RECONCILIATION AS OF NOVEMBER 30, 19XX

Checkbook Balance			Balance per Bank		
Ending Checkbook Bal.	$400		Ending Bank Stat. Bal.	$280	
			Add:		
			Deposits in Transit	180	
					$460
Deduct:			Deduct:		
Service Charge	15		Outstanding Checks	75	
Reconciled Balance	$385		Reconciled Balance	$385	
	====			====	

ES   Moderate

6.82: Construct a bank reconciliation for Barco Company as of
April 30, 19xx, from the following information:
a. Balance per bank statement $5,300
b. Deposit in transit   2,000
c. Checkbook balance   5,500
d. Outstanding checks   1,709
e. NSF check (debit memo)   200
f. Error on check.   Amount on the
    check was $87, the amount on the
    check stub was $78 in payment for
    office supplies   9
g. The bank collected a note
    receivable for Barco   300

Answer: BARCO COMPANY
               BANK RECONCILIATION AS OF APRIL 30, 19XX

        Checkbook Balance   Balance per Bank

        Ending Checkbook Bal. $5,500 Ending Bank Stat. Bal. $5,300
        Add: Add:
        Proceeds from a note   300 Deposit in Transit   2,000
                                 _____   _____
                                 $5,800 $7,300
        Deduct: Deduct:
        Error in recording ck.   9 Outstanding checks   1,709
        NSF Check   200   _____

        Reconciled Balance $5,591 Reconciled Balance $5,591
                               ======   ======

ES   Moderate

119

6.83: Indicate what effect each situation will have on the bank reconcilation process. Place the number of your choice beside the items listed.

1. Add to bank balance
2. Deduct from bank balance
3. Add to checkbook balance
4. Deduct from checkbook balance

_____a. $500 deposit in transit
_____b. $20 bank service charge
_____c. $50 NSF check
_____d.   Check written for $25 recorded as $52
_____e.   Check #225 outstanding for $100
_____f.   Check written for $70 recorded as $50.

Answer: a.   1
          b.   4
          c.   4
          d.   3
          e.   2
          f.   4

ES   Moderate

120

6.84: Prepare the appropriate journal entry(s) for the following items found on Arco Company's bank reconciliation of April 30, 19xx:
a. Deposits in transit $2,000
b. Outstanding checks   1,709
c. NSF check   200
d. Error on check. Amount on check stub was $78, the amount on the check was $87 for office supplies   9
e. The bank collected a note receivable   300

Answer: The following journal entries would be acceptable.

Accounts Receivable	200	
Cash		200

Office Supplies	9	
Cash		9

Cash	300	
Note Receivable		300

OR

Cash	91	
Accounts Receivable	200	
Office Supplies	9	
Note Receivable		300

ES Moderate

6.85: Prepare journal entries for the following petty cash fund transactions:
Aug. 1   Established a $50 petty cash fund.
    31   Replenished the petty cash fund. Currency and coins remaining were $8. Approved paid vouchers were: $6 donation expense, $9 postage expense, $12 office supplies expense, and $13 miscellaneous expense.

Answer:

Aug. 1	Petty Cash	50	
	Cash		50

Aug.31	Donation Expense	6	
	Postage Expense	9	
	Office Supplies Expense	12	
	Miscellaneous Expense	13	
	Cash Short and Over	2	
	Cash		42

ES Moderate

6.86: Prepare journal entries for the following petty cash fund
transactions:
Jul. 1   Established a $75 petty cash fund.
    9   Increased the petty cash fund to $100.
   31   Replenished the petty cash fund. Currency and coins
        remaining were $20. Approved paid vouchers were:
        $12 donation expense, $21 postage expense, $35
        office supplies expense and $15 miscellaneous
        expense.

Answer: Jul. 1 Petty Cash   75
                  Cash   75

        Jul. 9 Petty Cash   25
                  Cash   25

        Jul. 31 Donation Expense   12
                Postage Expense   21
                Supplies Expense   35
                Miscellaneous Expense   15
                  Cash Short and Over   3
                  Cash   80
        ES Difficult

6.87: Bjay's Bake Shop cash on hand in the cash register did not
      agree with the sales tape. Total cash sales from the sales
      tape were $1,400 while the total cash in the register was
      $1,300. Bjay keeps a $50 change fund in her shop.

      Required: Prepare the appropriate journal entry to record
                 the day's sales and the cash shortage.

Answer: Cash   1,250
          Cash Short and Over   150
            Sales   1,400
          ES Difficult

122

6.88: Discuss reasons why a manager would be concerned about developing a system of internal control over the cash receipts and cash payments of the business. Describe at least five company policies that would be included in an internal control system.

Answer: a. To safeguard the company's incoming cash receipts and cash payments from unauthorized transactions.
b. To promote honesty and ethics among company employees. Remove "temptation."
c. To maximize net income by reducing cash losses.

Policies:
a. Separate the various aspects of transactions among several employees.
b. Deposit all cash receipts in the bank on a daily basis.
c. Monthly bank reconciliations to be prepared by employees who do not have access to cash transactions.
d. Provide adequate paperwork backup for all transactions.
e. Make all payments over a threshold amount by check.
f. Restrict and bond persons authorized to sign checks.
g. Establish a controlled petty cash system.
ES   Moderate

6.89: Discuss the various steps and procedures included in the bank reconciliation process. What are the advantages in preparing a monthly bank reconciliation?

Answer: 1. Restrict the access to bank statements to authorized personnel. These people should not be persons handling cash or making disbursements.
2. Compare all cancelled checks with information in checkbook. Check amounts, payee, and endorsements.
3. Prepare a list of outstanding checks. Subtract the total from the bank statement balance.
4. Trace all deposits to the bank statement. Make a list of all deposits in transit and add the total to the bank statement balance.
5. Review all debit and credit memos. Adjust checkbook and book balance accordingly.
6. Compare adjusted balance per bank with adjusted balance per books. Investigate any differences and make necessary corrections.
7. Prepare journal entries for corrections, additions, and omissions to books.
8. Reconciliation procedure should be completed at least monthly to ensure accuracy of both the book's and the bank's records. Serves as an additional control over cash receipts and disbursements.
ES   Difficult

7. Payroll Concepts and Procedures: Employee Taxes

7.1: Another name for the Fair Labor Standards Act is:
a) Federal Insurance Contributions Act.
b) Federal Income Tax Act.
c) Federal Wages and Hour Law.
d) Federal Hourly Act.

Answer: (c)
MC   Easy

7.2: This law requires employers that are involved in interstate commerce to pay at least minimum rate of pay and establishes a regular 40-hour work week:
a) Federal Insurance Contributions Act.
b) Federal Income Tax Act.
c) Fair Labor Standards Act.
d) Fair Employment Act.

Answer: (c)
MC   Easy

7.3: Under the Fair Labor Standards Act, any hours that an employee works over 40 during a work week:
a) the employer pays no FICA tax.
b) the employee is paid time and a half.
c) the employer does not pay workers' compensation.
d) All of the above.

Answer: (b)
MC   Easy

7.4: Which of the following type of employers is exempt from the 40 hour standard?
a) Restaurants
b) Hotels
c) Construction companies
d) Both (a) and (b) are exempt.

Answer: (d)
MC   Easy

7.5: Restaurants and hotels can have a maximum standard work week before paying overtime:
a) up to 40 hours per week.   b) up to 50 hours per week.
c) up to 48 hours per week.   d) up to 44 hours per week.

Answer: (d)
MC   Moderate

7.6: A W-4 form is:
   a) used to compute the amount of FICA tax withheld.
   b) given to the employees at the end of each year to show total earnings, deductions, etc.
   c) used to determine the amount of federal income tax to withhold.
   d) None of the above.

Answer: (c)
   MC   Moderate

7.7: The Employee's Withholding Allowance Certificate is called:
   a) Form W-2.   b) Form W-3.
   c) Form W-4.   d) Form 8109.

Answer: (c)
   MC   Easy

7.8: The amount of federal income tax withheld is computed using:
   a) employee's income, number of allowances, and marital status.
   b) net earnings and form W-4.
   c) W-2 charts.
   d) FICA tax tables.

Answer: (a)
   MC   Moderate

7.9: The Federal Insurance Contributions Act is better known as:
   a) FIT.   b) workers' compensation.
   c) FICA.   d) FUTA.

Answer: (c)
   MC   Easy

7.10: The following pay FICA taxes:
   a) employees.   b) employers.
   c) self-employed.   d) All of the above.

Answer: (d)
   MC   Easy

7.11: There are two parts to FICA:
   a) old age benefits and workers' compensation.
   b) retirement and income tax withholdings.
   c) Social Security and Medicare.
   d) None of the above.

Answer: (c)
   MC   Moderate

7.12: The payroll register contains:
a) payroll information for the payroll period.
b) the total information for individual employees.
c) the ledger accounts for payroll.
d) all cumulative payroll information.

Answer: (a)
MC   Moderate

7.13: The payroll register does <u>not</u> contain:
a) payroll information for the payroll period.
b) net pay.
c) gross pay.
d) all cumulative payroll information for each individual employee.

Answer: (d)
MC   Moderate

7.14: Net pay is the same as:
a) gross pay.   b) take home pay.
c) before taxes pay.   d) pay before deductions.

Answer: (b)
MC   Moderate

7.15: All of the following are employee payroll withholdings except:
a) state income taxes.
b) federal income tax.
c) state unemployment tax.
d) medical insurance premium payments.

Answer: (c)
MC   Moderate

7.16: Which of the following would <u>not</u> typically be an employee payroll withholding?
a) Union dues
b) Purchases of savings bonds
c) Federal income tax
d) Unemployment taxes

Answer: (d)
MC   Moderate

7.17: To examine in detail the weekly payroll of all employees, one would look at the:
   a) W-2.
   b) W-4.
   c) payroll register.
   d) employee earnings record.

Answer: (c)
   MC   Moderate

7.18: The payroll register includes sections for recording:
   a) gross pay, deductions, and net pay.
   b) assets, liabilities, equity, revenues, and expenses.
   c) trade accounts receivable and short-term note receivables.
   d) accrued expenses, unearned revenues, and net pay.

Answer: (a)
   MC   Moderate

7.19: Net pay is equal to:
   a) hours worked * hourly wage.
   b) gross pay - payroll tax expense.
   c) gross pay - deductions.
   d) gross payroll - income taxes withheld.

Answer: (c)
   MC   Moderate

7.20: If Bob Rice's hourly wage is $8.00 and he worked 35 hours during the week, what is his gross pay for the week?
   a) $300   b) $320   c) $280   d) $250

Answer: (c)
   MC   Easy

7.21: Alice Green's hourly rate is $10.00, and she worked 44 during the week. Assuming an overtime rate of time and a half over 40 hours, Alice's gross pay is:
   a) $400.   b) $460.   c) $430.   d) $350.

Answer: (b)
   MC   Moderate

7.22: Joan works 48 hours as a waitress in a restaurant. Compute her weekly pay. Her hourly rate of pay is $4.00 per hour. Remember that overtime is over 44 hours.
   a) $192   b) $200   c) $210   d) $230

Answer: (b)
   MC   Moderate

7.23: Lucinda works 50 hours at a rate of pay of $5.50 per hour. She receives double pay over 40 hours. What is her gross pay?
a) $290.   b) $305.   c) $302.50   d) $275.

Answer: (c)
MC Moderate

7.24: The formula to compute gross earnings for an employee who earns $5.20 an hour, works 46 hours, and receives time and a half for all hours over 40 is:
a) ($5.20 * 46) + (6 * $5.20).
b) ($5.20 * 1.5 * 6) + ($5.20 * 40).
c) ($5.20 * 3) + ($5.20 * 40).
d) ($5.20 * 46 * 1.5).

Answer: (b)
MC Moderate

7.25: Joy Roy earns an hourly rate of $12 per hour. What would her gross earnings be if she worked 50 hours? (Assume an overtime rate of time and a half over 40 hours.)
a) $660   b) $600   c) $580   d) $550

Answer: (a)
MC Moderate

7.26: The Federal Insurance Contribution Act created a tax. This tax is also known as:
a) federal income tax and Medicare tax.
b) Social Security tax and state income tax.
c) compensation tax.
d) Social Security tax and Medicare tax.

Answer: (d)
MC Moderate

7.27: On December 1, 19xx, Patty Soreson does not have any FICA-Social Security tax withheld. What is the most likely reason?
a) Patty has already made over the FICA-Social Security limit for the year.
b) An error was made if no FICA-Social Security and FICA-Medicare was withheld.
c) Patty's number of allowance withholdings claimed was high.
d) Patty owes no federal income tax for the period.

Answer: (a)
MC Moderate

7.28: Which of the following is an optional payroll deduction?
   a) Union dues   b) Federal income taxes
   c) FICA   d) State income taxes

Answer: (a)
   MC   Moderate

7.29: Which of the following taxes has a maximum amount an
   employee must pay in a year?
   a) Federal income tax
   b) FICA-Social Security tax
   c) FICA-Medicare tax
   d) Both (a) and (c) are correct

Answer: (b)
   MC   Moderate

7.30: The amount of FICA-Social Security and FICA-Medicare taxes
   an employer must pay is:
   a) less than the amount withheld from the employee.
   b) not dependent the amount withheld from the employee.
   c) equal to the amount withheld from the employee.
   d) greater than the amount withheld from the employee.

Answer: (c)
   MC   Moderate

7.31: Mary Ross' cumulative earnings are $45,000, and her gross
   pay for the week is $500. If the FICA rates are Social
   Security 6.2% on $60,600 and Medicare 1.45%, what are her
   FICA-Social Security and FICA-Medicare taxes for the week?
   a) $31.00, $7.25   b) $310.00, $72.50
   c) $3.10, $0.73   d) $25.50, $8.00

Answer: (a)
   MC   Difficult

7.32: If Andy Cox's cumulative earnings prior to this pay period
   are $60,000 and his gross pay for the week is $1,000, what
   is his FICA-Social Security tax for this pay period?
   FICA-Social Security tax rate is 6.2% on $60,600.
   a) $37.20   b) $30.00   c) $0   d) $62.00

Answer: (a)
   MC   Moderate

7.33: If Jeff Crane's cumulative earnings before this pay period are $70,000 and he earned $500 this pay period, what amount will Jeff contribute to FICA? FICA tax rates are Social Security 6.2% on $60,600 and Medicare 1.45%.
    a) $32.05   b) $7.25
    c) $38.25   d) None of the above.

Answer: (b)
    MC   Moderate

7.34: Michael James earned $600 for the week. If his cumulative earnings are $53,000 prior to this pay period, how much FICA must his employer withhold from his earnings? FICA tax rates are Social Security 6.2% on $60,600 and Medicare 1.45%.
    a) $45.90   b) $33.50   c) $42.90   d) $0

Answer: (a)
    MC   Moderate

7.35: To compute FICA Social Security tax to be withheld:
    a) use the net earnings and number of allowances.
    b) use gross earnings, number of allowances, and marital status.
    c) use net earnings and form W-4.
    d) None of the above.

Answer: (d)
    MC   Moderate

7.36: Compute employee FICA taxes for the year on earnings of $42,000 at 6.2% Social Security and 1.45% Medicare.
    a) $3,213.00   b) $32,130.00
    c) $32,130.30   d) $321.30

Answer: (a)
    MC   Moderate

7.37: On January 7, 19xx, Earl Green earned $1,000 and has the following deductions: FICA: Social Security 6.2%, Medicare 1.45%; federal income tax $135.00; and state income tax $10.00. What is his net pay?
    a) $1,000.00   b) $878.50   c) $778.50   d) $645.00

Answer: (c)
    MC   Moderate

7.38: Allison Page earns $36,000 per year. What is her net pay for the month ended January 31, if FICA tax rates are 6.2% Social Security and 1.45% Medicare; federal income tax is 20%; and union dues are $100?
a) $2,680.10   b) $2,350.80   c) $2,070.50   d) $1,880.10

Answer: (c)
MC   Moderate

7.39: Posting the payroll entry comes from the:
a) payroll register.
b) journal.
c) employee's earnings record.
d) None of the above.

Answer: (b)
MC   Moderate

7.40: Compute net earnings on January 15, when total taxable pay equals $500.00. FICA Social Security tax rates are 6.2%, FICA Medicare rate is 1.45%, federal income tax $24.50, and state income tax $4.80.
a) $356.50   b) $432.45   c) $439.75   d) $463.55

Answer: (b)
MC   Moderate

7.41: What type of an account is Wages and Salaries Payable?
a) Asset   b) Liability   c) Revenue   d) Expense

Answer: (b)
MC   Moderate

7.42: The Office Salaries Expense account would be used to record:
a) net earnings for the office workers.
b) a credit to the amount owed to the office workers.
c) gross earnings for the office workers.
d) a debit for the amount of net pay owed to the office workers.

Answer: (c)
MC   Easy

7.43: Wages and Salaries Payable is:
a) debited when recording the payroll expense for the period.
b) debited when paying the employees at the end of the period.
c) credited when paying the employees at the end of the period.
d) an expense account.

Answer: (b)
MC   Moderate

7.44: What type of account is FICA-Social Security Tax Payable?
   a) Asset   b) Liability   c) Revenue   d) Expense

Answer: (b)
   MC   Easy

7.45: What type of account is FICA-Medicare Tax Payable?
   a) Asset   b) Liability   c) Revenue   d) Expense

Answer: (b)
   MC   Easy

7.46: What liability account is reduced when each employee is
   paid?
   a) Payroll Taxes Payable
   b) Federal Income Taxes Payable
   c) Wages and Salaries Expense
   d) Wages and Salaries Payable

Answer: (d)
   MC   Moderate

7.47: The employer records deductions from the employee's
   paycheck:
   a) as debits to expense accounts.
   b) as credits to liability accounts until paid.
   c) as debits to asset accounts until paid.
   d) as credits to capital accounts.

Answer: (b)
   MC   Moderate

7.48: A summary record of each person's earnings, deductions, and
   net pay is called:
   a) payroll register.
   b) W-4.
   c) employee individual earnings record.
   d) general journal.

Answer: (c)
   MC   Moderate

7.49: The amount of federal income tax withheld from an employee
   during the year is reported to the employee on a:
   a) W-4 form.   b) W-2 form.
   c) 1040 form.   d) 1099 form.

Answer: (b)
   MC   Moderate

7.50: The amount of FICA-Social Security and FICA-Medicare is
reported to the employee on a:
a) 1099 form   b) W-4   c) W-2   d) W-3

Answer: (c)
MC   Easy

7.51: Payroll is usually a minor expense in running a business.

Answer: False
TF   Moderate

7.52: The Fair Labor Standards Act is also called the Wages and
Hours Law.

Answer: True
TF   Moderate

7.53: Most high-level administrative employees are not exempt from
the Federal Wage and Hour Laws.

Answer: False
TF   Moderate

7.54: An allowance or exemption represents a certain amount of a
person's income that will be considered nontaxable.

Answer: True
TF   Moderate

7.55: Form W-4 is used in conjunction with FICA.

Answer: False
TF   Moderate

7.56: The wage bracket tables are found in Circular E of the
Employer's Tax Guide.

Answer: True
TF   Moderate

7.57: A worker can usually claim one allowance for him/herself.

Answer: True
TF   Easy

7.58: FICA-Social Security has no base limit.

Answer: False
TF   Moderate

7.59: FICA provides for medical benefits after age 65.

Answer: True
     TF Moderate

7.60: Medicare (hospital insurance) is not a part of FICA.

Answer: False
     TF Moderate

7.61: The two parts of FICA are Social Security (Old Age Survivors and Disability Insurance) and Medicare (hospital insurance).

Answer: True
     TF Moderate

7.62: The employer is required to pay for the cost of injury for the employee for nonrelated job accidents.

Answer: False
     TF Moderate

7.63: Workers' compensation insurance is to protect employees against losses due to injury or death incurred while on the job.

Answer: True
     TF Moderate

7.64: When an employee's earnings are greater than FICA base rate during the calendar year, no more FICA-Social Security tax is deducted from earnings.

Answer: True
     TF Moderate

7.65: A W-4 form and a Withholding Allowance Certificate are the same thing.

Answer: True
     TF Moderate

7.66: The more allowances a person claims, the less FICA tax paid.

Answer: False
     TF Difficult

7.67: All states use the same percent for the state tax rate.

Answer: False
TF Moderate

7.68: The amount of federal income tax withheld is less when more allowances are claimed.

Answer: True
TF Moderate

7.69: The payroll information for a pay period is found in the payroll register.

Answer: True
TF Moderate

7.70: Net pay and gross pay mean the same.

Answer: False
TF Moderate

7.71: Gross pay is the amount that the employee takes home.

Answer: False
TF Easy

7.72: Payroll Tax Payable is credited for the amount of net pay.

Answer: False
TF Moderate

7.73: Regular earnings are equal to total earnings less deductions.

Answer: False
TF Moderate

7.74: In the payroll register, the amount recorded in the taxable earnings: unemployment column is the tax being paid by the employer.

Answer: False
TF Difficult

7.75: In the payroll register, the amount recorded in the taxable earnings: FICA (Social Security and Medicare) column is the amount of earnings that will be taxed for FICA.

Answer: True
TF Difficult

7.76: The FICA tax rate has been the same for many years.

Answer: False
TF Easy

7.77: Like FICA-Social Security, the federal income tax has a cutoff point where there is no longer federal income tax withheld.

Answer: False
TF Moderate

7.78: The employee's individual earnings record contains the information about an employee's gross earnings, deductions, and net pay for each payroll period.

Answer: True
TF Moderate

7.79: A separate checking account for payroll may be maintained for larger firms.

Answer: True
TF Moderate

7.80: Calculate the total wages earned for each employee (assume an overtime rate of time and a half over 40 hours):

a. Diane Brown earns $12 per hour and worked 42 hours in one week.
b. Gene Corn earns $16 per hour and worked 48 hours in one week.

Answer: a. $516

b. $832
ES Moderate

7.81: Compute the net pay for each employee listed below. Assume FICA tax rate is: Social Security 6.2% on $60,600; Medicare 1.45%; federal income tax is 20%; state income tax is 5%; and union dues are $10.

	Cumulative Pay	This Week's Pay
C. Jones	$35,000	$1,000
K. Holmes	60,000	1,500

Answer: C. Jones $ 663.50
        K. Holmes $1,056.05
        ES   Moderate

7.82: Compute the net pay for each employee. FICA tax rate is: Social Security 6.2% on $60,600; Medicare 1.45%; federal income tax is 15%; state income tax is 5%; and medical insurance is $100 per employee.

	Cumulative Pay	This Week's Pay
Eric Ross	$63,000	$2,000
Tim Painter	51,000	3,000

Answer: Eric Ross Net Pay $1,471.00

        Tim Painter Net Pay $2,070.50

        ES   Moderate

7.83: From the following information, please complete the chart for gross earnings for the week. Assume an overtime rate of time and a half over 40 hours.

	Hourly Rate	No. of Hours Worked	Gross Earnings
Ron James	$7	44	_____
John David	8	35	_____
Jerry Charles	9	43	_____

Answer: Ron James gross pay   = $322.00

        John David gross pay   = $280.00

        Jerry Charles gross pay   = $400.50
        ES   Moderate

7.84: Dill Corporation records show the following information.

	Cumulative Earnings Before Payroll	Weekly Salary	Dept.
Paulette Lynn	$60,000	$1,000	Sales
Patricia Jean	40,000	2,000	Office
Polly Renee	65,000	1,900	Sales

Assume the following:
a. FICA: Social Security, 6.2% on $60,600; Medicare, 1.45%.
b. Each employee contributes $40 per week for union dues.
c. State income tax is 5% of gross pay.
d. Federal income tax is 20% of gross pay.

Prepare a general journal payroll entry.

Answer:		
Sales Salaries Expense	2,900	
Office Salaries Expense	2,000	
FICA-Social Security Pay.		161.20
FICA-Medicare Pay.		71.05
Federal Inc. Tax Pay.		980.00
State Inc. Tax Pay.		245.00
Union Dues Pay.		120.00
Salaries Pay.		3,322.75

ES Difficult

7.85: Prepare a general journal payroll entry for Lincoln Market using the following information.

	Cumulative Earnings Before Payroll	Weekly Salary	Dept.
Sam Evans	$20,000	$ 500	Office
Marianne Sall	40,000	800	Sales
Ben Jay	61,000	1,000	Office

Assume the following:
a. FICA: Social Security, 6.2% on $60,600; Medicare, 1.45%.
b. Federal income tax is 15% of gross pay.
c. Each employee pays $10 per week for medical insurance.

Answer:		
Office Salaries Expense	1,500	
Sales Salaries Expense	800	
FICA-Social Security Pay.		80.60
FICA-Medicare Pay.		33.35
Federal Inc. Tax Pay.		345.00
Medical Ins Pay.		30.00
Salaries Pay.		1,811.05

ES Difficult

7.86: Define and state the purpose of FICA.

Answer: Federal Insurance Contributions Act (FICA) helps fund the payments related to:
1. monthly retirement benefits for those over 62 years of age.
2. medical benefits after age 65.
3. benefits for workers who have become disabled.
4. benefits for families of deceased workers who were covered by the Federal Social Security Act.

Each year rates are set for Social Security. Employers must match the contributions of each employee. In 1994 the rate was set at 6.2 percent on $60,600. For Medicare the rate is 1.45 percent.
ES Moderate

7.87: What is the purpose of the Fair Labor Standards Act?

Answer: The purpose of the Fair Labor Standards Act is to set the regulations an employer must follow. Some of the regulations are:
a. A worker will receive a minimum hourly rate of pay, and the maximum number of hours a worker will work during a week at the regular rate of pay is 40 hours.

b. At least time and a half must be paid to the worker for hours worked in excess of 40 hours. Exceptions are employees of restaurants, hotels, and the like who have maximum hours of up to 44 before overtime pay is required.

c. The law also deals with minimum wage, child labor restrictions, and equal pay regardless of sex.
ES Moderate

8. The Employers's Tax Responsibilities: Principles...

8.1: Form SS-4 is used by the:
   a) employee to file state income tax returns.
   b) employer to file for an identification number.
   c) employer to file SUTA tax.
   d) employer to file FICA tax.

Answer: (b)
   MC   Moderate

8.2: The payroll taxes the employer is responsible for are:
   a) FICA, SUTA, and FUTA.
   b) FICA, FIT, and SIT.
   c) FICA, workers' compensation, and FIT.
   d) None of the above.

Answer: (a)
   MC   Moderate

8.3: FICA for the employer is calculated by:
   a) multiplying the individual earnings by the FICA tax
   rates.
   b) multiplying the Taxable Earnings: FICA columns by the
   FICA tax rates.
   c) using the charts provided.
   d) None of the above.

Answer: (b)
   MC   Easy

8.4: The Federal Unemployment Tax is:
   a) paid by the employers.
   b) paid by employees.
   c) paid by unemployed workers.
   d) All of the above.

Answer: (a)
   MC   Easy

8.5: FUTA tax is paid on the:
   a) first $52,000 of employee earnings.
   b) first $7,000 of employer earnings.
   c) first $52,000 of employer earnings.
   d) first $7,000 of employee earnings.

Answer: (d)
   MC   Moderate

8.6: Federal Unemployment Tax must be paid:
   a) quarterly when the amount owed is less than $100.00.
   b) monthly when the amount owed is greater than $100.00.
   c) yearly when the amount owed is greater than $100.00.
   d) quarterly when the amount owed is greater than $100.00.

Answer: (d)
   MC   Difficult

8.7: A merit-rating plan:
   a) creates ideal employee evaluation plans.
   b) raises unemployment rates substantially.
   c) is for responsible employees.
   d) reduces the employer's state unemployment tax rate if
   low unemployment is maintained.

Answer: (d)
   MC   Moderate

8.8: To compute the FICA tax owed by the employer, the employer
   would use the _____ columns of the payroll register:
   a) FICA-Social Security and FICA-Medicare Withholdings.
   b) FICA-Social Security and FICA-Medicare Expense.
   c) FIT Withholdings.
   d) FICA-Social Security and FICA-Medicare Taxable Earnings.

Answer: (d)
   MC   Moderate

8.9: Which of the following statements is false?
   a) Payroll Tax Expense is an expense account
   b) FICA-Social Security Tax Payable increases on the credit
   side of the account
   c) Payroll Tax Expense increases on the debit side of the
   account
   d) SUTA Tax Payable increases on the debit side of the
   account

Answer: (d)
   MC   Moderate

8.10: Federal tax deposits are:
   a) paid to an authorized commercial depository.
   b) paid to a Federal Reserve Bank.
   c) not paid directly to the IRS.
   d) All of the above.

Answer: (d)
   MC   Moderate

8.11: The IRS rule to determine whether an employer makes deposits monthly or semi-weekly for 941 taxes is called:
   a) look forward period rule.
   b) look back period rule.
   c) the eighth monthly period.
   d) None of the above.

Answer: (b)
   MC   Difficult

8.12: Which taxes are considered 941 taxes?
   a) FICA, FUTA, SUTA   b) FICA and SIT
   c) FICA and FIT   d) None of the above.

Answer: (c)
   MC   Moderate

8.13: Form 8109 is:
   a) a federal tax deposit coupon.
   b) used when paying SUTA tax.
   c) sent directly to the IRS.
   d) All of the above.

Answer: (a)
   MC   Difficult

8.14: The State Unemployment Tax Payable is:
   a) a liability account with a debit balance.
   b) an expense account with a debit balance.
   c) a liability account that increases on the credit side.
   d) an expense account that increases on the credit side.

Answer: (c)
   MC   Easy

8.15: Federal Unemployment Tax yearly report is:
   a) Form W-2.   b) Form 941.
   c) Form 940EZ.   d) Form W-3.

Answer: (c)
   MC   Easy

8.16: The Federal Income Tax withheld from employees and FICA Tax quarterly reporting form is:
   a) Form 940.   b) Form 941.
   c) Form W-4.   d) None of the above.

Answer: (b)
   MC   Moderate

8.17: The percentage of FICA-Medicare multiplied by taxable
      earnings on the 941 is:
      a) 12.4%.   b) 1.45%.   c) 6.2%.   d) 2.9%.

Answer: (d)
        MC   Moderate

8.18: Form 941 is filed:
      a) annually.
      b) quarterly.
      c) during an eighth-monthly period.
      d) All of the above depending on the amount owed.

Answer: (b)
        MC   Moderate

8.19: Which form is used to report FICA taxes for the employer and
      employee, and federal income taxes for the employee?
      a) Form 940EZ   b) Form 941
      c) Form W-4   d) None of the above

Answer: (b)
        MC   Easy

8.20: This form contains information about gross earnings and is
      given to the employee by January 31.
      a) Form W-2   b) Form W-3   c) Form SS-4   d) Form W-4

Answer: (a)
        MC   Moderate

8.21: This form is sent to the Social Security Administration by
      February 28. It reports total wages, FICA tax withheld,
      etc., for the previous year.
      a) Form W-2   b) Form W-3   c) Form SS-4   d) Form 940

Answer: (b)
        MC   Moderate

8.22: The employer's annual Federal Unemployment Tax return is:
      a) Form 940EZ.   b) Form 941.
      c) Form W-4.   d) Form 8109.

Answer: (a)
        MC   Moderate

8.23: Form 940 is filed:
   a) annually.
   b) quarterly.
   c) during an eighth-monthly period.
   d) All of the above depending on the amount owed.

Answer: (a)
   MC Moderate

8.24: FICA (Social Security and Medicare) and unemployment taxes
   are similar in that they:
   a) are both paid by the employee.
   b) have the same maximum taxable wage base.
   c) are a specified percent of federal income tax
   withholdings.
   d) are either totally or partially a tax expense to the
   employer.

Answer: (d)
   MC Moderate

8.25: Merit rating plans apply to:
   a) federal unemployment taxes.
   b) state unemployment taxes.
   c) FICA taxes.
   d) All of the above.

Answer: (b)
   MC Moderate

8.26: Payroll Tax Expense includes all the following except:
   a) FICA taxes (Social Security and Medicare).
   b) federal unemployment taxes.
   c) state unemployment taxes.
   d) federal and state income taxes.

Answer: (d)
   MC Moderate

8.27: The account for Payroll Tax Expense includes all of the
   following except:
   a) withholdings of taxes from all employees.
   b) FICA taxes (Social Security and Medicare) paid by the
   employer for the latest payroll period.
   c) unemployment taxes for the year to date.
   d) employer payroll taxes for the year to date.

Answer: (a)
   MC Moderate

8.28: Which of the following is a tax paid by both employee and employer?
   a) FICA taxes (Social Security and Medicare)
   b) FUTA tax
   c) Federal income tax
   d) Excise tax

Answer: (a)
   MC Moderate

8.29: An employee has gross earnings of $500 and withholdings of $37 FICA (Social Security and Medicare), and $50 for income taxes. The employer pays $37 for FICA (Social Security and Medicare), $10 for SUTA, and $4 for FUTA. The total cost of this employee to the employer is:
   a) $547.   b) $551.   c) $587.   d) $589.

Answer: (b)
   MC Difficult

8.30: JoLynne Thomas has gross earnings of $300 and withholdings of $20 for FICA (Social Security and Medicare) and $40 for income taxes. The employer pays $20 for FICA (Social Security and Medicare) and $2.40 for FUTA. The total cost for employee JoLynne Thomas incurred by the employer is:
   a) $342.40.   b) $300.00.   c) $322.40.   d) $325.00.

Answer: (c)
   MC Difficult

8.31: Reggie's earnings during the month of May were $2,000. His earnings for the year prior to May were $6,800. Reggie's employer is subject to federal unemployment taxes of 0.8% and state unemployment taxes of 5.4% on the first $7,000. The employer's unemployment payroll tax expense for the months prior to May and for the month of May respectively, are:
   a) $42.16 and $1.24.   b) $421.60 and $12.40.
   c) $421.60 and $1.24.   d) $421.60 and $124.

Answer: (b)
   MC Difficult

8.32: Jane's earnings during the month of March were $1,500. Her earnings for the year prior to March were $5,500. Jane's employer is subject to state unemployment of 2.0% and federal unemployment taxes of 0.8% on the first $7,000. The employer's unemployment payroll tax expense for the months prior to March and for the month of March respectively are:
   a) $154 and $42.   b) $154 and $56.40.
   c) $154 and $36.40.   d) $154 and $154.

Answer: (a)
   MC Difficult

8.33: The Night Watch Company payroll for June includes the following data:

Gross salaries $30,000

Salaries subject to FICA: 30,000

  6.2% Social Security

  1.45% Medicare

Salaries subject to:

  FUTA 0.8%   8,000

  SUTA 2.7%   8,000

The employer's payroll tax for the period would be:
a) $280.   b) $2,295.   c) $2,575.   d) $2,875.

Answer: (c)
MC   Moderate

8.34: Model Train Company's payroll for July includes the following data:

Gross salaries $40,000

Salaries subject to FICA:

  6.2% Social Security   35,000

  1.45% Medicare   40,000

Salaries subject to:

  0.8% FUTA   2,000

  2.0% SUTA   2,000

The employer's payroll tax for the period would be:
a) $2,096.   b) $2,226.   c) $3,206.   d) $2,806.

Answer: (d)
MC   Moderate

8.35: The general journal entry to record the monthly payroll tax would include:
a) a debit to Salaries Expense.
b) a credit to Salaries Payable.
c) a debit to Salaries Payable.
d) a debit to Payroll Tax Expense.

Answer: (d)
MC   Moderate

8.36: The entry to record the employer's payroll taxes would include:
a) a debit to Payroll Taxes Expense.
b) a credit to FICA-Social Security Taxes Payable and FICA-Medicare Taxes Payable.
c) a credit to State and Federal Unemployment Tax Payable.
d) All the above.

Answer: (d)
MC   Moderate

8.37: The entry to record the accrual of federal unemployment tax would include:
   a) a credit to FUTA Tax Payable.
   b) a debit to Federal Tax Expense.
   c) a credit to Payroll Tax Expense.
   d) None of the above.

Answer: (a)
   MC   Moderate

8.38: The entry to record the payroll taxes would include:
   a) a debit to Payroll Tax Expense.
   b) a debit to State Unemployment Taxes Payable.
   c) a debit to Salaries Payable.
   d) a debit to Salaries Expense for the net pay.

Answer: (a)
   MC   Moderate

8.39: The entry to record the payroll tax expense would include:
   a) a credit to Federal Income Taxes Payable.
   b) a credit to Cash.
   c) a credit to FICA (Social Security and Medicare) Taxes Payable.
   d) a credit to Wages Payable.

Answer: (c)
   MC   Moderate

8.40: The employer's total FICA, SUTA, and FUTA tax is recorded as:
   a) a debit to Payroll Tax Expense.
   b) a credit to Payroll Tax Expense.
   c) a credit to Payroll Tax Payable.
   d) a debit to Payroll Tax Payable.

Answer: (a)
   MC   Moderate

8.41: The entry to record the employer's payroll tax is:
   a) debit Payroll Taxes Payable, credit FICA (Social Security and Medicare), SUTA, FUTA Payable.
   b) debit Payroll Taxes Expense, credit FICA (Social Security and Medicare), FUTA, SUTA Payable.
   c) debit FICA (Social Security and Medicare), SUTA, FUTA Payable, credit Payroll Taxes Payable.
   d) debit FICA (Social Security and Medicare), SUTA, FUTA payable, credit Payroll Taxes Expense.

Answer: (b)
   MC   Moderate

8.42: The entry to record the payment of federal income taxes withheld from employees and FICA taxes would be:
a) credit Cash, debit FICA-Social Security Payable, FICA-Medicare Payable, and Federal Income Tax Payable.
b) debit Cash, credit FICA-Social Security Payable, FICA-Medicare Payable, and Federal Income Tax Payable.
c) credit Cash, credit FICA-Social Security Payable, FICA-Medicare Payable, and Federal Income Tax Payable.
d) None of the above.

Answer: (a)
MC   Moderate

8.43: When paying FUTA, the entry would be:
a) debit Cash, credit FUTA payable.
b) debit FUTA Expense, credit Cash.
c) debit FUTA Payable, credit Cash.
d) debit Cash, credit FUTA Expense.

Answer: (c)
MC   Moderate

8.44: When paying SUTA, the entry would be:
a) debit SUTA Expense, credit Cash.
b) debit Cash, credit SUTA Expense.
c) debit Cash, credit SUTA Payable.
d) debit SUTA Payable, credit Cash.

Answer: (d)
MC   Moderate

8.45: Russell Bear's cumulative earnings before this pay period were $6,200; gross for the week is $500. How much of this week's pay is subject to taxes for SUTA and FUTA? The rates are SUTA, 5.4% and FUTA, 0.8% with a base of $7,000.
  a) $300   b) $500   c) $6,700   d) $0

Answer: (b)
MC   Moderate

8.46: John Grey's cumulative earnings before this pay period were $6,900; gross pay for the week is $300. How much of this week's pay is subject to taxes for FUTA and SUTA?
  a) $300   b) $100   c) $0   d) $6,900

Answer: (b)
MC   Moderate

8.47: The premium for workers' compensation insurance is based on:
   a) cost of workers' compensation last year.
   b) actual payroll last year.
   c) actual payroll this year.
   d) None of the above.

Answer: (d)
   MC   Moderate

8.48: Workers' Compensation Insurance is:
   a) paid by the employer to protect the employee against
   job-related injury or death.
   b) paid by the employee to protect him/her against
   job-related accidents or death.
   c) paid by the employer to protect the employee against
   non-job-related injury or death.
   d) paid by the employee to protect him/her against
   non-job-related accidents and death.

Answer: (a)
   MC   Moderate

8.49: If Darin Manufacturing has the following two grades of
   workers, what is the estimated premium that Darin will need
   to pay?
         Office: $100,000 total payroll, premium rate $.15 per
                   $100 of gross pay.
         Factory: $200,000 total payroll, premium rate $.90 per
                   $100 of gross pay.
   a) $2,050.   b) $1,950.   c) $1,800.   d) $150.

Answer: (b)
   MC   Moderate

8.50: The journal entry to record the estimated advance premium
   payment for workers' compensation is:
   a) Cash
           Prepaid Insurance, Workers' Compensation
   b) Prepaid Insurance, Workers' Compensation
           Cash
   c) Workers' Compensation Insurance Expense
           Cash
   d) Workers' Compensation Insurance Payable
           Cash

Answer: (b)
   MC   Moderate

8.51: An SS-4 is used for the employer to secure a tax break.

Answer: False
   TF   Moderate

8.52: Payroll Tax Expense is the account the employer uses for the employer's payroll taxes (FICA, FUTA, and SUTA).

Answer: True
TF   Moderate

8.53: Taxable FICA Social Security and Medicare earnings * FICA rates = employer's FICA tax.

Answer: True
TF   Moderate

8.54: The Federal Unemployment Tax Act was established to allow the federal government to monitor state unemployment programs.

Answer: True
TF   Moderate

8.55: Generally, employers can take a credit against the FUTA tax for contributions paid into the state unemployment funds.

Answer: True
TF   Moderate

8.56: Maximum tax credit allowed against FUTA is 6.2%.

Answer: False
TF   Moderate

8.57: A merit-rating plan increases state unemployment tax rates no matter how infrequently unemployment occurs.

Answer: False
TF   Moderate

8.58: FUTA tax is generally paid monthly.

Answer: False
TF   Moderate

8.59: An employer can usually claim a credit on his/her state unemployment taxes for the amount of taxes paid to the federal fund.

Answer: False
TF   Moderate

8.60: Employers are responsible for deducting FUTA tax from the employees' earnings.

Answer: False
TF Moderate

8.61: Most states have a state unemployment tax of 7.65%.

Answer: False
TF Moderate

8.62: An employer can reduce the state unemployment tax rate by providing steady employment for the employees.

Answer: True
TF Moderate

8.63: When federal tax deposits are mailed within three days after the due date, they are considered to be late.

Answer: True
TF Moderate

8.64: The Payroll Tax Expense is recorded at the time the payroll is recorded.

Answer: True
TF Moderate

8.65: Businesses will make their payroll tax deposits either monthly or semi-weekly when paying Form 941 taxes.

Answer: True
TF Moderate

8.66: A deposit must be made when filing the W-2 form.

Answer: False
TF Moderate

8.67: Form 8109 is used to make deposits.

Answer: True
TF Moderate

8.68: Form 940EZ is used to file the annual FUTA tax report.

Answer: True
TF Moderate

8.69: The cost of worker's compensation insurance must be estimated and paid in advance by the employer.

Answer: True
    TF Moderate

8.70: The premium rate for workers' compensation is based on $100.00 of weekly payroll.

Answer: True
    TF Moderate

8.71: Each state is responsible for administering an unemployment program.

Answer: True
    TF Moderate

8.72: The W-2 is the Wage and Tax Statement.

Answer: True
    TF Easy

8.73: The individual employee earnings are summarized on the W-3 form.

Answer: True
    TF Moderate

8.74: The W-3 is also known as the Transmittal of Income and Tax Statements.

Answer: True
    TF Moderate

8.75: The W-3 is filed along with copies of the W-2 forms.

Answer: True
    TF Moderate

8.76: The 940 is filed quarterly.

Answer: False
    TF Moderate

8.77: 940 taxes can be deposited on Form 8109.

Answer: True
    TF Moderate

8.78: The balance due on Form 941 should never be more than $100.

Answer: False
　　　　TF Difficult

8.79: If an employee leaves an employer during the year, the employer must give a W-2 within 30 days of the request.

Answer: True
　　　　TF Difficult

8.80: Using the information below, determine the amount of the payroll tax expense for Forget's. In your answer list the amounts for FICA (Social Security and Medicare), SUTA, and FUTA.

Employee	Gross Pay
J. Gross	$1,000
P. James	500
Q. Quan	600

Assume: FICA tax rates are Social Security 6.2% and Medicare 1.45%; state unemployment tax rate is 5.0%; and federal unemployment tax rate is 0.8%. All employees have earned less than $7,000.

Answer:

FICA-Social Security	$130.20
FICA-Medicare	30.45
SUTA	105.00
FUTA	16.80

	$282.45
	=======

　　　ES Moderate

8.81: Using the information provided below, prepare a journal entry to record the payroll tax expense for Russ' Pottery.

Employee	Gross Pay	Cumulative Earnings Prior to this Payroll
Site	$600	$20,000
Byte	500	4,000
Light	700	70,000

Assume: FICA tax rates are Social Security 6.2% on $60,600 and Medicare 1.45%; state unemployment tax rate is 2%; and federal unemployment tax rate is 0.8%, both on the first $7,000.

Answer:

Payroll Tax Expense	108.30	
FICA-Social Security Payable		68.20
FICA-Medicare Payable		26.10
SUTA Tax Payable		10.00
FUTA Tax Payable		4.00

　　ES Difficult

8.82: Information for Las Vegas Laundry Company for the first week in November is as follows:

Employees' gross wages	$100,000
Taxable earning for FICA-	
Social Security	70,000
Medicare	100,000
Taxable earning subject to federal and state unemployment taxes	20,000
Federal income tax withheld	20,000

Assume the following tax rates:

FICA: Social Security	6.2% on	$60,600
FICA: Medicare	1.45%	
Federal unemployment	0.8% on	$7,000
State unemployment	2.0% on	$7,000

Required: Prepare the following journal entries for the period:

    a. The payroll entry.
    b. The payroll expense entry.

Answer: a.

Salaries Expense	100,000	
FICA-Social Security Pay		4,340
FICA-Medicare Pay		1,450
Federal Inc. Tax Pay		20,000
Salaries Pay		74,210

    b.

Payroll Tax Expense	6,350	
FICA-Social Security Pay		4,340
FICA-Medicare Pay		1,450
SUTA Tax Pay		400
FUTA Tax Pay		160

ES Moderate

8.83: McEnroe Shoes payroll data for the second week of October includes the following:

Employees' gross earnings	$200,000
Taxable earnings for FICA:	
Social Security	150,000
Medicare	200,000
Taxable earnings for federal	
and state unemployment taxes	10,000

Assume the following tax rates:

FICA: Social Security	6.2% on	$60,600
Medicare	1.45%	
Federal unemployment	0.8% on	$7,000
State unemployment	1.5% on	$7,000
Federal income tax	20.0 percent	

Required: Prepare the general journal entries to record:
    a. Payroll for the period.
    b. Employer's payroll taxes.

Answer: a.

Salaries Expense	200,000	
FICA-Social Security Pay		9,300
FICA-Medicare Pay		2,900
Fed. Inc. Tax Pay		40,000
Salaries Pay		147,800

b.

Payroll Tax Expense	12,430	
FICA-Social Security Pay		9,300
FICA-Medicare Pay		2,900
SUTA Tax Pay		150
FUTA Tax Pay		80

ES Moderate

8.84: From the following data, determine the FUTA tax liability for Basil Company for the first quarter of 19xx. FUTA tax rate is 0.8% on the first $7,000 of earnings. Assume all quarters have the same number of pay periods.

Employees	Gross Pay Per Week
J. Kline	$600
P. Ross	300
R. Jones	800

Answer:

J. Kline	$ 7,000
P. Ross	3,900
R. Jones	7,000

	$17,900 * 0.8% = $143.20
	=======

ES Difficult

155

8.85: Record in general journal the payroll tax entry for the week ended July 3, 19xx. Use the following information gathered to make the entry for Tasty Company.

Employee	Cumulative Earnings Before Weekly Payroll	Gross Pay For Week
J. Iris	$8,000	500
L. Rose	6,800	300
A. Lilly	6,000	200

FICA tax rate is Social Security 6.2% on $60,600, and Medicare 1.45%. Federal unemployment is 0.8% on $7,000. The merit rating for Tasty Company is 5.6%.

Answer: Payroll Tax Expense   102.10
          FICA-Social Security Pay   62.00
          FICA-Medicare Pay   14.50
          FUTA Tax Pay   3.20
          SUTA Tax Pay   22.40
       ES Moderate

8.86: From the following data, estimate the annual advance premium for workers' insurance and record it in general journal form.

Type of Work	Estimated Payroll	Rate per $100
Office	$40,000	$ .18
Factory	60,000	1.60
Sales	30,000	1.00

Answer: Prepaid Workers' Compensation Insurance   1,332
           Cash   1,332
       ES Moderate

8.87: Estimate the annual advance premium for workers' compensation insurance and record it in general journal form using the following data provided.

Type of Work	Estimated Payroll	Rate Per $100
Sales	$10,000	$1.10
Office	5,000	.25
Nursing Staff	80,000	2.00

Answer: Prepaid Workers' Compensation Ins.   1,722.50
           Cash   1,722.50
       ES Moderate

8.88: Explain the purpose of workers' compensation and discuss the premium cost to the employer.

Answer: Workers' Compensation is insurance provided by an employer to protect its employees against loss due to injury or death related to employment. The premium of workers' compensation insurance is based on the total estimated gross payroll and the rate is determined by past injury experience in that type of position. The rate stated per $100 of payroll is then multiplied by the estimated gross payroll. At the end of the year, if the estimated amount is not equal to the actual amount, an adjustment is made.
ES Moderate

8.89: The Uptown Bank Credit Card Company has a significant increase in business each spring-due to a large increase in new applicants from graduating college students. Each spring, subsequently, 50 temporary workers are hired for a 12-week period, working 40 hours per week at $7 per hour, and then they are laid off. Uptown's permanent employment total is 500 workers. Because of these yearly layoffs, Uptown's state unemployment merit tax rate is 9%. If the number of layoffs could be reduced, the merit tax rate could be reduced to 4.1%.

As the payroll specialist for Uptown, you have been asked to evaluate the following:
1. Should Uptown stop hiring temporary employees and ask its full time workers to work overtime to handle the extra load?
2. Should Uptown get its temporary employees from a temporary employment agency and therefore not be subject to the extra taxes?
What information would you need to evaluate the above?

Answer: 1. Use regular employees on overtime basis:
a. Would regular employees be willing to work the overtime hours?
b. What would be the total additional cost (regular pay plus overtime pay to use regular workers?)
c. What is the total cost of using temporary employees? (Hourly wages plus benefits plus increase in taxes over the lower amount.)
d. What is the continuing availability of quality temporary workers? What training would have to be provided? What is the cost of training?

2. Use temporary employment agency:
a. What is the total cost of using the agency? (Worker's hourly wage plus fee charged by the agency.)
b. What is the availability of quality workers through the agency?
c. What training would have to be provided?
d. What is the cost of training?
ES Difficult

9. Special Journals: Sales and Cash Receipts

9.1: Generally, the revenue account for a merchandising firm is:
    a) Gross Profit.   b) Gross Sales.
    c) Net Sales.   d) Sales.

Answer: (d)
    MC   Easy

9.2: Merchandise companies that buy goods from manufacturers or suppliers for resale to other sellers are:
    a) wholesalers.
    b) independent purchasing agents.
    c) retailers.
    d) conglomerates.

Answer: (a)
    MC   Easy

9.3: Merchandise companies that buy goods from wholesalers for resale to consumers are:
    a) wholesalers.
    b) independent purchasing agents.
    c) retailers.
    d) conglomerates.

Answer: (c)
    MC   Easy

9.4: The total of all cash and credit sales equals:
    a) gross sales.   b) net sales.
    c) net income.   d) gross profit.

Answer: (a)
    MC   Easy

9.5: Gross sales equals:
    a) net sales plus gross profit.
    b) gross profit less net income.
    c) the total of cash and credit sales.
    d) net income plus gross profit.

Answer: (c)
    MC   Easy

9.6: Which account is a contra revenue account with a debit balance for returned goods?
   a) Sales Returns and Allowances
   b) Sales Discount
   c) Credit period
   d) Discount period

Answer: (a)
   MC   Easy

9.7: Which account is used by management to keep track of customer dissatisfaction?
   a) Sales Returns and Allowances
   b) Sales Discount
   c) Sales
   d) Cost of Goods Sold

Answer: (a)
   MC   Easy

9.8: Which contra revenue account has a debit balance and is used to record cash discounts for early payment by a customer?
   a) Sales Returns and Allowances
   b) Sales Discount
   c) Sales
   d) Cost of Goods Sold

Answer: (b)
   MC   Easy

9.9: The period of time customers are allowed to pay their bills and still be eligible for a discount is the:
   a) credit period.   b) discount period.
   c) closing period.   d) due date.

Answer: (b)
   MC   Moderate

9.10: The amount of time the customer is allowed to repay the bill is the:
   a) discount period.   b) closing period.
   c) credit period.   d) due date.

Answer: (c)
   MC   Moderate

9.11: The credit period is the:
   a) opening date.
   b) days allowed for the customer to pay the bill.
   c) discount period.
   d) closing date.

Answer: (b)
   MC   Easy

9.12: Credit terms of n/10, EOM means that:
a) if the bill is paid by the end of the month, a discount will be granted.
b) the bill is due 10 days before the end of the month.
c) if the bill is paid 10 days after the end of the month, a discount is allowed.
d) the bill is due 10 days after the end of the month and no discount is allowed.

Answer: (d)
MC Moderate

9.13: Credit terms of 1/10, n/30 mean that:
a) 1% discount is allowed if the bill is paid within 10 days, or the entire amount is due within 30 days.
b) a discount is allowed if the bill is paid within 30 days.
c) a discount is allowed if the bill is paid after 10 days
d) a 1% discount is allowed if the customer pays the bill within 30 days.

Answer: (a)
MC Moderate

9.14: Sales discounts are allowed only on:
a) credit sales to customers.
b) freight.
c) sales tax.
d) All of the above.

Answer: (a)
MC Moderate

9.15: Sales discount is computed on:
a) sales to customers.   b) sales tax and freight.
c) returned merchandise.   d) All of the above.

Answer: (a)
MC Moderate

9.16: The total reached after subtracting sales returns and allowances and sales discounts is called:
a) net purchases.   b) sales.
c) net sales.   d) sales returns.

Answer: (c)
MC Easy

9.17: The normal balance of the sales discount account is:
   a) a debit.
   b) a credit.
   c) it doesn't have a normal balance.
   d) zero.

Answer: (a)
   MC   Moderate

9.18: The normal balance of the sales returns and allowances account is:
   a) a debit.
   b) a credit.
   c) zero.
   d) it does not have a normal balance.

Answer: (a)
   MC   Easy

9.19: An advantage of using special journals is to:
   a) decrease recordings.
   b) group similar transactions.
   c) decrease posting.
   d) All of the above.

Answer: (d)
   MC   Moderate

9.20: Accounts of a single type are kept in this ledger:
   a) supplemental ledger.   b) additional ledger.
   c) subsidiary ledger.   d) None of the above.

Answer: (c)
   MC   Moderate

9.21: When using a subsidiary ledger, the Accounts Receivable account in the general ledger is called the:
   a) master account.   b) subsidiary account.
   c) receivable account.   d) controlling account.

Answer: (d)
   MC   Easy

9.22: When merchandise is sold on account, it would be recorded in the:
   a) cash receipts journal.   b) purchases journal.
   c) sales journal.   d) cash payments journal.

Answer: (c)
   MC   Easy

9.23: The sales journal is used for:
   a) recording cash receipts.
   b) recording purchases of merchandise.
   c) recording credit sales.
   d) recording cash sales.

Answer: (c)
   MC   Easy

9.24: When a customer pays on account, the transaction would be
      recorded in the:
   a) cash receipts journal.   b) purchases journal.
   c) sales journal.   d) cash payments journal.

Answer: (a)
   MC   Easy

9.25: Recording to the accounts receivable ledger is done:
   a) daily.   b) monthly.
   c) when completed.   d) when requested.

Answer: (a)
   MC   Moderate

9.26: The purpose of the accounts receivable subsidiary ledger is:
   a) to help manage the accounts of multiple credit
      customers.
   b) to keep a running balance of each customer's account.
   c) to provide supporting information for the general ledger
      control account.
   d) All of the above.

Answer: (d)
   MC   Moderate

9.27: Sales Tax Payable is a:
   a) liability account with a debit balance.
   b) liability account with a credit balance.
   c) contra asset account with a debit balance.
   d) contra asset account with a credit balance.

Answer: (b)
   MC   Easy

9.28: Sales Returns and Allowances is a:
   a) revenue account with a credit balance.
   b) cost of goods sold account with a debit balance.
   c) contra revenue account with a debit balance.
   d) contra revenue account with a credit balance.

Answer: (c)
   MC   Moderate

9.29: This form is used to inform customers that the amount of goods returned or amount allowed for damages has been deducted:
  a) debit memorandum.
  b) credit memorandum.
  c) credit document.
  d) credit allowance.

Answer: (b)
  MC   Easy

9.30: A credit memorandum is sent to a customer for the purpose of:
  a) informing the customer an amount has been deducted from the account.
  b) informing the customer an amount has been added to the account.
  c) both (a) and (b).
  d) neither (a) nor (b).

Answer: (a)
  MC   Moderate

9.31: A listing of customers and their ending balances is called:
  a) a list of the receivables.
  b) a schedule of accounts receivable.
  c) a customer list.
  d) a chart of customers.

Answer: (b)
  MC   Easy

9.32: Barbara's Bakery reports net sales of $15,000. If Sales Returns and Allowances are $1,500 and Sales Discounts are $150, what are gross sales?
  a) $13,000   b) $13,350   c) $16,650   d) $13,500

Answer: (c)
  MC   Moderate

9.33: Cris Car Dealership reports gross sales of $25,000. If Sales Returns and Allowances are $1,200 and Sales Discounts are $800, what are the net sales?
  a) $23,000   b) $27,000   c) $26,200   d) $25,000

Answer: (a)
  MC   Easy

9.34: Flat Tire Company sold $200 of tires to a charge customer, terms 2/10, n/30. Which entry is required to record this transaction?
   a) Debit Cash for $194, credit Tire Sales for $194
   b) Debit Accounts Receivable for $200, credit Tire Sales for $200
   c) Debit Accounts Receivable for $194, debit Sales Discount for $6, and credit Tire Sales for $200
   d) Debit Accounts Receivable for $204, credit Tire Sales for $204

Answer: (b)
   MC   Easy

9.35: Flora's Flowers sold a $50 bouquet to a charge customer, terms 2/10, n/30. Flora should record this transaction as follows:
   a) debit Cash $50; credit Sales $50.
   b) debit Accounts Receivable $50; credit Sales $50.
   c) debit Accounts Receivable $49; debit Sales Discounts $1; credit Sales $50.
   d) debit Sales $50; credit Accounts Receivable $50.

Answer: (a)
   MC   Easy

9.36: Gina's Flower Shop received payment in full for goods sold within the discount period on a $1,000 sales invoice, terms 1/10, n/30. Which entry records this transaction?
   a) Debit Accounts Receivable, credit Flower Sales for $1,000
   b) Debit Cash, credit Accounts Receivable for $990
   c) Debit Cash for $990, debit Sales Discount for $10, and credit Accounts Receivable for $1,000
   d) Debit Cash for $990, debit Sales Discount for $10, and credit Flower Sales for $1,000

Answer: (c)
   MC   Moderate

9.37: Mary's Antique Shop sold goods for $400 plus 5% sales tax to a charge customer, terms n/30. Which entry is required to record this transaction?
   a) Debit Accounts Receivable, credit Antique Sales for $420
   b) Debit Cash for $400, and credit Antique Sales for $400
   c) Debit Accounts Receivable for $400, credit Antique Sales for $400
   d) Debit Accounts Receivable, $420, credit Sales Tax Payable, $20, and credit Antique Sales, $400

Answer: (d)
   MC   Difficult

9.38: Peter Strong Company received payment in full within the credit period for goods sold for $400 plus 5 percent sales tax. Terms of the sale were n/30. Which entry is required to record this transaction?
  a) Debit Accounts Receivable 400, credit Sales, $420
  b) Debit Cash, $400, credit Sales, $400
  c) Debit Cash, $400, credit Sales, $420.
  d) Debit Cash, $420, credit Accounts Receivable, $420.

Answer: (d)
  MC Difficult

9.39: P. Panda Shop sold goods for $300 to a charge customer. The customer returned for credit $120 worth of goods. Which entry is required to record the return transaction?
  a) Debit Sales Returns and Allowances $120, credit Accounts Receivable for $120
  b) Debit Sales Returns and Allowances for $120, credit Sales for $120
  c) Debit Sales $120, credit Sales Returns and Allowances $120
  d) Debit Accounts Receivable, credit Sales Returns and Allowances for $120

Answer: (a)
  MC Moderate

9.40: Molly's Craft Shop sold goods for $450 to a charge customer. The customer returned for credit $100 worth of goods. Terms of the sale were 2/10, n/30. If the customer pays the amount within the discount period, what is the amount the customer should pay?
  a) $441   b) $450   c) $350   d) $343

Answer: (d)
  MC Moderate

9.41: Sam Abels returned $100 of merchandise to Boost Buy Company. His original purchase was $400, with terms 2/10, n/30. If Sam pays the balance of his account within the discount period, how much should he pay?
  a) $294   b) $292   c) $300   d) $306

Answer: (a)
  MC Moderate

9.42: Which of the following is a reason for a business to use special journals?
   a) It is more efficient and less time consuming to separate transactions into special journals and record each type in its own journal.
   b) A business saves time in posting.
   c) It is possible to use several different people to journalize and do the necessary postings.
   d) All of the above.

Answer: (d)
   MC   Easy

9.43: Which of the following statements about subsidiary ledgers is most accurate?
   a) The subsidiary ledger accounts will never equal the control account in the general ledger.
   b) The accounts receivable ledger is a book of accounts that provides supporting detail for Accounts Receivable.
   c) The subsidiary ledger accounts will equal the amount in the Sales account.
   d) None of the above.

Answer: (b)
   MC   Moderate

9.44: Benny's Violin Company sold goods to a charge customer. The transaction would be recorded in:
   a) the cash receipts journal.
   b) the general journal.
   c) the sales journal.
   d) some other journal.

Answer: (c)
   MC   Easy

9.45: Pipefitting Company accepted the return of goods previously sold to a charge customer. The transaction would be recorded in:
   a) the cash receipts journal.
   b) the general journal.
   c) the sales journal.
   d) some other journal.

Answer: (b)
   MC   Easy

9.46: Jolly Giant accepted the return of goods from a customer. The transaction would be recorded in:
   a) the cash receipts journal.
   b) the general journal.
   c) the sales journal.
   d) some other journal.

Answer: (b)
   MC   Easy

9.47: Patty Cakes Company received a payment for one-half of the amount owed from a charge customer. The transaction would be recorded in:
   a) the cash receipts journal.
   b) the general journal.
   c) the sales journal.
   d) some other journal.

Answer: (a)
   MC   Easy

9.48: Accounts Receivable would appear as a credit in the:
   a) cash receipts journal.
   b) cash disbursement journal.
   c) sales journal.
   d) None of the above.

Answer: (a)
   MC   Easy

9.49: Sales Discounts would appear as a debit in:
   a) the cash receipts journal.
   b) the general journal.
   c) the sales journal.
   d) some other journal.

Answer: (a)
   MC   Moderate

9.50: Cash would appear in the credit column in:
   a) the cash receipts journal.
   b) the general journal.
   c) the sales journal.
   d) some other journal.

Answer: (d)
   MC   Easy

9.51: Sales discounts are usually not an incentive for the customer to pay early.

Answer: False
   TF   Easy

9.52: The normal balance of Sales Discounts is a credit.

Answer: False
      TF Easy

9.53: Sales Returns and Allowances provide a record of customers' dissatisfaction.

Answer: True
      TF Easy

9.54: Gross Sales equals all the cash and credit sales made by a business for a specific period.

Answer: True
      TF Moderate

9.55: The Sales Returns and Allowances account could be used by management to determine if customers were returning goods at a higher rate than usual.

Answer: True
      TF Moderate

9.56: Sales Discounts is a contra revenue account with a debit balance that accumulates the cash discounts customers are granted.

Answer: True
      TF Difficult

9.57: The time a customer is granted to pay the bill is the discount period.

Answer: False
      TF Easy

9.58: Terms of 2/10, n/30 means that a customer is allowed a 10% discount in 30 days.

Answer: False
      TF Easy

9.59: Credit terms whereby the customer is granted credit until the 10th day of the following month are n/10, EOM.

Answer: True
      TF Moderate

9.60: Credit terms remain the same from company to company.

Answer: False
TF Moderate

9.61: All customers always take cash discounts when available.

Answer: False
TF Moderate

9.62: Net Sales is computed by adding Gross Sales, Sales
Discounts, and Sales Returns and Allowances.

Answer: False
TF Moderate

9.63: Credit terms of 3/10 permit the customer to deduct 3% of the
sale if payment is made within 10 days.

Answer: True
TF Easy

9.64: Gross profit equals gross sales minus total expenses.

Answer: False
TF Moderate

9.65: Cash receipts are recorded in the Sales Journal.

Answer: False
TF Easy

9.66: All merchandise firms are required to use special journals
under GAAP.

Answer: False
TF Moderate

9.67: Firms that use special journals can eliminate the general
journal.

Answer: False
TF Difficult

9.68: A special journal requires more posting than the general
journal because the general journal has special column
totals.

Answer: False
TF Moderate

9.69: The controlling account is found in the subsidiary ledger and it summarizes or controls the general ledger account.

Answer: False
    TF Moderate

9.70: Two examples of subsidiary ledgers are the accounts receivable ledger and the accounts payable ledger.

Answer: True
    TF Easy

9.71: A special ledger for the controlling account in the general ledger would be called a subsidiary ledger.

Answer: True
    TF Easy

9.72: Accounts in the accounts receivable subsidiary ledger are usually organized alphabetically.

Answer: True
    TF Easy

9.73: When merchandise is sold on account, the transaction is recorded in the cash receipts journal.

Answer: False
    TF Moderate

9.74: A controlling account is a listing of all the customers and the account balances.

Answer: False
    TF Moderate

9.75: A sales invoice is a bill for the sale.

Answer: True
    TF Easy

9.76: Recording to the accounts receivable ledger should be performed at the end of the month.

Answer: False
    TF Moderate

9.77: Posting to the general ledger from the special journals should be done at the end of the month.

Answer: True
TF   Moderate

9.78: Sales Tax Payable is an owner's equity account with a credit balance.

Answer: False
TF   Moderate

9.79: All receipts of cash should be recorded in the Cash Receipts Journal.

Answer: True
TF   Easy

9.80: Proving the accuracy of the transactions in the special journals is done by crossfootings.

Answer: True
TF   Moderate

9.81: Match the following terms with their definitions or descriptions.

1. _____ Accounts receivable subsidiary ledger
2. _____ Cash receipts journal
3. _____ Controlling account-Accounts Receivable
4. _____ Credit memorandum
5. _____ Credit period
6. _____ Discount period
7. _____ Gross sales

a. The revenue earned from the sale of merchandise to customers.
b. The process of proving the total debit and credit columns of a special journal.
c. A business form sent to a customer indicating the seller is reducing the amount owed.
d. A special journal that records all receipts of cash.
e. A period shorter than the credit period to encourage early payment by customers.
f. Length of time allowed for payment of goods sold on account.
g. The Accounts Receivable account in the general ledger.
h. A book or file of the individual records of amounts owed by credit customers.

Answer: 1. h   5. f
2. d   6. b
3. g   7. e
4. c   8. a

ES   Moderate

9.82: Match the following with their definitions or descriptions.
1. _____ Merchandise
2. _____ Net Sales
3. _____ Retailers
4. _____ Sales discount
5. _____ Sales invoice
6. _____ Sales journal
7. _____ Sales Returns and Allowances
8. _____ Special journal
9. _____ Subsidiary ledger
10. _____ Sundry

a. Miscellaneous accounts columns in a special journal.
b. A journal used to record similar kinds of transactions.
c. Contra revenue account for price adjustments allowed to customers.
d. The bill sent to a customer requesting payment for a sale on credit.
e. Buy goods from wholesalers for resale to customers.
f. Goods available for resale to customers.
g. Gross sales less returns and sales discounts.
h. Contra revenue account that records discounts granted to customers for early payment.
i. A special journal used to record sales made on credit.
j. A ledger that contains accounts of a single type, such as the accounts receivable subsidiary ledger.

Answer: 1. f   6. i
        2. g   7. c
        3. e   8. b
        4. h   9. j
        5. d   10. a

ES Moderate

9.83: Use the following information to answer the questions below:

Sales $20,000
Sales Discount   200
Sales Returns and Allowances   1,000
Purchases Returns and Allow.   50

a. The Net Sales are _____.

Answer: a. $18,800

ES Easy

173

9.84: Match the following to the four journal entries. Each entry may have more than one number, and can be used more than once.
1. Journalized into Sales Journal.
2. Journalized into Cash Receipts Journal.
3. Record immediately to Subsidiary Ledger.
4. Record in General Journal.

a. _____ Sold merchandise on account to P. Holmes.
b. _____ Received check from P. Holmes.
c. _____ Cash sales.
d. _____ Issued credit memorandum to S. Mitchell.

Answer: a. 1,3
b. 2,3
c. 2
d. 4,3

ES Easy

9.85: Finch Furniture Company sold K. Daniels a bedroom set for $2,500 plus sales tax of 6%. Terms of the sale are 1/10, n/30. Date of the sale was May 22, date of the payment was June 1.

Required: Determine the amount K. Daniels should pay Finch Furniture on June 1. Show your computations.

$ _____

Answer: $2,625
ES Moderate

9.86: Morris Jewelry Store sold R. Alexander a diamond engagement ring for $2,000 plus sales tax of 5%. Terms of the sale are n/30. Date of the sale was April 12, date of the payment was May 12. On April 15, R. Alexander received an allowance for a flaw in the ring, $500.

Required: Determine the amount R. Alexander should pay Morris Jewelry Store on May 12.

$_____

Answer: $1,575
ES Difficult

9.87: The following are selected transactions for M. Thorp. For each transaction indicate the account(s) to be debited and the account(s) to be credited. Also indicate in which of the following journals each transaction will be recorded: Sales Journal (S), Cash Receipts Journal (CR), or General Journal (GJ).

Account(s) Debit	Account(s) Credit	Journal		
_____	_____	_____	a.	Sold merchandise on account to S. Book.
_____	_____	_____	b.	M. Thorp invested additional cash in the business.
_____	_____	_____	c.	Received payment from S. Book. No discount was given.
_____	_____	_____	d.	Made a cash sale.
_____	_____	_____	e.	Accepted a return from T. Mills for credit.

Answer:

	Debit	Credit	Journal
a.	Accts. Rec./ S. Book	Sales	S
b.	Cash	M. Thorp, Cap.	CR
c.	Cash	Accts. Rec./ S. Book	CR
d.	Cash	Sales	CR
e.	Sales Returns and Allowances	Accts. Rec./ T. Mills	GJ

ES   Moderate

175

9.88: The following are selected transactions for B. Simms. For each transaction indicate the account(s) to be debited and the account(s) to be credited. Also indicate in which of the following journals each transaction will be recorded: Sales Journal (S), Cash Receipts Journal (CR), or General Journal (GJ).

Account(s) Debit	Account(s) Credit	Journal		
============	==========	=======		
_____	_____	_____	a.	Sold store supplies for cash to A. Cate as a special service.
_____	_____	_____	b.	B. Simms invested additional cash in the business.
_____	_____	_____	c.	Sold merchandise to J. Kate on account.
_____	_____	_____	d.	Made a cash sale.
_____	_____	_____	e.	Accepted a return from J. Kate for credit.
_____	_____	_____	f.	Received payment in full from J. Kate.

Answer:

	Debit	Credit	Journal
a.	Cash	Supplies	CR
b.	Cash	B. Simms, Cap.	CR
c.	Accts. Rec./ J. Kate	Sales	S
d.	Cash	Sales	CR
e.	Sales Returns and Allowances	Acct. Rec./ J. Kate	GJ
f.	Cash	Acct. Rec./ J. Kate	CR

ES Moderate

9.89: The following is a list of columns from the cash receipts journal and the sales journal.
   a. Accounts Receivable Credit
   b. Accounts Receivable Debit
   c. Sales Credit
   d. Cash Debit
   e. Sundry Credit
   f. Sales Discount Debit
   g. Sales Tax Payable Credit

Required: 1. Indicate the column letter each of the following transactions would use.
2. Indicate in which journal the transactions would be recorded by placing an (S) for Sales Journal, and a (CR) for Cash Receipts Journal.

Column(s)   Journal
==========   =======

_____ _____ 1. Bill Bark invested $8,000 in his company.
_____ _____ 2. Cash sales amounted to $5,000.
_____ _____ 3. Sold merchandise on account, $300 plus sales tax.
_____ _____ 4. Received cash payment from charge customer, no discount.
_____ _____ 5. Received cash payment from charge customer, less discount.

Answer: **Column(s)   Journal**
             =========   =======
   1.   d, e   CR
   2.   d, c   CR
   3.   b, c, g   S
   4.   d, a   CR
   5.   d, f, a   CR

ES Difficult

177

9.90: The following is a list of columns from the cash receipts journal, sales journal, and general journal.
  a. Accounts Receivable Credit
  b. Accounts Receivable Debit
  c. Sales Credit
  d. Cash Debit
  e. Sundry Credit
  f. Sales Discount Debit
  g. Sales Tax Payable Credit
  h. Debit Column, General Journal
  i. Credit Column, General Journal

Required:
1. Indicate the column letter each of the following transactions would use.
2. Indicate in which journal the transaction would be recorded by placing an (S) for Sales Journal, a (CR) for Cash Receipts Journal, and a (GJ) General Journal.

Column(s)	Journal	
_____	_____	1. Sold equipment to Sam for $5,000 cash.
_____	_____	2. Sold merchandise on account, $600 plus sales tax.
_____	_____	3. Cash sales $400, not subject to sales tax.
_____	_____	4. Customer returned $200 of goods from transaction 2.
_____	_____	5. Received cash payment from charge customer less discount. See transactions 2 and 4.

Answer:

	Column(s)	Journal
1.	d, e	CR
2.	b, g, c	S
3.	d, c	CR
4.	h, i	GJ
5.	d, a, f	CR

ES Difficult

178

9.91: Define and compare the accounts receivable ledger with the controlling account, Accounts Receivable.

Answer: Accounts receivable ledger is a group of accounts that contains, in alphabetical order, the individual records of amounts owed by various credit customers. Daily postings are made to the customer's account updating the current balances.

Accounts Receivable controlling account, located in the general ledger, shows a firm the total amount of money owed to it. Monthly postings are made to the account.

Both the accounts receivable ledger and the controlling account, Accounts Receivable, are reconciled at the end of the month by preparing a schedule of accounts receivable.
ES Moderate

9.92: Compare a discount period and a credit period.

Answer: Credit period is the length of time allowed for payment of goods sold on account. Customers are encouraged to pay their bills within this time frame to maintain a good credit rating.

Discount period is shorter than the credit period to encourage early payment of bills. Customers are given an incentive to make payments shortly after invoicing.

Terms such as 2/10, n/30 demonstrate the discount period and the credit period. The discount period is 10 days and the credit period is 30 days. If the customer pays the bill within 10 days, the customer will receive a 2% discount or if the customer pays the bill within 30 days, a good credit will be maintained.
ES Moderate

10. Special Journals: Purchases and Cash Payments

10.1: Foung brings merchandise into his clothing store for resale to customers. Which journal would Foung use to record this transaction if the merchandise was acquired on credit?
a) Sales
b) Cash Payments
c) Purchases
d) Cash Receipts

Answer: (c)
MC   Easy

10.2: What type of account is Purchases?
a) Liability   b) Revenue   c) Asset   d) Cost

Answer: (d)
MC   Easy

10.3: What type of account is Purchases Returns and Allowances?
a) Liability
b) Asset
c) Contra cost
d) Contra revenue

Answer: (c)
MC   Easy

10.4: If Foung sends back damaged merchandise for credit, it would be a:
a) Sales Returns and Allowances.
b) Sales Discounts.
c) Purchases Discounts.
d) Purchases Returns and Allowances.

Answer: (d)
MC   Easy

10.5: What type of account is Purchases Discounts?
a) Liability
b) Asset
c) Contra revenue
d) Contra cost

Answer: (d)
MC   Easy

10.6: What type of account is Freight-In?
a) Liability
b) Asset
c) Contra cost
d) Cost

Answer: (d)
MC   Easy

10.7: The term F.O.B. means:
   a) free on board.
   b) freight or bill.
   c) freight order billing
   d) None of the above.

Answer: (a)
   MC   Easy

10.8: The term used when the seller is responsibile for the cost of freight to the purchaser is:
   a) F.O.B. shipping point.
   b) F.O.B. destination.
   c) freight-in.
   d) purchase invoice.

Answer: (b)
   MC   Moderate

10.9: The term used when the purchaser is responsible for the cost of freight is:
   a) F.O.B. shipping point.
   b) F.O.B. destination.
   c) freight-in.
   d) purchase invoice.

Answer: (a)
   MC   Moderate

10.10: Foung is required to pay the freight costs on merchandise brought into his clothing store. The freight terms are:
   a) F.O.B. shipping point.
   b) F.O.B. destination.
   c) Neither (a) nor (b).
   d) Both (a) and (b).

Answer: (a)
   MC   Moderate

10.11: When the term F.O.B. shipping point is used, title passes:
   a) when goods reach halfway point.
   b) when goods reach the destination.
   c) when goods are shipped.
   d) when the goods are unpacked by the buyer.

Answer: (c)
   MC   Moderate

10.12: A form used internally for requesting the purchase department to buy goods is a:
   a) purchase invoice.
   b) sales invoice.
   c) purchase requisition.
   d) receiving report.

Answer: (c)
   MC   Easy

181

10.13: The business form used for placing orders for goods from the supplier is a:
   a) purchase invoice for the buyer.
   b) sales invoice for the buyer.
   c) purchase invoice for the seller.
   d) purchase order.

Answer: (d)
   MC   Easy

10.14: The account used to record the buyer's shipping costs is:
   a) Purchase Discounts.
   b) Purchase Returns and Allowances.
   c) Freight-In.
   d) Accounts Payable.

Answer: (c)
   MC   Easy

10.15: The invoice sent to the purchaser from the seller for merchandise the purchaser bought is called a:
   a) purchase invoice for the buyer.
   b) sales invoice for the buyer.
   c) purchase invoice for the seller.
   d) purchase order.

Answer: (a)
   MC   Easy

10.16: A form completed at the time the shipment arrives is the:
   a) purchase invoice.   b) sales invoice.
   c) purchase order.   d) receiving report.

Answer: (d)
   MC   Easy

10.17: The business form used to verify the purchase order, invoice, and receiving report before approval and payment is made is the:
   a) receiving report.   b) purchase order.
   c) invoice approval form.   d) purchase requisition.

Answer: (c)
   MC   Moderate

10.18: What would be the correct order of events for the purchase of goods?
a) Purchase order, purchase requisition, receiving report, invoice approval form
b) Purchase requisition, purchase order, receiving report, invoice approval form
c) Invoice approval form, purchase order, purchase requisition, purchase invoice
d) Purchase requisition, purchase invoice, purchase order, invoice approval form

Answer: (b)
MC Difficult

10.19: Which special journal is used to record merchandise or other items bought on account?
a) Sales journal
c) Purchases journal
b) Cash receipts journal
d) Cash payments journal

Answer: (c)
MC Moderate

10.20: The amounts owed to creditors are listed alphabetically for purchases on account in the:
a) accounts payable subsidiary ledger.
b) controlling account in the general ledger.
c) accounts receivable subsidiary ledger.
d) purchases journal.

Answer: (a)
MC Easy

10.21: Amounts are posted to the Accounts Payable Subsidiary Ledger:
a) at the end of the month.
b) daily.
c) when financial statements are being prepared.
d) whenever the accountant has some spare time.

Answer: (b)
MC Easy

10.22: After an amount has been recorded from the purchases journal to the accounts payable subsidiary ledger:
a) the purchase order number is placed in the post reference column in the accounts payable ledger.
b) a check mark is placed in the post reference column in the purchases journal.
c) an account number is placed in the post reference column in the ledger.
d) a check mark is placed in the post reference column in the accounts payable subsidiary ledger.

Answer: (b)
MC Moderate

10.23: Purchases returns and allowances would be recorded in the:
   a) purchases journal.
   b) sales returns and allowances journal.
   c) cash payments journal.
   d) general journal.

Answer: (d)
   MC   Easy

10.24: The post reference column in the accounts payable subsidiary ledger:
   a) tells what document was used to prepare the entry.
   b) tells what day the information was recorded.
   c) tells the amount that was recorded.
   d) tells which journal page the information comes from.

Answer: (d)
   MC   Moderate

10.25: When a debit memorandum for returned merchandise for Norma Co. is recorded and posted, the entry is:
   a) debit Purchases Returns and Allowances, credit Accounts Payable in the general ledger.
   b) debit Accounts Payable, credit Purchases.
   c) debit Accounts Payable Norma Co. in the accounts payable subsidiary ledger, debit Accounts Payable in the general ledger, credit Purchases Returns and Allowances.
   d) debit Purchases, credit Accounts Payable.

Answer: (c)
   MC   Moderate

10.26: This account is used to record the amount that the buyer returns for credit or price adjustment:
   a) Purchases Discounts.
   b) Purchases Returns and Allowances.
   c) Freight-In.
   d) Accounts Payable.

Answer: (b)
   MC   Easy

10.27: A general ledger account that records the discount given by suppliers for early payment is:
   a) Purchase Discount.
   b) Purchase Return and Allowance.
   c) Trade Discount.
   d) Accounts Payable.

Answer: (a)
   MC   Easy

10.28: The special journal used to record all transactions involving payment of cash is:
  a) Sales journal.
  b) Cash Receipts journal.
  c) Purchases journal.
  d) Cash Payments journal.

Answer: (d)
  MC   Moderate

10.29: At the end of the month, the Sundry column total is posted to:
  a) Sundry account in the general ledger.
  b) a miscellaneous account in the general ledger.
  c) each asset account.
  d) is not posted.

Answer: (d)
  MC   Moderate

10.30: A list of creditors with ending balances is called:
  a) a Schedule of Accounts Receivable.
  b) a Schedule of Accounts Payable.
  c) a list of suppliers.
  d) a trade list.

Answer: (b)
  MC   Moderate

10.31: Discounts which reduce the price for customers who buy items for resale or to produce other goods are:
  a) purchase discounts.
  b) purchases returns and allowances.
  c) trade discounts.
  d) cash discounts.

Answer: (c)
  MC   Moderate

10.32: Which account is the controlling account for the amounts owed to individual creditors?
  a) Accounts Payable in the subsidiary ledger
  b) Accounts Receivable in the general ledger
  c) Accounts Receivable in the subsidiary ledger
  d) Accounts Payable in the general ledger

Answer: (d)
  MC   Difficult

10.33: The main source for preparing the schedule of accounts payable is the:
a) purchase journal.
b) accounts payable general ledger account.
c) trial balance.
d) accounts payable subsidiary ledger.

Answer: (d)
MC Moderate

10.34: Which of the following discounts is not recorded and is not a general ledger account?
a) Sales discount   b) Purchase discount
c) Trade discount   d) Cash discount

Answer: (c)
MC Easy

10.35: Certain groups of buyers are granted a reduction in price to make it possible for them to resell merchandise and earn a profit. The reduction in price is referred to as a:
a) trade discount.   b) sales discount.
c) wholesale discount.   d) purchasers discount.

Answer: (a)
MC Moderate

10.36: What is the net price of the merchandise if the list price is $800, trade discount is 40%, and the terms are 2/10, EOM?
a) $784   b) $800   c) $580   d) $480

Answer: (d)
MC Moderate

10.37: Orange Drink Company offers a trade discount of 25%. If the list price is $1,200, the trade discount amount would be:
a) $300.   b) $900.   c) $200.   d) $400.

Answer: (a)
MC Moderate

10.38: Barnie's Crafe on May 31 has the following account balances:
Sales $10,000
Sales Returns and Allowances   1,000
Purchases   7,000
Freight-In   500
Purchases Returns and Allow.   1,000
Purchases Discounts   700
Net purchases for the period are:
a) $4,300.   b) $6,300.   c) $5,300.   d) $5,800.

Answer: (c)
MC Moderate

10.39: The entry to record a purchase of $1,000 on account, terms of 2/10, n/30, would include a:
a) debit to Purchases Discount for $20.
b) debit to Accounts Payable for $1,000.
c) credit to Accounts Payable for $1,000.
d) credit to Cash, $1,000.

Answer: (c)
MC   Easy

10.40: Foung returned $200 of merchandise within the discount period. The entry to record the return is:
a) debit to Purchases for $200, credit Accounts Payable for $200.
b) debit to Purchases for $200, credit Purchases Returns and Allowances for $200.
c) debit to Accounts Payable for $200, credit Purchases Returns and Allowances for $200.
d) debit to Accounts Payable for $200, credit Purchases Discount for $200.

Answer: (c)
MC   Moderate

10.41: The entry to record a payment on a $900 account within the 1% discount period would include a:
a) debit to Accounts Payable for $900.
b) debit to Accounts Payable for $891.
c) credit to Purchases for $909.
d) debit to Cash for $891.

Answer: (a)
MC   Moderate

10.42: Barben Company made payment in full within the discount period on a $2,000 invoice, terms 2/10, n/30. The entry to record this transaction includes a:
a) debit to Accounts Payable, $1,960, credit to Purchases Discount, $40, and credit to Cash, $2,000.
b) debit to Accounts Payable, $2,000, credit to Purchases Discount, $40, and credit to Cash, $1,960.
c) debit to Accounts Payable, $2,000, credit to Cash, $2,000.
d) debit to Cash, $2,000, credit to Accounts Payable, $2,000.

Answer: (b)
MC   Moderate

10.43: On June 15, the Gravel Company purchased $700 of merchandise on account from the Ditch Company, terms 4/10, n/30. The goods were shipped F.O.B. shipping point. The freight charge of $40 was paid by Ditch Company and added to the invoice. The amount to record in the Purchases account is:
   a) $700.   b) $740.   c) $672.   d) $712.

Answer: (a)
   MC   Moderate

10.44: On March 30, Rose's Flowers purchased $1,000 of merchandise on account from the Grower's Company, terms 1/10, n/30. The goods were shipped F.O.B. shipping point. The freight charge of $80 was paid by Grower's Company and added to the invoice. The amount to record in the Accounts Payable account is:
   a) $1,000.   b) $990.   c) $1,080.   d) $1,070.

Answer: (c)
   MC   Moderate

10.45: Green Acres purchased $4,000 merchandise. The invoice for $4,100 included $100 freight with terms 3/15, n/30. Merchandise in the amount of $300 was returned. If the invoice was paid within the discount period, how much cash was paid?
   a) $3,980   b) $3,689   c) $3,977   d) $3,726

Answer: (b)
   MC   Difficult

10.46: Red Ink purchased merchandise for $1,000 plus freight of $60 with terms 2/10, n/30. Merchandise in the amount of $200 was returned. If the invoice was paid within the discount period, Purchases Discount would be credited for:
   a) $16.   b) $21.20.   c) $17.20   d) $20.

Answer: (a)
   MC   Moderate

10.47: Purple Plum made two purchases during the period: $800 from Blue Company, F.O.B. shipping point, total freight $50; and $500 from Green Company, F.O.B. destination, total freight $70. The Freight-In account at the end of the period will be:
   a) $70.   b) $120.   c) $50.   d) $20.

Answer: (c)
   MC   Moderate

10.48: When a debit memo is issued, an entry is made to:
   a) debit Cash, credit Accounts Payable.
   b) debit Accounts Payable, credit Purchases Returns and Allowances.
   c) debit Accounts Payable, credit Purchases Discount.
   d) debit Accounts Payable, credit Purchases.

Answer: (b)
   MC Difficult

10.49: A debit memo for the return of merchandise is recorded in the:
   a) sales journal.   b) purchases journal.
   c) general journal.   d) cash payments journal.

Answer: (c)
   MC Moderate

10.50: Payment on account for merchandise would be recorded in the:
   a) sales journal.   b) purchases journal.
   c) general journal.   d) cash payments journal.

Answer: (d)
   MC Moderate

10.51: Every transaction in a purchases journal includes:
   a) a credit to Cash.
   b) a credit to Purchases Discount.
   c) a credit to Accounts Payable.
   d) a debit to Sales Discount.

Answer: (c)
   MC Moderate

10.52: Supplies are debited to the purchases account.

Answer: False
   TF Moderate

10.53: Purchases of merchandise for cash are recorded in the purchases journal.

Answer: False
   TF Easy

10.54: The Purchases Returns and Allowances account normally has a debit balance.

Answer: False
   TF Moderate

10.55: The Purchases Discount account normally has a credit balance and is a Contra Cost account.

Answer: True
     TF Moderate

10.56: Trade discounts are recorded in the cash payments journal along with purchases discounts.

Answer: False
     TF Moderate

10.57: The account Freight-In accumulates the shipping costs to the buyer.

Answer: True
     TF Moderate

10.58: When the terms are F.O.B. shipping point, the purchaser is responsible for the cost of shipping from the seller's shipping point to the purchaser's location.

Answer: True
     TF Moderate

10.59: Shipping costs are sometimes prepaid by the seller and the cost is added to the sales invoice.

Answer: True
     TF Easy

10.60: A purchase requisition is sent to the supplier when ordering merchandise.

Answer: False
     TF Moderate

10.61: Payment for merchandise should not be made until approval is given.

Answer: True
     TF Easy

10.62: The receiving report is prepared when the goods are received after the shipment has been inspected.

Answer: True
     TF Easy

10.63: The seller issues a debit memorandum when granting a reduction in price to a customer.

Answer: False
TF Easy

10.64: Purchases Discounts and Freight-In are both contra cost accounts with a credit balance.

Answer: False
TF Difficult

10.65: The buyer issues a debit memorandum to indicate that a previous purchase amount is being reduced because goods were returned or an allowance was requested.

Answer: True
TF Moderate

10.66: The selling price of merchandise is called the cost of goods sold.

Answer: False
TF Easy

10.67: The seller's sales invoice is the purchaser's purchase invoice.

Answer: True
TF Easy

10.68: Payments of cash are recorded in the cash receipts journal.

Answer: False
TF Easy

10.69: A cash disbursement journal and a cash payments journal are the same thing.

Answer: True
TF Easy

10.70: A list showing the ending balances owed to individual creditors is called a Schedule of Accounts Payable.

Answer: True
TF Moderate

10.71: Trade discounts and purchase discounts are given to the purchaser from the supplier for early payment on account.

Answer: False
TF Moderate

10.72: Discounts are not taken on freight costs.

Answer: True
TF Moderate

10.73: Trade discounts are recorded in the journal.

Answer: False
TF Moderate

10.74: The Sundry debit column total is posted at the end of the accounting period.

Answer: False
TF Easy

10.75: Amounts are posted to the general ledger but not to the subsidiary ledger.

Answer: False
TF Easy

10.76: The controlling account is found in the subsidiary ledger for all accounts payable.

Answer: False
TF Difficult

10.77: A buyer may not receive both a trade discount and a cash discount.

Answer: False
TF Moderate

10.78: The accounts payable column total is posted to the accounts payable general ledger account at the end of the month.

Answer: True
TF Moderate

10.79: Individual amounts are recorded during the month to the accounts payable ledger.

Answer: True
TF Moderate

10.80: Clockworks has the following selected accounts. Use this information to answer the questions below.

Freight-In	$ 100
Purchases Discount	500
Purchases Returns and Allow.	600
Purchases	5,000
Beginning Inventory	1,000
Ending Inventory	1,500

a. Net purchases are _____.

b. Total cost of goods purchased is _____.

Answer: a. $3,900

b. $4,000
ES Moderate

10.81: Mary's Pie Company has the following selected accounts. Use this information to answer the questions below.

Sales Returns and Allowances $	300
Sales Discounts	200
Purchases	3,000
Sales	8,000
Purchases Discount	300
Freight-In	600
Beginning Inventory	8,000
Ending Inventory	8,500

a. Net purchases are _____.

b. Total cost of goods purchased is _____.

Answer: a. $2,700

b. $3,300
ES Moderate

10.82: On June 15, K. Finch purchased merchandise for her furniture store. The invoice was for $10,500 plus freight, $800, terms 3/10, n/30. On June 20, K. Finch returned $300 of merchandise for credit. On June 30, K. Finch paid the amount owed. Answer the following questions.

a. The debit to Purchases on June 15 is _____.

b. The credit to Accounts Payable on June 15 is _____.

c. The credit to Purchases Returns and Allowances on June 20 is _____.

d. The credit to Cash on June 30 is _____.

e. The credit to Purchases Discount on June 30 is _____.

Answer: a. $10,500

b. $11,300

c. $300

d. $11,000

e. $0
ES Moderate

10.83: On May 6, R. Alexander purchased merchandise for his jewelry store. The invoice was for $80,000 plus freight of $1,500, terms 1/15, n/30. On May 10, R. Alexander returned merchandise for $15,000 credit. On May 19, R. Alexander paid the amount owed. Answer the following questions:

a. The credit to Accounts Payable on May 6 is _____.

b. The debit to Freight-In on May 6 is _____.

c. The debit to Accounts Payable on May 10 is _____.

d. The credit to Purchases Discount on May 19 is _____.

e. The credit to Cash on May 19 is_____.

Answer: a. $81,500

b. $1,500

c. $15,000

d. $650

e. $65,850
ES Moderate

10.84: Given below are the transactions for B. Showers Company. For each transaction state the account(s) to be debited and account(s) to be credited and indicate the journal in which each transaction should be recorded. Indicate (P) for purchase journal, (CP) for cash payments, or (GJ) for general journal in the column headed journal.

Debit	Credit	Journal	
======	======	=======	
Supplies	Accts. Pay.	P	0. Purchased supplies on account
_____	_____	_____	a. Purchased merchandise on account.
_____	_____	_____	b. Paid utilities expense.
_____	_____	_____	c. Purchased merchandise for cash.
_____	_____	_____	d. Returned one-half of goods purchased in a.
_____	_____	_____	e. Showers made a withdrawal of cash.
_____	_____	_____	f. Purchased store equipment on account.
_____	_____	_____	g. Paid for purchases in a., less return within the period.

Answer:

	Debit	Credit	Journal
	======	======	=======
a.	Purchases	Accts. Pay.	P
b.	Utilities Exp.	Cash	CP
c.	Purchases	Cash	CP
d.	Accts. Pay.	Purchase Returns and Allowances	GJ
e.	Withdrawals	Cash	CP
f.	Store Equip.	Accts. Pay.	P
g.	Accts. Pay.	Purchases Dis. Cash	CP

ES   Moderate

10.85: Given below are the transactions for G. Turner Company. For each transaction state the account(s) to be debited and account(s) to be credited and indicate the journal in which each transaction should be recorded. Indicate (P) for purchase journal, (CP) for cash payments journal, or (GJ) for general journal.

Debit	Credit	Journal	
Supplies	Cash	CP	0. Purchased supplies for cash.
_____	_____	_____	a. Withdrew $500 in cash from the business.
_____	_____	_____	b. Paid salaries expense, $800.
_____	_____	_____	c. Purchased merchandise for cash, $2,500.
_____	_____	_____	d. Purchased merchandise on account, $4,000.
_____	_____	_____	e. Returned $1,000 of goods purchased in d.
_____	_____	_____	f. Paid two months' rent in advance, $600.
_____	_____	_____	g. Paid for purchases in d., less discount and return.

Answer:

	Debit	Credit	Journal
a.	Withdrawals	Cash	CP
b.	Salaries Exp.	Cash	CP
c.	Purchases	Cash	CP
d.	Purchases	Accts. Pay.	P
e.	Accts. Pay.	Purchases Ret. and Allowances	GJ
f.	Prepaid Rent	Cash	CP
g.	Accts. Pay.	Purchases Dis. Cash	CP

ES Moderate

196

10.86: Below are listed several books of original entry. Indicate the journal in which each transaction should be recorded by placing the letters representing the appropriate journal in the space provided.

CP   Cash payments journal
CR   Cash receipts journal
P   Purchases journal
GJ   General journal

0. __CP__   Paid weekly salaries.

a. _____   Purchased merchandise on account.

b. _____   Gave customer credit on account for merchandise returned.

c. _____   Owner invested additional cash in the business.

d. _____   Sold merchandise on account.

e. _____   Received credit on account from a supplier for merchandise returned.

f. _____   Purchased office equipment on account.

g. _____   Sold merchandise for cash.

h. _____   Paid for goods purchased in a.

i. _____   Owner withdrew cash from the business.

j. _____   Paid for advertising expense.

Answer: a.   P
        b.   GJ
        c.   CR
        d.   S
        e.   GJ
        f.   P
        g.   CR
        h.   CP
        i.   CP
        j.   CP
        ES   Easy

10.87: Below are listed several books of original entry. Indicate the journal in which the following transactions should be recorded by placing the letters representing the appropriate journal in the space provided.

CP Cash payments journal
CR Cash receipts journal
P Purchases journal
S Sales journal
GJ General journal

0. __CP__ Owner's cash withdrawal

a. _____ Owner invested cash in new business.

b. _____ Paid for one year insurance in advance.

c. _____ Sold merchandise on account.

d. _____ Purchased merchandise on account.

e. _____ Received credit on account from a supplier for merchandise returned.

f. _____ Sold merchandise for cash.

g. _____ Received payment for merchandise sold on account.

h. _____ Paid for goods purchased in d.

i. _____ Paid cash for merchandise purchased.

j. _____ Paid for cleaning services.

Answer: a. CR
        b. CP
        c. S
        d. P
        e. GJ
        f. CR
        g. CR
        h. CP
        i. CP
        j. CP
        ES Easy

10.88: Compare and contrast the controlling account Accounts
Payable to the accounts payable ledger. Discuss why the
balance of the controlling account, Accounts Payable, does
not equal the sum of the accounts payable ledger during the
month.

Answer: Both the control account, Accounts Payable, and the accounts
payable ledger have normal credit balances and must be
balanced to each other at the end of the month. They both
represent the amount owed to creditors. The control account
contains summary entries made at the month end from the
purchases journal, cash payments journal, and the general
journal. The accounts payable ledger is a book or file that
lists alphabetically the amounts owed to creditors from
purchases on account. Information is posted daily from the
purchases journal, cash payments, and general journal to
provide the current status of the accounts balances.

The control account and the accounts payable ledger balance
will not agree during the month because the control account
is posted from the totals of the purchases and cash payment
journals, but the accounts payable ledger is posted daily to
individual creditors.
ES Moderate

10.89: Explain the difference between F.O.B. shipping point and
F.O.B. destination.

Answer: F.O.B. destination means the seller pays or is responsible
for the cost of freight to purchaser's location or
destination.

F.O.B. shipping point means the buyer or purchaser pays or
is responsible for the shipping costs from seller's shipping
point to purchaser's location.
ES Easy

11. The Combined Journal

11.1: The method used that records revenue when it is earned and records expenses when they are incurred is:
   a) the cash method.   b) the standard method.
   c) the accrual method.   d) None of the above.

Answer: (c)
   MC   Moderate

11.2: The basis of accounting whereby revenue is recorded when cash is received and expenses are recorded when paid is:
   a) the cash basis of accounting.
   b) the accrual basis of accounting.
   c) the current basis of accounting.
   d) the matching basis of accounting.

Answer: (a)
   MC   Moderate

11.3: The cash basis method may be used because:
   a) it is simple.
   b) it applies the matching principles concept.
   c) it is required for companies with inventory.
   d) it does not require an understanding of business.

Answer: (a)
   MC   Moderate

11.4: Revenue is recorded only when the cash is received under the:
   a) cash method.   b) current price method.
   c) accrual method.   d) combined basis.

Answer: (a)
   MC   Moderate

11.5: The method that records expenses when paid, and revenue when cash is received, with adjustments for long-term assets, is:
   a) cash method.
   b) modified cash-basis method.
   c) accrual method.
   d) None of the above.

Answer: (b)
   MC   Moderate

11.6: What type of business would not use a modified cash-basis
       method of accounting?
       a) Professional services   b) Accounting services
       c) Department store   d) Architects

Answer: (c)
        MC   Moderate

11.7: The method that is used when a company has inventory is:
      a) cash method.
      b) modified cash-basis method.
      c) accrual method.
      d) None of the above.

Answer: (c)
        MC   Moderate

11.8: When using the modified cash system, which accounts would
      not be listed in the chart of accounts?
      a) Supplies Expense
      b) Accounts Receivable
      c) Federal Income Tax Payable
      d) None of the above.

Answer: (b)
        MC   Moderate

11.9: Net income using the cash basis method equals:
      a) revenue (earned) plus expenses (incurred).
      b) revenue (cash received) plus expenses (paid).
      c) revenue (cash received) minus expenses (paid).
      d) revenue (earned) minus expenses (incurred).

Answer: (c)
        MC   Easy

11.10: To calculate net income using the cash basis, you would:
       a) subtract expenses (paid) from revenue (cash received).
       b) subtract expenses (incurred) from revenue (received).
       c) add revenue (earned) and expenses (incurred).
       d) add revenue (cash received) and expenses (cash paid).

Answer: (a)
        MC   Easy

11.11: Which of the following accounts are treated the same under
       the modified cash-basis and the accrual basis?
       a) Equipment   b) Accounts Receivable
       c) Professional Fees   d) Inventory

Answer: (a)
        MC   Moderate

201

11.12: A chart of accounts would include which of these under both
the modified cash-basis and the accrual basis?
a) Building
b) Accounts Payable
c) FUTA Taxes Payable
d) Inventory

Answer: (a)
MC   Moderate

11.13: The difference in the Chart of Accounts under the cash basis
and modified cash-basis method is reflected in which
account?
a) Accumulated Depreciation
b) Professional Fees
c) Telephone Expense
d) None of the above.

Answer: (a)
MC   Moderate

11.14: A combined journal is used to replace the general journal in
order to:
a) reveal more information about a transaction.
b) save time in journalizing, recording, and posting.
c) require more posting time.
d) All the above.

Answer: (b)
MC   Moderate

11.15: An advantage a combined journal has over the general journal
is that it:
a) does not require an understanding of accounting.
b) eliminates the need of a general ledger.
c) saves time in posting, recording and journalizing.
d) reveals more information about a transaction.

Answer: (c)
MC   Moderate

11.16: When using a combined journal, the bank balance can be
calculated:
a) only at the end of the month.
b) only at the end of the week.
c) after totals are proved.
d) at any time.

Answer: (d)
MC   Moderate

11.17: When can the cash balance be calculated if a combined
       journal is being used?
       a) Only after the totals are posted
       b) After any transaction
       c) Only when the bank account is reconciled
       d) Only at the end of the period

Answer: (b)
        MC   Moderate

11.18: To prove the combined journal, the total debits must equal:
       a) the cash paid.   b) the cash received.
       c) total credits.   d) the Sundry column.

Answer: (c)
        MC   Easy

11.19: How is a combined journal proved?
       a) By comparing total cash paid out with the total cash
       received
       b) By comparing the total debits with the total credits
       c) By comparing the Sundry column with the Cash column
       d) By comparing the total debits with the cash received

Answer: (b)
        MC   Moderate

11.20: The total of the Sundry column is:
       a) posted on a daily basis.
       b) posted as a total at the end of the month.
       c) not posted.
       d) None of the above.

Answer: (c)
        MC   Moderate

11.21: The posting reference symbol "X" means:
       a) posting to subsidiary ledger.
       b) no posting necessary.
       c) posting to owner's equity.
       d) None of the above.

Answer: (b)
        MC   Moderate

11.22: Instead of using subsidiary ledgers, the modified cash-basis
       might use:
       a) memorandum records.   b) special records.
       c) combined schedules.   d) special ledgers.

Answer: (a)
        MC   Moderate

11.23: How do companies using a modified cash-basis keep information about receivables or payables?
  a) Subsidiary ledgers   b) Special journals
  c) Memorandum records   d) No records required

Answer: (c)
   MC   Moderate

11.24: Under the cash basis method, the owner's portion of FICA, as well as FUTA and SUTA tax, is:
  a) not recorded until paid.
  b) recorded when incurred.
  c) recorded when IRS rules indicate.
  d) withheld from employees.

Answer: (a)
   MC   Moderate

11.25: The entry to record the payment of FUTA and SUTA tax for the employer using the modified cash-basis method would be:
  a) debit Payroll Tax Expense, credit Cash.
  b) debit FUTA Tax Payable, credit Cash.
  c) debit SUTA Tax Payable, credit Cash.
  d) debit Cash, credit Payroll Tax Expense.

Answer: (a)
   MC   Moderate

11.26: The entry to record the payment of FICA Tax and Federal Income Tax and the employer FUTA, SUTA and FICA taxes under the modified-cash basis method would be:
  a) debit Employee Federal Income Tax Payable; FICA Tax Payable, credit Cash.
  b) debit Employer Federal Income Tax Payable; FICA Tax Payable, credit Cash.
  c) debit Employee Federal Income Tax Payable; FICA Tax Payable, Payroll Tax Expense, credit Cash.
  d) None of the above.

Answer: (c)
   MC   Difficult

11.27: In an accounting department where a division of labor is needed:
  a) the combined journal would be used.
  b) more specialized journals would be used.
  c) only a general journal would be used.
  d) None of the above.

Answer: (b)
   MC   Moderate

11.28: If several persons work in an accounting department, recording transactions would most likely be more efficient if:
a) all transactions are recorded in a general journal.
b) various specialized journals are used.
c) a combined journal is used.
d) transactions are recorded directly in the general ledger.

Answer: (b)
MC Moderate

11.29: When a type of transaction occurs frequently, the accountant may set up in the combined journal:
a) groups of accounts.   b) special accounts.
c) special columns.   d) None of the above.

Answer: (c)
MC Moderate

11.30: The purpose of special columns in a combined journal is to:
a) save posting time   b) save journalizing time
c) save recording time   d) All the above.

Answer: (d)
MC Moderate

11.31: Which amounts in the combined journal should be posted daily under the accrual method?
a) Accounts Payable   b) Cash
c) Sales   d) Purchases

Answer: (a)
MC Moderate

11.32: Which posting reference symbol will be used in the ledger when posting from the combined journal?
a) The account number that the amount is posted to
b) CJ (page number)
c) J (page number)
d) X

Answer: (b)
MC Moderate

11.33: What does the X mean under the column total in a combined journal?
a) Total of column is posted last.
b) Total of column is posted daily.
c) Total of column is not posted.
d) Not enough information to answer.

Answer: (c)
MC Moderate

11.34: When using a combined journal, adjusting and closing entries
are recorded:
a) in the general journal.
b) in the Sundry column of the combined journal.
c) in special journals.
d) are not recorded when a combined journal is used.

Answer: (b)
MC   Easy

11.35: Adjusting and closing entries for a company using a combined
journal are:
a) not required.
b) recorded in the general journal.
c) recorded in special columns.
d) recorded in the Sundry columns of the combined journal.

Answer: (d)
MC   Moderate

11.36: The rent paid for the month would be recorded in the
combined journal under:
a) a special column called Miscellaneous Expense.
b) a special column called Supplies Expense.
c) a special column called Accounts Receivable.
d) the Sundry column.

Answer: (d)
MC   Moderate

11.37: Dr. Luther deposited $5,000 cash in her dental practice.
She uses a combined journal under a modified cash system.
How would this transaction be recorded?
a) Debit Luther, Capital $5,000 in the Sundry column,
credit Cash $5,000
b) Debit Cash $5,000, credit Professional Fees $5,000
c) Debit Professional Fees $5,000, credit Cash $5,000
d) Credit Luther, Capital $5,000 in the Sundry column,
debit Cash $5,000 on the Cash column.

Answer: (d)
MC   Easy

11.38: George Smythe transferred $3,000 of furniture from his home to his office's patient waiting room. How would this transaction be recorded in a combined journal under the modified cash system?
a) Credit Smythe, Capital $3,000 in the Sundry column, debit Furniture $3,000 in the Sundry column
b) Debit Smythe, Capital $3,000 in the Sundry column, credit Furniture $3,000 in the Sundry column
c) Debit Cash $3,000, credit Smythe, Capital $3,000 in the Sundry column
d) Debit Supplies $3,000 in the Sundry column, credit Smythe, Capital $3,000 in the Sundry column

Answer: (a)
MC   Moderate

11.39: Barry's Services completed $800 of services for the Seymour Company on account. Barry uses a combined journal under the accrual system. This transaction would be recorded under which of the following headings?
a) Accounts Receivable $800 debit, Service Fees $800 credit
b) Accounts Receivable $800 credit, Service Fees $800 debit
c) The transaction would not be recorded until the cash is received.
d) Memo, Sundry column $800 debit, Service Fees $800 credit

Answer: (a)
MC   Moderate

11.40: R. Holmes billed a client $1,500 for legal services. How would this transaction be recorded in a combined journal under the modified cash system?
a) Cash debit $1,500, Fees Earned credit $1,500
b) Fees Earned debit $1,500, Accounts Receivable credit $1,500
c) Accounts Receivable debit $1,500, Fees Earned credit $1,500
d) The transaction would not be recorded until the cash is received.

Answer: (d)
MC   Moderate

11.41: Zuber's accounting firm purchased a small amount of supplies for $1,000 on credit. This transaction would be recorded in a combined journal under a modified cash system as follows:
a) debit Supplies $1,000, credit Cash $1,000.
b) debit Supplies $1,000, credit Accounts Payable $1,000.
c) debit Accounts Payable $1,000, credit Zuber, Capital $1,000 in the Sundry column.
d) The transaction would not be recorded until the cash is paid.

Answer: (d)
MC   Moderate

11.42: Paul's Speedy Printing owes but has not paid $200 rent due at the end of the month. This obligation would be recorded in a combined journal under the accrual method as follows:
  a) debit Rent Expense $200 in the Sundry column, credit Rent Payable $200 in the Sundry column.
  b) credit Rent Expense $200 in the Sundry column, credit Cash $200.
  c) debit Prepaid Rent $200 in the Sundry column, credit Rent Payable $200 in the Sundry column.
  d) This transaction will not be recorded until the cash is paid.

Answer: (a)
   MC   Moderate

11.43: W. Neal collected $500 earned from his consulting clients for work performed during the prior year. How would this collection be recorded in a combined journal under the modified cash system?
  a) Cash debit $500, Fees Earned credit $500
  b) Fees Earned debit $500, Cash credit $500
  c) Cash debit $500, Accounts Receivable credit $500
  d) Accounts Receivable debit $500, Fees Earned credit $500

Answer: (a)
   MC   Moderate

11.44: C. Shlaes collected $300 on account for engineering consulting services. She should record this collection in a combined journal under the modified cash system as follows:
  a) debit Cash $300, credit Accounts Receivable $300.
  b) debit Fees Earned $300, credit Accounts Receivable $300.
  c) debit Cash $300, credit Fees Earned $300.
  d) debit Fees Earned $300, credit Cash $300.

Answer: (c)
   MC   Moderate

11.45: Ben's Tax Company owes $100 expense for the weekly cleaning service. Ben should record this transaction in a combined journal under the modified cash system as follows:
  a) debit Cleaning Expense $100 in the Sundry column, credit Accounts Payable $100.
  b) debit Cleaning Expense $100 in the Sundry column, credit Cash $100.
  c) debit Cash $100, credit Cleaning Expense $100 in the Sundry column.
  d) None of the above.

Answer: (d)
   MC   Moderate

11.46: Dr. Amjoy withdrew $400 cash for personal use. How would this transaction be recorded in a combined journal under the modified cash system?

    a) Debit Amjoy, Capital $400 in the Sundry column, credit Cash $400
    b) Debit Withdrawals $400 in the Sundry column, credit Cash $400
    c) Debit Salary Expense $400 in the Sundry column, credit Cash $400
    d) Debit Cash $400, credit Withdrawals $400 in the Sundry column

Answer: (b)
    MC Moderate

11.47: Bill's Bikes opened a new store and paid $6,000 cash for new bicycles for inventory for resale. How should Bill record this transaction in a combined journal under the modified cash system?
    a) Purchases debit $6,000, Cash credit $6,000
    b) Supplies debit $6,000, Cash credit $6,000
    c) Debit Cost of Goods Sold $6,000 in the Sundry column, credit Cash $6,000
    d) Bill cannot use modified cash system for merchandise inventory type business.

Answer: (d)
    MC Moderate

11.48: Sally's Beauty Shop uses a combined journal under a modified cash system. How should she record the cash payment of $700 for beauty cream to be resold to her customers?
    a) Debit Supplies $700, credit Cash $700
    b) Debit Purchases $700, credit Cash $700
    c) Debit Miscellaneous Expense $700, credit Cash $700
    d) Sally cannot use modified cash system for merchandise inventory type business.

Answer: (d)
    MC Moderate

11.49: Laun Cher Co. issued a payroll check to an employee who earned gross wages of $700. Withholdings included FICA of $53 and FIT of $140. The payment would be recorded in a combined journal under the modified cash system as follows:
    a) debit Salary Expense $700, credit Cash $700.
    b) debit Withdrawals $700, credit Cash $700.
    c) debit Salary Expense $700, credit FICA-Social Security Tax Payable $35, FICA-Medicare Payable $18, credit FIT Payable $140, and credit Cash $507.
    d) Cher cannot use modified cash system to record payment of payroll.

Answer: (c)
    MC Difficult

11.50: Abby Smith earned wages of $500 for one week. Her withholdings included FICA $38, and FIT $100. Her employer would record the payment in a combined journal under the modified cash system as follows:
a) debit Salary Expense $500, credit FICA-Social Security Payable $25, credit FICA-Medicare Payable $13, credit FIT Payable $100, and credit Cash $362.
b) the employer cannot use modified cash system to record payment of payroll.
c) debit Salary Expense $500, credit Cash $500.
d) debit Employee Withdrawals $500, credit FICA-Social Security $25, FICA-Medicare $13, credit FIT $100, and credit Cash $362.

Answer: (a)
MC Difficult

11.51: Dr. Sligh Faux paid $200 FICA taxes withheld from employees and $500 FIT taxes withheld plus Faux's share of FICA-Social Security and FICA-Medicare. This transaction should be recorded in a combined journal under the modified cash system as follows:
a) debit Payroll Tax Expense $700, credit Cash $700.
b) debit Payroll Tax Expense $900, credit Cash $900.
c) debit Payroll Tax Payable $900, credit Cash $900.
d) debit Payroll Tax Expense $200, debit FICA-Social Security Payable $150, debit FICA-Medicare Payable $50, debit FIT Payable $500, credit Cash $900.

Answer: (d)
MC Difficult

11.52: Payroll taxes withheld from employees during the period were $500 FICA and $900 FIT. The entry to record the payment of the taxes withheld and the employer's share in a combined journal under the modified cash system would be:
a) debit Payroll Tax Expense $1,200, credit Cash $1,200.
b) debit Payroll Tax Expense $500, debit FICA-Social Security Payable $400, debit FICA-Medicare Payable $100, debit FIT Payable $900, credit Cash $1,900.
c) debit Payroll Tax Expense $1,900, credit Cash $1,900.
d) debit Payroll Tax Payable $1,900, credit Cash $1,900.

Answer: (b)
MC Difficult

11.53: The headings in the combined journal used by G. Gruen
Consultants include debit and credit columns under Sundry,
Cash, Accounts Receivable, Accounts Payable, Office
Equipment, and Medical Fees. Which accounting system is
Gruen using?
a) Cash basis
b) Modified cash
c) Accrual basis
d) Cannot be determined from the information presented.

Answer: (c)
MC   Moderate

11.54: Bea's Buttons used the following columns in her business's
combined journal: Sundry, Cash, Supplies Expense, Sales,
Salary Expense, FICA-Social Security Payable, FICA-Medicare
Payable, and FIT Payable. Which acccounting system is Bea
using?
a) Accrual basis   b) Cash basis
c) Modified cash   d) Fiduciary basis

Answer: (c)
MC   Moderate

11.55: Rita Karl invested $2,000 cash and $3,000 of office
equipment in her new advertising agency business. The
transaction would be recorded in a combined journal under
the accrual basis, as follows:
a) debit Cash $2,000, debit Office Equipment $3,000, credit
Karl, Capital $5,000.
b) debit Karl, Capital $5,000, credit Office Equipment
$3,000, credit Cash $2,000.
c) debit Investment $5,000, credit Karl, Capital $5,000.
d) debit Sundry $5,000, credit Karl, Capital $5,000.

Answer: (a)
MC   Moderate

11.56: Barbara's Bakery sold $300 of rolls to Tommy's Sandwich Shop
on account. Barbara records this transaction in a combined
journal under the accrual basis as follows:
a) debit Sales $300, credit Accounts Receivable $300.
b) debit Cash $300, credit Sales $300.
c) debit Accounts Receivable $300, credit Sales $300.
d) debit Accounts Payable $300, credit Sales $300.

Answer: (c)
MC   Easy

11.57: Chicken Feathers Ribbon Co. uses a combined journal under
the modified cash-basis. How should a purchase on account
of $1,000 of ribbons for resale be recorded?
  a) Debit Supplies $1,000, credit Accounts Payable $1,000
  b) Debit Supplies $1,000, credit Cash $1,000
  c) Debit Purchases $1,000, credit Accounts Payable $1,000
  d) None of the above.

Answer: (d)
  MC Easy

11.58: At the beginning of the month, Seymour's Rack Co. paid
$3,600 cash for a one-year fire insurance policy. How would
one month's insurance expense be recorded in a combined
journal under the accrual basis?
  a) Debit Insurance Expense $300 in the Sundry column and
  credit Prepaid Insurance $300 in the Sundry column
  b) Debit Insurance Expense $3,600 and credit Prepaid
  Insurance $3,600 in the Sundry column
  c) Debit Insurance Expense $300 in the Sundry column,
  credit Cash $300
  d) Cannot record this transaction in a combined journal.

Answer: (a)
  MC Moderate

11.59: The combined journal is a book of original entry.

Answer: True
  TF Easy

11.60: The combined journal does not have the same advantages when
journalizing and posting entries as the special journals.

Answer: False
  TF Moderate

11.61: The pure cash basis method is the easiest to follow because
of federal and state laws.

Answer: False
  TF Moderate

11.62: The hybrid method is the same as the modified cash-basis
method.

Answer: True
  TF Moderate

11.63: Under the modified cash-basis method, the amount paid for equipment in one year cannot be treated as an expense of the period.

Answer: True
TF   Moderate

11.64: The hybrid method shows the small amounts of supplies purchased as an expense.

Answer: True
TF   Moderate

11.65: To avoid distorting the financial reports, the modified cash-basis makes adjustments for depreciation, purchases of insurance, and large amounts of supplies.

Answer: True
TF   Difficult

11.66: The combined journal can replace the general journal and save time posting and journalizing.

Answer: True
TF   Easy

11.67: The combined journal would be used for a business that has a large number of different transactions.

Answer: False
TF   Moderate

11.68: A general journal is not used with the combined journal.

Answer: True
TF   Easy

11.69: The Sundry columns in the combined journal are used to record transactions that do not have a special column.

Answer: True
TF   Moderate

11.70: The Accounts Payable debit column in the combined journal is used to record amounts owed to creditors.

Answer: False
TF   Easy

11.71: The combined journal could have a special column for Sales Tax Payable.

Answer: True
TF   Easy

11.72: When a combined journal is used, it replaces special journals such as the sales journal, etc.

Answer: True
TF   Moderate

11.73: The headings for the combined journal are designed to meet the individual needs of each business.

Answer: True
TF   Easy

11.74: Accounts that are used the least in the business should have a special column.

Answer: False
TF   Easy

11.75: The total of the Sundry columns is posted at the end of the month.

Answer: False
TF   Moderate

11.76: The Sales column of the combined journal is used to record both charge and cash sales under the accrual basis.

Answer: True
TF   Moderate

11.77: When using the cash method for accounting, inventory is adjusted at the end of the period.

Answer: False
TF   Moderate

11.78: When the combined journal is used, the cash balance can be determined easily.

Answer: True
TF   Moderate

11.79: When using the combined journal, the cash balance can only be determined at the end of the month.

Answer: False
TF Moderate

11.80: Under the cash basis system, FUTA and SUTA are considered liability accounts.

Answer: False
TF Difficult

11.81: The Sundry columns can be used for recording adjusting and closing entries in the combined journal.

Answer: True
TF Moderate

11.82: An (X) below the total column in the combined journal means the column total is not posted.

Answer: True
TF Moderate

11.83: An (X) in the post reference column means the amount has already been posted.

Answer: False
TF Moderate

11.84: Payroll Tax Expense is used to record the employer's payroll taxes.

Answer: True
TF Moderate

11.85: Sales Tax Payable is an expense account.

Answer: False
TF Easy

11.86: To prove the journal means that debits and credits equal.

Answer: True
TF Moderate

11.87: The combined journal for Dr. Dealer has the following
headings with appropriate columns for recording debits and
credits: Cash, Explanation, Sundry, Professional Fees,
Supplies Expense.

The following is a partial chart of accounts of Dr. Dealer:

111 Cash   411 Professional Fees
121 Medical Equipment   511 Rent Expense
312 Dealer, Withdrawals   515 Telephone Expense
                                   520 Supplies Expense

Indicate, in the spaces provided below, the account numbers
and the debit and credit amounts for the following
transactions applying the modified cash-basis.

	Debit		**Credit**		
Account	Amount	Account	Amount		
===============		===============			
<u>511</u>	<u>$3</u>	<u>111</u>	<u>$3</u>	0.	Paid office rent $3
___	___	___	___	a.	Paid telephone bill $1
___	___	___	___	b.	Personal withdrawals $2
___	___	___	___	c.	Paid cash for dental supplies $2
___	___	___	___	d.	Cash receipts from patients $9
___	___	___	___	e.	Paid cash for medical equipment $4

Answer:

	Debit		**Credit**	
	========		=======	
0.	511	$3	111	$3
a.	515	$1	111	$1
b.	312	$2	111	$2
c.	520	$2	111	$2
d.	111	$9	411	$9
e.	121	$4	111	$4
ES	Moderate			

216

11.88: The combined journal for Al's Tax Service has the followig headings with appropriate columns for recording debits and credits: Cash, Explanation, Sundry, Professional Fees, Supplies Expense.

The following is a partial chart of accounts of Al's Tax Service:

111	Cash	312	Al, Withdrawals
121	Office Equipment	411	Professional Fees
211	Accounts Payable	511	Rent Expense
311	Al, Capital	515	Telephone Expense
		520	Supplies Expense

Indicate, in the spaces below, the account numbers and the debit and credit amounts for the following transactions under the modified cash-basis.

Debit		Credit		
Account	Amount	Account	Amount	
511	$2	111	$2	0. Paid equipment rental fee $2
___	___	___	___	a. Received but did not pay the bill for utilities $1
___	___	___	___	b. Personal withdrawal $3
___	___	___	___	c. Purchased office supplies on account $7
___	___	___	___	d. Cash receipts from clients $8
___	___	___	___	e. Collected cash for service previously performed $3
___	___	___	___	f. Paid for supplies purchased on (c) above

Answer:

	Debit		Credit	
0.	511	$2	111	$2
a.	No entry			
b.	312	$3	111	$3
c.	No entry			
d.	111	$8	411	$8
e.	111	$3	411	$3
f.	520	$7	111	$7
ES	Moderate			

11.89: The combined journal for Gill's Guide Service has the following column headings with appropriate dividers for recording debits and credits: Cash, Explanation, Sundry, Salary Expense, FICA Payable, and FIT Payable.

The following is a partial chart of accounts of Gill's Tax Service:

111	Cash	411	Guide Fees
114	Prepaid Insurance	513	Salaries Expense
211	FICA Tax Payable	514	Payroll Tax Expense
212	Federal Income Tax Payable	520	Camping Supplies

Indicate in the spaces provided the account numbers and the debit and credit amounts for the following transactions under the modified cash-basis.

Debit		Credit		
Account	**Amount**	**Account**	**Amount**	
===============		===============		
111	$10	411	$10	0. Received cash from customers $10
___	_	___	_	a. Paid for camping supplies $2
___	_	___	_	b. Paid three months' premium for insurance $3
___	_	___	_	c. Gave a refund to a customer $1
___	_	___	_	d. Paid the payroll. Gross pay $7, FICA $1, FIT $2
___	_	___	_	
___	_	___	_	e. Paid FICA and FIT tax from payroll (d) above. Don't forget Gill's share of the FICA.
___	_	___	_	
___	_	___	_	

Answer:

	Debit		**Credit**	
	=====		======	
0.	111	$10	411	$10
a.	520	$2	111	$2
b.	114	$3	111	$3
c.	411	$1	111	$1
d	513	$7	211	$1
			212	$2
			111	$4
e.	514	$1		
	211	$1		
	212	$2	111	$4
ES	Moderate			

218

11.90: The combined journal for Larry's Lawn Service has the following headings with appropriate columns for indicating debits and credits: Cash, Explanation, Sundry, Fees, Salary Expense, FICA Payable, and FIT Payable.

The following is a partial chart of accounts of Larry's Lawn Service:

111	Cash	513	Salaries Expense
211	FICA Tax Payable	514	Payroll Tax Expense
212	Federal Income Tax Payable	520	Mowing Supplies Expense
411	Mowing Fees	525	Rental Expense

Indicate, in the format below, the account numbers and the debit and credit amounts for the following transactions under the modified cash-basis.

Debit		**Credit**		
Account	Amount	Account	Amount	
==============		==============		
111	$7	411	$7	0. Received cash from customer $7
___	__	___	__	a. Paid for mowing supplies $4
___	__	___	__	b. Paid three months' rental on tractor $3
___	__	___	__	c. Received a refund for supplies $1
___	__	___	__	d. Paid the payroll. Gross pay $10, FICA $1, FIT $2
___	__	___	__	
___	__	___	__	e. Paid the FICA and FIT from (d) above. Don't forget the employer's share of FICA.
___	__	___	__	
___	__	___	__	

Answer:

	Debit		**Credit**	
	=====		======	
0.	111	$7	411	$7
a.	520	$4	111	$4
b.	525	$3	111	$3
c.	111	$1	520	$1
d.	513	$10	211	$1
			212	$2
			111	$7
e.	514	$1		
	211	$1		
	212	$2	111	$4

ES   Moderate

11.91: The combined journal for Betty's Beauty Boutique has the following headings with appropriate columns for indicating debits and credits: Explanation, Sundry, Cash, Accounts Receivable, Accounts Payable, Supplies Expense, and Fees Earned.

The following is a partial chart of accounts of Betty's Beauty Boutique:

111	Cash	121	Equipment
112	Accounts Receivable	211	Accounts Payable
113	Supplies	311	Betty's Capital
115	Prepaid Insurance	411	Beauty Fees

Indicate, in the format below, the account numbers and the debit and credit amounts for the following transactions under the accrual basis.

Debit		Credit		
Account	Amount	Account	Amount	
111	$9			0. Betty invested $9 cash and $3 of equipment in the business.
121	$3	311	$12	
___	___	___	___	a. Purchased supplies on account $2
___	___	___	___	b. Collected from cash customer $5
___	___	___	___	c. Paid insurance for three years in advance $3
___	___	___	___	d. Provided services on account $4
___	___	___	___	e. Collected from customer in (d) $4
___	___	___	___	f. Paid on account for (a) above $1

Answer:

	Debit		Credit	
0.	111	$9		
	121	$3	311	$12
a.	113	$2	211	$2
b.	111	$5	411	$5
c.	115	$3	111	$3
d.	112	$4	411	$4
e.	111	$4	112	$4
f.	211	$1	111	$1

ES   Moderate

11.92: The combined journal for Detroit Auto Supplies has the following headings with appropriate columns for indicating debits and credits: Explanation, Sundry, Cash, Accounts Receivable, Accounts Payable, Purchases, and Sales.

The following is a partial chart of accounts for Detroit Auto Supplies:

111 Cash
112 Accounts Receivable
115 Prepaid Insurance
121 Equipment

211 Accounts Payable
311 Detroit, Capital
411 Sales
513 Purchases
515 Insurance Expense

Indicate, in the form below, form, the account numbers and the debit and credit amounts for the following transactions under the accrual basis.

Debit		**Credit**		
Account	Amount	Account	Amount	
111	$8	311	$10	0. D. Detroit invested $8 cash and $2 of equipment in the business.
121	$2			
___	___	___	___	a. Paid insurance for three years in advance $3
___	___	___	___	b. Purchased merchandise on account for resale $4
___	___	___	___	c. Collected from cash customers $7
___	___	___	___	d. Sales on account $3
___	___	___	___	e. Collected from customers in (d) above $2
___	___	___	___	f. Paid on account for (b) above $2
___	___	___	___	g. One year of the policy purchased in (a) expired

Answer:

	Debit		**Credit**	
	=====		======	
0.	111	$8		
	121	$2	311	$10
a.	115	$3	111	$3
b.	513	$4	211	$4
c.	111	$7	411	$7
d.	112	$3	411	$3
e.	111	$2	112	$2
f.	211	$2	111	$2
g.	515	$1	115	$1

ES Moderate

11.93: Bill Bungee opened Bungee Jumping Enterprises and also sold jumping accessories. The combined journal for Bungee has the following headings with appropriate columns for indicating debits and credits: Explanation, Sundry, Cash, Accounts Receivable, Accounts Payable, Purchases and Sales.

The following is a partial chart of accounts of Bungee Jumping Enterprises:

111	Cash	211	Accounts Payable
112	Accounts Receivable	311	Bungee, Capital
115	Prepaid Insurance	411	Sales
121	Equipment	513	Purchases
		515	Insurance Expense

Indicate in the form below, the account numbers and the debit and credit amounts for the following transactions under the accrual basis.

Debit		Credit		
Account	**Amount**	**Account**	**Amount**	
111	$9			
121	$3	311	$12	0. Bungee invested $9 cash and $3 of equipment in the business.
___	__	___	__	a. Paid insurance for two years in advance $2
___	__	___	__	b. Purchased on account jumping accessories for resale to customers $5
___	__	___	__	c. Collected from bungee jumping cash customers $6
___	__	___	__	d. Sold products to customers on account $2
___	__	___	__	e. Collected from customers charged in (d) $1
___	__	___	__	f. Paid on account (b) $3
___	__	___	__	g. One year of the two-year policy purchased in (a) expired

Answer:

	Debit		**Credit**	
	=====		======	
0.	111	$9		
	121	$3	311	$12
a.	115	$2	111	$2
b.	513	$5	211	$5
c.	111	$6	411	$6
d.	112	$2	411	$2
e.	111	$1	112	$1
f.	211	$3	111	$3
g.	515	$1	115	$1

ES   Moderate

11.94: Discuss the major features of (a) accrual basis accounting, (b) cash basis accounting, and (c) modified cash-basis accounting.

Answer: a. Accrual basis accounting is based on the matching principle. Revenue is recorded when it is earned, and expenses are recorded when they are incurred.
  b. In the cash basis of accounting, revenue is recorded when the cash is received and expenses are recorded when the cash is paid.
  c. The modified cash-basis is a combination of the cash basis and accrual basis method. Revenue is recorded when the cash is received and expenses are recorded when the cash is paid out. Exceptions include:
    1. Long-lived assets such as buildings and equipment are treated under the accrual basis.
    2. Advance payments for insurance and large purchases of supplies are treated the same under the accrual basis and the modified cash-basis.
  ES Moderate

11.95: Discuss the purpose of combined journals and describe some of their features.

Answer: The combined journal is a special journal that can replace the general journal and special journals, thereby saving journalizing and posting labor. It is particularly useful for smaller businesses with a limited number of daily transactions.

Combined journals combine the features of the sales, cash payments, cash receipts, purchases, and general journals. Specialized columns with appropriate headings can be included to suit the individual needs of the business. Debit and credit columns for Cash, Accounts Receivable, Accounts Payable, Sundry, Purchases, Revenue, and various commonly-used expenses may be included.
ES Moderate

12. Preparing a Worksheet for a Merchandise Company

12.1: The goods a company has available to sell to customers are called:
   a) supplies.
   b) merchandise inventory.
   c) purchases.
   d) sales of goods.

Answer: (b)
   MC   Moderate

12.2: Merchandise inventory is:
   a) goods a company plans to sell to its customers.
   b) a current asset on the balance sheet.
   c) an important item on a merchandise company's financial statements.
   d) All the above.

Answer: (d)
   MC   Easy

12.3: In the perpetual inventory system the inventory balance is:
   a) updated only at the end of the period.
   b) updated at the beginning of the period.
   c) continually updated throughout the year.
   d) None of the above.

Answer: (c)
   MC   Moderate

12.4: In the periodic inventory system the inventory balance is:
   a) updated only at the end of the period.
   b) updated at the beginning of the period.
   c) continually updated throughout the year.
   d) None of the above.

Answer: (a)
   MC   Moderate

12.5: The perpetual inventory system is used when the company has:
   a) high volume and low unit prices.
   b) a high variety of merchandise and high unit prices.
   c) low volume and high unit prices.
   d) low variety and low unit prices.

Answer: (c)
   MC   Difficult

12.6: The periodic inventory system is most likely to be used when the company has:
   a) high volume and low unit prices.
   b) a variety of merchandise and low unit prices.
   c) low volume and high unit prices.
   d) low variety and high unit prices.

Answer: (b)
   MC   Difficult

12.7: An account used in a periodic inventory method to record buying of merchandise for resale is called:
   a) sales.   b) purchases.
   c) supplies.   d) beginning inventory.

Answer: (b)
   MC   Moderate

12.8: The dollar amount determined by a physical count of merchandise on hand at the end of the period is called:
   a) beginning inventory.   b) ending inventory.
   c) periodic inventory.   d) perpetual inventory.

Answer: (b)
   MC   Moderate

12.9: This amount does not change during the period and is added to Purchases when computing the cost of goods available for sale:
   a) beginning inventory.   b) ending inventory.
   c) periodic inventory.   d) perpetual inventory.

Answer: (a)
   MC   Difficult

12.10: Beginning Inventory is $65, Net Purchases are $1,000, and Sales Returns and Allowances are $200. Goods Available for Sale is:
   a) $1,065   b) $865
   c) $1,000   d) None of the above

Answer: (a)
   MC   Moderate

12.11: The formula for Cost of Goods Sold is:
   a) ending inventory - net purchases + beginning inventory.
   b) net purchases + ending inventory - beginning inventory.
   c) ending inventory + beginning inventory - purchases.
   d) beginning inventory + net purchases - ending inventory.

Answer: (d)
   MC   Difficult

12.12: Beginning Inventory is $100, Net Purchases are $1,000, and Ending Inventory is $100. Cost of Goods Sold is:
    a) $1,200   b) $1,000   c) $800   d) $900

Answer: (b)
    MC   Moderate

12.13: This amount is calculated on an inventory sheet using the physical count of merchandise in stock:
    a) beginning inventory.   b) ending inventory.
    c) periodic inventory.   d) perpetual inventory.

Answer: (b)
    MC   Moderate

12.14: The ending inventory for the period will become:
    a) the beginning inventory next period.
    b) sales next period.
    c) a periodic inventory.
    d) a perpetual inventory.

Answer: (a)
    MC   Easy

12.15: The beginning inventory for the current period is:
    a) a periodic inventory.
    b) a perpetual inventory.
    c) the beginning inventory last period.
    d) the ending inventory last period.

Answer: (d)
    MC   Easy

12.16: To adjust the Merchandise Inventory account, the first step is:
    a) debit Merchandise Inventory, credit Capital for the ending inventory balance.
    b) debit Capital, credit Merchandise Inventory for the ending inventory balance.
    c) debit Merchandise Inventory, credit Income Summary for the beginning inventory balance.
    d) debit Income Summary, credit Merchandise Inventory for the beginning inventory balance.

Answer: (d)
    MC   Difficult

12.17: The second step for adjusting Merchandise Inventory is:
a) debit Merchandise Inventory, credit Income Summary for the ending inventory balance.
b) debit Income Summary, credit Merchandise Inventory for the ending inventory balance.
c) debit Merchandise Inventory, credit Capital for the beginning inventory balance.
d) debit Capital, credit Merchandise Inventory for the beginning inventory balance.

Answer: (a)
MC Difficult

12.18: What type of account is Unearned Rent?
a) Asset   b) Liability   c) Revenue   d) Expense

Answer: (b)
MC Difficult

12.19: Rental Income is what type of account?
a) Asset   b) Liability   c) Revenue   d) Expense

Answer: (c)
MC Moderate

12.20: What is the normal balance for Unearned Rent?
a) Debit   b) Credit
c) Zero   d) Depends on circumstances

Answer: (b)
MC Moderate

12.21: Unearned Rent results because:
a) no fee has been paid, but the service is complete.
b) the fee is earned but not collected.
c) the fee has been collected before the service has been provided.
d) the fee has been paid and the service is complete.

Answer: (c)
MC Moderate

12.22: As the unearned rent is earned:
a) the liability account is decreased and the revenue account is increased.
b) the liability account is increased and the revenue account is decreased.
c) the liability account is decreased and the revenue account is not affected.
d) the liability account is not affected and the revenue account is decreased.

Answer: (a)
MC Difficult

12.23: An example of unearned revenue would be:
a) potential sale of merchandise.
b) purchase of merchandise on account.
c) legal fees collected after work is performed.
d) subscriptions collected in advance for a magazine.

Answer: (d)
MC   Moderate

12.24: The first two columns of a worksheet are used for:
a) adjustments.   b) journalizing.
c) the trial balance.   d) posting.

Answer: (c)
MC   Easy

12.25: The second two columns of a worksheet are used for:
a) the trial balance.   b) the income statement.
c) the balance sheet.   d) adjustments.

Answer: (d)
MC   Easy

12.26: The account Mortgage Payable:
a) shows increases in the amount of debt owed on a mortgage.
b) shows decreases in the amount of debt owed on a mortgage.
c) is a liability account.
d) All of the above.

Answer: (d)
MC   Moderate

12.27: Unearned rent would be reported on the:
a) balance sheet.
b) income statement.
c) owner's equity statement.
d) not reported until earned.

Answer: (a)
MC   Moderate

12.28: The account category "other expense" could be used to record:
a) an operating expense for interest expense.
b) an operating expense for interest incurred.
c) a non-operating expense for interest incurred.
d) None of the above.

Answer: (c)
MC   Moderate

12.29: What financial report shows the amount for Freight-In?
   a) Income Statement
   b) Balance Sheet
   c) Statement of Owner's Equity
   d) Trial Balance

Answer: (a)
   MC   Moderate

12.30: The adjustment for supplies used would be:
   a) debit Supplies, credit Supplies Expense.
   b) debit Supplies Used, credit Cash.
   c) debit Supplies Expense, credit Supplies.
   d) debit Supplies, credit Cash.

Answer: (c)
   MC   Moderate

12.31: The adjustment for accrued salaries would be:
   a) debit Salaries Expense, credit Salaries Payable.
   b) debit Salaries Payable, credit Salaries Expense.
   c) debit Salaries Expense, credit Cash.
   d) debit Salaries Payable, credit Cash.

Answer: (a)
   MC   Moderate

12.32: Which inventory appears in the balance sheet column of the work sheet?
   a) Beginning inventory
   b) Ending inventory
   c) Combination of beginning and ending inventories
   d) Inventory does not appear on the balance sheet

Answer: (b)
   MC   Difficult

12.33: The next step in the accounting cycle after preparing an unadjusted trial balance is to:
   a) prepare the financial statements.
   b) complete the worksheet.
   c) journalize the adjusting entries in the general journal.
   d) prepare the closing journal entries.

Answer: (b)
   MC   Easy

12.34: The Balance Sheet columns on the worksheet prepared for the Andretti Company had subtotals as follows: debit column, $14,000, and credit column, $14,600. This information indicates that:
a) the company incurred a net income of $600.
b) the company incurred a net loss of $600.
c) an error was made when preparing the adjustments in the worksheet.
d) a mathematical error was made in the worksheet.

Answer: (b)
MC   Moderate

12.35: The Balance Sheet columns on a worksheet have subtotals as follows: debit column, $1,000, and credit column, $900. This indicates that:
a) the company incurred a net loss of $100.
b) the company earned a net income of $100.
c) there was an error in the Adjustments columns.
d) there was an error in the Balance Sheet columns.

Answer: (b)
MC   Moderate

12.36: Accumulated Depreciation-Buildings should be shown on the:
a) income statement as an expense.
b) balance sheet as a current liability.
c) balance sheet as a contra account to Buildings.
d) balance sheet as a contra account to the owner's capital account.

Answer: (c)
MC   Easy

12.37: An account never used in an adjusting entry is:
a) Consulting Fees-Revenue.
b) Interest Payable.
c) Accumulated Depreciation.
d) Building.

Answer: (d)
MC   Moderate

12.38: On July 1, Ball Company received $4,800 for two years' rent in advance from Smithson Co. The December 31 adjusting entry Ball should make is:
a) debit Rent Income, credit Unearned Rent $2,400.
b) debit Cash, credit Rent Income $2,400.
c) debit Unearned Rent, credit Rent Expense $1,200.
d) debit Unearned Rent, credit Rent Income $1,200.

Answer: (d)
MC   Moderate

12.39: Barb's Bakery paid $480 on a one-year insurance policy on September 1, 19xx. The entry included a debit to Prepaid Insurance. The adjusting entry on December 31 would include a:

a) debit to Prepaid Insurance for $160, and a credit to Cash for $160.
b) debit to Insurance Expense for $120, and a credit to Prepaid Insurance for $120.
c) debit to Insurance Expense for $160, and credit to Prepaid Insurance for $160.
d) debit to Cash for $320, and credit to Prepaid Insurance for $320.

Answer: (c)
MC   Moderate

12.40: Hobbler Realty paid $3,600 rent on a building in advance for three years on October 31, 19xx. The amount that should be apportioned as rent expense for the balance of the year is:
a) $1,200.   b) $200.   c) $1,800.   d) $400.

Answer: (b)
MC   Moderate

12.41: An adjusting entry at the end of the period would <u>not</u> be caused by which of the following transactions that took place during the period?
a) Purchase of equipment
b) Payment of this month's rent
c) Purchase of a three-year insurance policy
d) Performing a service that was paid for in a previous period

Answer: (b)
MC   Easy

12.42: Under a periodic inventory system, cost of goods sold is computed by:
a) deducting the cost of the ending inventory from the net cost of purchases.
b) deducting the cost of the ending inventory from the cost of merchandise available for sale.
c) deducting the cost of the beginning inventory from the cost of merchandise available for sale.
d) adding the net cost of purchases to the cost of the ending inventory.

Answer: (b)
MC   Easy

12.43: Cost of Goods Sold is $200, Net Purchases are $400, and Ending Inventory is $300. Beginning Inventory was:
   a) $500.   b) $100.   c) $200.   d) $300.

Answer: (b)
   MC   Difficult

12.44: When completing a worksheet:
   a) the ending inventory amount appears in the Income Statement debit column.
   b) the beginning inventory amount appears in the Income Statement debit column.
   c) the ending inventory amount appears in the Unadjusted Trial Balance debit column of the worksheet.
   d) the beginning inventory amount appears in the Balance Sheet debit column of the worksheet.

Answer: (b)
   MC   Moderate

12.45: In preparing a worksheet, the $600 balance of Siesta, Drawing account was extended as a debit to the Income Statement columns. This procedure will:
   a) overstate net income $600.
   b) understate net income $600.
   c) overstate net income $1,200.
   d) understate net income $1,200.

Answer: (b)
   MC   Moderate

12.46: Beginning and ending inventories are $650 and $700, respectively. The Income Statement debit and credit columns of the worksheet total $2,700 and $2,800, respectively, not including the amounts for beginning and ending inventories. The net income or loss for the period is:
   a) $150 net income.   b) $150 net loss.
   c) $100 net income.   d) $100 net loss.

Answer: (a)
   MC   Difficult

12.47: The beginning inventory was properly extended as a debit in the income statement columns of a worksheet. However, the $3,000 ending inventory was debited in the income statement columns and credited in the balance sheet columns. This procedure would:
   a) cause the worksheet to be out of balance.
   b) overstate net income by $3,000.
   c) overstate net income by $6,000.
   d) understate net income by $6,000.

Answer: (d)
   MC   Difficult

12.48: Beginning and ending inventories for Alnight Stores are
$6,000 and $4,000, respectively. The debit amounts (not
including inventory) in the income statement columns of the
worksheet total $14,000, and the credit amounts (not
including inventory) total $15,500. The firm has:
  a) net income of $6,500.   b) net loss of $6,500.
  c) net loss of $500.   d) net income of $500.

Answer: (c)
  MC Difficult

12.49: Net Sales are $2,125, Sales Discounts are $50, and Purchase
Discounts are $100. Gross sales are:
  a) $2,275   b) $1,975   c) $2,175   d) $2,050

Answer: (c)
  MC Moderate

12.50: The formula for determining Net Sales is:
  a) Gross Sales - Purchase Discounts - Purchases Returns and
  Allowances.
  b) Gross Sales + Sales Discounts - Sales Returns and
  Allowances.
  c) Gross Sales - Sales Discounts - Sales Returns and
  Allowances.
  d) Gross Sales + Sales Returns and Allowances - Sales
  Discounts.

Answer: (c)
  MC Difficult

12.51: Which of the following items appears as a credit in the
income statement columns of the worksheet?
  a) Sales Returns and Allowances
  b) Purchases Discounts
  c) Accumulated Depreciation
  d) Sales Discounts

Answer: (b)
  MC Moderate

12.52: Ending merchandise inventory is subtracted when calculating
the cost of goods sold.

Answer: True
  TF Moderate

12.53: The Income Summary account does not have a normal balance.

Answer: True
  TF Moderate

12.54: The Income Summary account normal balance is a credit.

Answer: False
     TF Moderate

12.55: The ending inventory figure is shown on the balance sheet.

Answer: True
     TF Moderate

12.56: The income statement shows beginning inventory as a part of cost of goods sold.

Answer: True
     TF Moderate

12.57: When adjustments are made, the beginning inventory figure is transferred to the Income Summary account.

Answer: True
     TF Difficult

12.58: The Income Summary account does not have a normal balance.

Answer: True
     TF Moderate

12.59: In the periodic inventory system, it is not necessary to take a physical inventory at the end of the period.

Answer: False
     TF Moderate

12.60: The ending inventory is assumed to be sold, therefore it is subtracted from cost of goods sold.

Answer: False
     TF Difficult

12.61: Unearned Rent is one type of unearned revenue.

Answer: True
     TF Easy

12.62: Revenue is recognized when earned under the accrual system.

Answer: True
     TF Moderate

12.63: An adjustment to Prepaid Insurance would not normally be made until the end of two years.

Answer: False
TF   Moderate

12.64: When the adjustment is made for depreciation, both the Depreciation Expense account and Accumulated Depreciation account are increased.

Answer: True
TF   Moderate

12.65: The amount of supplies used causes an increase in supplies and decrease in expense.

Answer: False
TF   Moderate

12.66: The category Other Income can be used to report rental income.

Answer: True
TF   Moderate

12.67: It is necessary to record beginning inventory when using the periodic inventory system.

Answer: True
TF   Moderate

12.68: An adjustment is made on the worksheet when the periodic inventory system is used.

Answer: True
TF   Moderate

12.69: To record the adjustment for supplies on the worksheet, a credit is made to Supplies for the beginning supply balance, and a debit for the same amount is made to Income Summary.

Answer: False
TF   Difficult

12.70: No adjustment is ever made to Unearned Revenue.

Answer: False
TF   Difficult

12.71: A periodic inventory system is less efficient than a perpetual system when there is a high unit price per item.

Answer: True
TF Moderate

12.72: Adjustments are journalized before recording them in the worksheet.

Answer: False
TF Moderate

12.73: The balance in the inventory account is updated under the periodic inventory method at the end of the period.

Answer: True
TF Moderate

12.74: The beginning and ending inventories are combined to come up with the balance sheet inventory amount.

Answer: False
TF Difficult

12.75: Merchandise Inventory account is a Cost of Goods Sold account.

Answer: False
TF Moderate

12.76: Mortgage Payable is a liability account.

Answer: True
TF Easy

12.77: Unearned Rent is found on the Balance Sheet.

Answer: True
TF Moderate

12.78: Purchases is a permanent account.

Answer: False
TF Moderate

12.79: The ending inventory is found on the worksheet in the balance sheet columns.

Answer: True
TF Moderate

12.80: Interest expense is usually found under the caption Other Expense.

Answer: True
TF Moderate

12.81: Unearned Rent is an asset account.

Answer: False
TF Moderate

12.82: The cost of goods on hand in a company to <u>begin</u> an accounting period.

Answer: Beginning merchandise inventory
MA Easy

12.83: The cost of goods that remain unsold at the end of the accounting period. It is an asset on the new balance sheet.

Answer: Ending merchandise inventory
MA Easy

12.84: A liability account showing amount owed on a mortgage.

Answer: Mortgage payable
MA Easy

12.85: An inventory system that, at the <u>end</u> of each accounting period, calculates the cost of the unsold goods on hand.

Answer: Periodic inventory system
MA Easy

12.86: An inventory system that keeps <u>continual track</u> of each type of inventory by recording units on hand at beginning, units sold, and the current balance after each sale or purchase.

Answer: Perpetual inventory system
MA Easy

12.87: A liability account that records receipt of payment for goods or services in advance of delivery.

Answer: Unearned revenue
MA Easy

12.88: Indicate the normal balance of each of the following
accounts:
a. Purchases Returns and Allowances
b. Merchandise Inventory (beginning of the period)
c. Freight-In
d. Payroll Tax Expense
e. Purchases Discount
f. Sales Discount
g. FICA-Social Security Tax Payable
h. Unearned Revenue

Answer: a. Credit
b. Debit
c. Debit
d. Debit
e. Credit
f. Debit
g. Credit
h. Credit
ES Moderate

12.89: Calculate (a) net sales, (b) cost of goods sold, (c) gross
profit, and (d) net income from the following:

Sales	$2,200	Beginning Inventory	$ 65
Sales Discount	50	Net purchases	1,320
Sales Rets. and		Ending Inventory	51
Allowances	25	Operating Expenses	360

Answer:

Sales		$2,200
Deduct:		
Sales Discounts	$50	
Sales Returns and Allowances	25	
		75
Net Sales		$2,125
Cost of Goods Sold:		
Beginning Inventory	$ 65	
Net Purchases	1,320	
Goods Available for Sale	$1,385	
Ending Inventory	51	
Cost of Goods Sold		1,334
Gross Profit on Sales		$ 791
Less:		
Operating Expense		360
Net Income		$ 431

ES Moderate

238

12.90: Brady Company's unadjusted trial balance includes the
following:

Cash	$2,100
Unearned Legal Fees	600
Legal Fees Revenue	7,200

The accounting department has been notified that legal
services in the amount of $400 have been performed for
clients who had previously paid in advance. Prepare the
appropriate adjusting entry.

Answer: Unearned Legal Fees   400
    Legal Fees Revenue   400
   ES   Moderate

12.91: Moore and Company purchased merchandise costing $4,000.
Calculate the cost of goods sold under the following
different situations:
a.   Beginning inventory $400 and no ending inventory.
b.   Beginning inventory $500 and a $600 ending inventory.
c.   No beginning inventory and a $300 ending inventory.

Answer:

	a.	b.	c.
Beginning inventory	$ 400	$ 500	$ 0
Purchases	4,000	4,000	4,000
	$4,400	$4,500	$4,000
Less ending inventory	0	600	300
Cost of goods sold	$4,400	$3,900	$3,700
	======	======	======

ES   Moderate

12.92: Below is a partial worksheet for Holmes Company:

Account	Trial Balance Dr.	Cr	Adjustments Dr.	Cr.	Adj. Trial Bal. Dr.	Cr.
Inventory	11					
Store Supplies	10					
Store Equip.	20					
Accum. Dep. Store Equip.		6				
Salaries Payable						
Income Summary						
Salary Expense	10					
Depn. Expense						

Record the appropriate adjusting entries using the information below. Holmes uses the periodic inventory method:

Merchandise Inventory-ending: $13
Store supplies on hand   4
Depreciation on store equip.   4
Accrued salaries   2

Answer:

Account	Trial Balance Dr.	Cr.	Adjustments Dr.	Cr.	Adj. Trial Bal. Dr.	Cr.
Inventory	11		13	11	13	
Store Supplies	10			6	4	
Store Equip.	20				20	
Accum.Dep. Store Eq.		6		4		10
Salaries Payable				2		2
Income Summary			11	13	11	13
Salary Expense	10		2		12	
Depn. Expense			4		4	
Store Sup. Expense			6		6	

ES Moderate

12.93: The column totals for the partially completed worksheet for the Westley Company are shown below. Complete the columns and label the net income or net loss for the period.

	INCOME STATEMENT DEBIT	CREDIT	BALANCE SHEET DEBIT	CREDIT
SUBTOTALS	75	70	100	105

Answer:

	INCOME STATEMENT DEBIT	CREDIT	BALANCE SHEET DEBIT	CREDIT
SUBTOTALS	75	70	100	105
NET LOSS		5	5	
	75	75	105	105
	===============		===============	

ES   Moderate

12.94: Calculate the missing amounts. Each case is a distinct and separate business problem.

	Case A	Case B	Case C
Sales	32	38	48
Beg. Inventory	20	14	20
Purchases	16	(d)	(f)
Ending Inventory	(a)	18	16
Cost of Goods Sold	26	20	(g)
Gross Profit	(b)	(e)	22
Expense	8	10	14
Net Income or Loss	(c)	8	8

Answer:

CASE A	CASE B	CASE C
a. 10	d. 24	f. 22
b. 6	e. 18	g. 26
c. 2		

ES   Moderate

12.95: Discuss the reasons a company would consider using a periodic inventory system.

Answer: The periodic inventory system is often used by companies selling a variety of merchandise with low unit prices. A perpetual system is not considered by some to be economical when large numbers of low unit price items are purchased and sold on a daily basis unless the system is computerized. The record keeping aspects of a periodic system are relatively simple. A firm records costs and quantities purchased which are later compared to the quantities remaining on hand at the end of the accounting period. In this way, the cost of the units sold during the period can be calculated.
ES   Moderate

12.96: Explain why figures for beginning and ending inventory are not combined on the Income Summary line of the worksheet.

Answer: Both the beginning and ending inventory figures are inserted in the Income Statement columns. The beginning figure is used at the end of the accounting period and is part of the cost of goods available for sale. The ending figure is subtracted from the cost of goods available for sale when calculating the cost of goods sold.
ES   Moderate

13. Completion of Accounting Cycle for a Merchandise Co.

13.1: Prepare the income statement from the:
   a) general journal.   b) combined journal.
   c) worksheet.   d) balance sheet.

Answer: (c)
   MC   Easy

13.2: The correct worksheet columns to use for preparing the
      income statement are the:
   a) adjustments columns.
   b) income statement columns.
   c) adjusted trial balance columns.
   d) trial balance columns.

Answer: (b)
   MC   Moderate

13.3: Use the inside columns on the income statement for:
   a) subtotaling.   b) debits.
   c) credits.   d) adjustments.

Answer: (a)
   MC   Moderate

13.4: Use the outside column on the income statement for:
   a) summarizing revenues and expenses.
   b) reporting net income from operations.
   c) reporting net income.
   d) All of the above.

Answer: (d)
   MC   Moderate

13.5: Net sales are:
   a) gross sales - sales discounts - sales returns and
   allowances.
   b) gross sales + sales discounts + sales returns and
   allowances.
   c) revenue + sales discounts + sales returns and
   allowances.
   d) gross sales - sales discounts + sales returns and
   allowances.

Answer: (a)
   MC   Moderate

13.6: Net Sales + Sales Discounts + Sales Returns and Allowances
determines:
a) net income.
b) net income from operations.
c) gross profit.
d) gross sales.

Answer: (d)
MC   Moderate

13.7: Net purchases are:
a) total purchases - purchases discounts + purchases
returns and allowances.
b) total purchases - purchases discounts - purchases
returns and allowances.
c) total purchases - purchases discounts + purchases
discounts + purchases returns and allowances.
d) None of the above.

Answer: (b)
MC   Moderate

13.8: The difference between net purchases and net cost of
purchases is:
a) Freight-In is added to net purchases to get net cost of
purchases.
b) Freight-In is subtracted from net purchases to get net
cost of purchases.
c) ending inventory is subtracted.
d) Sales Returns and Allowances is added.

Answer: (a)
MC   Moderate

13.9: To calculate gross profit:
a) subtract Freight-In from net purchases.
b) subtract ending inventory from cost of goods available
for sale.
c) subtract cost of goods sold from net sales.
d) add freight to net purchases.

Answer: (c)
MC   Moderate

13.10: Gross profit is the difference between:
a) net income and operating expenses.
b) net sales and cost of goods sold.
c) revenues and operating expenses.
d) revenues and cost of goods sold plus operating expenses.

Answer: (b)
MC   Moderate

13.11: Net purchases plus freight-in is:
    a) gross profit.   b) net cost of purchases.
    c) gross purchases.   d) None of the above.

Answer: (b)
    MC Easy

13.12: The calculation of net purchases does not include:
    a) purchases returns and allowances.
    b) purchases discounts.
    c) purchases.
    d) freight-out.

Answer: (d)
    MC Moderate

13.13: The income statement lists regular business expenses under
the heading:
    a) current expenses.   b) operating debts.
    c) liabilities.   d) operating expenses.

Answer: (d)
    MC Moderate

13.14: Which of the following is not an operating expense?
    a) cost of goods sold   b) advertising expense
    c) freight-out   d) general office expenses

Answer: (a)
    MC Moderate

13.15: Which one of the following is used to calculate cost of
goods sold but not goods available for sale:
    a) purchases.
    b) freight-in.
    c) beginning merchandise inventory.
    d) ending merchandise inventory.

Answer: (d)
    MC Moderate

13.16: Goods available for sale include:
    a) ending inventory.
    b) sales returns and allowances.
    c) beginning inventory.
    d) selling expenses.

Answer: (c)
    MC Easy

13.17: The income statement lists expenses directly related to the selling activity under which heading?
   a) Selling expenses   b) Administrative expenses
   c) Cost of goods sold   d) Current expenses

Answer: (a)
   MC   Moderate

13.18: Which of the following is not an administrative expense?
   a) Office salaries
   b) Depreciation expense on the office equipment
   c) Sales persons' commissions
   d) Office manager's salary

Answer: (c)
   MC   Moderate

13.19: Paper used to wrap customers' purchases is a(n):
   a) selling expense.   b) administrative expense.
   c) cost of goods sold.   d) other expense.

Answer: (a)
   MC   Easy

13.20: Freight-out is a (an):
   a) selling expense.
   b) administrative expense.
   c) other expense.
   d) cost of goods purchased expense.

Answer: (a)
   MC   Easy

13.21: A merchandise company's interest expense is a(n):
   a) selling expense.   b) administrative expense.
   c) contra-revenue.   d) other expense.

Answer: (d)
   MC   Easy

13.22: Rental income earned by a merchandise company is:
   a) included in gross sales.
   b) added to gross profit.
   c) other income.
   d) subtracted from administrative expenses.

Answer: (c)
   MC   Easy

13.23: A classified balance sheet includes all of the following
       except:
       a) current assets.   b) plant and equipment.
       c) revenues.   d) current liabilities.

Answer: (c)
       MC Moderate

13.24: Which of the following is on a classified balance sheet?
       a) A. Finkel, Capital   b) Mortgage Payable
       c) Cash   d) All of the above.

Answer: (d)
       MC Moderate

13.25: Current assets are:
       a) cash and other assets that will not be used during the
       year.
       b) cash and other assets that will be used during the year.
       c) cash and other assets that will be converted or consumed
       during the normal operating cycle of the company or one
       year, whichever is longer.
       d) cash and assets that will be converted or consumed
       during the normal operating cycle or one year, whichever is
       shorter.

Answer: (c)
       MC Easy

13.26: All of the following are current assets except:
       a) accounts receivable.   b) store equipment.
       c) merchandise inventory.   d) prepaid insurance.

Answer: (b)
       MC Easy

13.27: Plant and equipment are:
       a) liabilities used to generate net income.
       b) cash and accounts receivable.
       c) long-lived assets used in the production or sales of
       goods or services.
       d) cash and assets that will be converted or used during
       the normal operating cycle of the company or one year,
       whichever is longer.

Answer: (c)
       MC Moderate

13.28: Which of the following is under the heading Plant and Equipment on a classified balance sheet?
a) Store Equipment
b) Office Machines
c) Accumulated Depreciation on Office Machines
d) All of the above.

Answer: (d)
MC   Easy

13.29: Accounts payable is a(n):
a) current liability.   b) long-term liability.
c) current asset.   d) operating expense.

Answer: (a)
MC   Easy

13.30: A landlord collected six months' rent in advance from a tenant. This would be classified as a(n):
a) current asset.   b) other income.
c) revenue.   d) current liability.

Answer: (d)
MC   Moderate

13.31: Long-term liabilities are debts or obligations not yet due that will be paid:
a) usually within one year or shorter.
b) usually after one year or longer.
c) within one business cycle or shorter.
d) None of the above.

Answer: (b)
MC   Moderate

13.32: Mortgage Payable amounts due in two years are:
a) long-term liabilities.   b) current liabilities.
c) current assets.   d) owner's equity.

Answer: (a)
MC   Easy

13.33: Mortgage Payable amounts due within one year are:
a) expenses.   b) revenue.
c) long-term liabilities.   d) current liabilities.

Answer: (d)
MC   Moderate

13.34: Adjusting entries on the worksheet:
   a) are journalized and posted to the ledger.
   b) are posted directly to the ledger.
   c) are closed to the income summary account.
   d) affect only balance sheet accounts.

Answer: (a)
   MC   Easy

13.35: The second set of columns on a worksheet are used for:
   a) recording reversing entries.
   b) the adjusted trial balance.
   c) determining adjusting entries.
   d) All of the above.

Answer: (c)
   MC   Easy

13.36: The capital account in the ledger agrees with the balance
   sheet:
   a) after the adjusting entries have been posted.
   b) after the closing entries have been posted.
   c) after the income statement has been prepared.
   d) after posting the reversing entries.

Answer: (b)
   MC   Difficult

13.37: After the closing entries have been posted:
   a) the temporary accounts are zeroed out.
   b) the capital account includes the current net profit or
   loss.
   c) the post-closing trial balance is prepared.
   d) All the above.

Answer: (d)
   MC   Moderate

13.38: The amount shown in the adjusted trial balance for
   merchandise inventory under the adjusting entry approach is:
   a) the cost of goods sold.
   b) net purchases.
   c) the beginning merchandise inventory.
   d) the ending merchandise inventory.

Answer: (d)
   MC   Moderate

13.39: Under the adjusting approach, the income summary amount in the income statement debit column on the worksheet is:
a) the ending merchandise inventory.
b) cost of goods sold.
c) the beginning merchandise inventory.
d) total purchases.

Answer: (c)
MC   Moderate

13.40: When the adjusting entry method is used to update merchandise inventory, the amount shown in the adjustments credit column for merchandise inventory on the worksheet is:
a) ending merchandise inventory.
b) beginning merchandise inventory.
c) total purchases.
d) cost of goods sold.

Answer: (b)
MC   Moderate

13.41: The adjusting entry for the beginning and ending merchandise inventory requires a debit and a credit, respectively, to:
a) cost of goods available for sale and sales.
b) the capital account and income summary.
c) income summary.
d) cost of goods sold and goods available for sale.

Answer: (c)
MC   Moderate

13.42: The goals of closing entries include:
a) closing out all permanent accounts.
b) closing out the capital account to income summary.
c) clearing the temporary accounts and updating capital.
d) closing out only the current asset accounts.

Answer: (c)
MC   Moderate

13.43: After the closing entries are posted to the ledger:
a) all the temporary accounts have zero balances.
b) merchandise inventory has a zero balance.
c) the capital account has a zero balance.
d) All of the above.

Answer: (a)
MC   Moderate

13.44: Reversing entries are general journal entries that:
   a) are the same as the adjusting entries.
   b) are used by all businesses.
   c) only affect income statement accounts.
   d) None of the above.

Answer: (d)
   MC   Difficult

13.45: Reversing entries occur at the beginning of the accounting period. The primary objective of reversing entries is to:
   a) correct errors.
   b) simplify the bookkeeping associated with accruals from the prior period.
   c) transfer the balance of the expense accounts to the capital account and set the accounts equal to zero.
   d) place the expenses for the current period in the proper accounts.

Answer: (b)
   MC   Moderate

13.46: Which of the following would be the basis for a reversing entry?
   a) Depreciation of building
   b) Accrual of interest expense
   c) Allocation of prepaid rent in the current period
   d) Correction of an error

Answer: (b)
   MC   Difficult

13.47: Reverse which of the following adjustments under the reversing option?
   a) The adjustment to record depreciation expense
   b) The adjustment to allocate prepaid insurance to the current period
   c) The adjustment to accrue salaries payable
   d) The adjustment to determine supplies expense for the period

Answer: (c)
   MC   Difficult

13.48: Which of the following could appear in an adjusting entry, closing entry, and reversing entry?
   a) Professional Fees
   b) Salaries Payable
   c) Depreciation Expense, Buildings
   d) Accumulated Depreciation, Buildings

Answer: (b)
   MC   Difficult

13.49: Interest income could appear in which entry(ies)?
  a) Adjusting   b) Reversing
  c) Closing   d) All of the above.

Answer: (d)
  MC   Difficult

13.50: If no adjustments are needed for the Wong Company:
  a) the post-closing trial balance will be identical to its trial balance.
  b) the adjusted trial balance will be identical to its post-closing trial balance.
  c) the trial balance will be identical to its adjusted trial balance.
  d) the trial balance, adjusted trial balance, and post-closing trial balance will be identical.

Answer: (c)
  MC   Moderate

13.51: If the income statement column subtotals for the debit and credit columns on the worksheet are $2,000 and $2,800, respectively, the company has:
  a) a net loss of $800.
  b) a net income of $800.
  c) incurred an error because the columns are out of balance.
  d) a net income of $2,800.

Answer: (b)
  MC   Moderate

13.52: If the balance sheet subtotals for the debit and credit columns on the worksheet are $4,000 and $3,200, respectively, the company has:
  a) a net loss of $800.
  b) a net income of $800.
  c) a balance sheet that is out of balance.
  d) a net income of $3,200.

Answer: (b)
  MC   Moderate

13.53: Under what circumstances will the subtotals of the last two columns of a worksheet be equal?
  a) Under no circumstances.
  b) Under all circumstances, if there are no arithmetical errors.
  c) when net income/net loss is zero.
  d) When there are no adjustments entered into the worksheet.

Answer: (c)
  MC   Moderate

13.54: The closing entry for the $2,000 balance of the Sales account includes:
  a) a debit to Sales for $2,000.
  b) a credit to Sales for $2,000.
  c) a debit to Income Summary for $2,000.
  d) None of the above.

Answer: (a)
  MC   Easy

13.55: The closing entry for the $700 balance of Wages Expense includes:
  a) a credit to Income Summary for $700.
  b) a debit to Income Summary for $700.
  c) a debit to Wages Expense for $700.
  d) None of the above.

Answer: (b)
  MC   Easy

13.56: The Income Summary account has total debit and credit postings of $3,000 and $2,200, respectively. The entry to close the Income Summary account would include:
  a) a debit to Capital for $2,200.
  b) a credit to Capital for $3,000.
  c) a debit to Capital for $800.
  d) a credit to Capital for $800.

Answer: (c)
  MC   Difficult

13.57: The adjusting entry for Packard Company's depreciation expense:
  a) should be reversed.
  b) should not be reversed.
  c) reversing entry is optional.
  d) None of the above.

Answer: (b)
  MC   Difficult

13.58: The columns on an income statement are called debit and credit columns.

Answer: False
  TF   Moderate

13.59: Operating expenses that are not related to the selling of goods are administrative expenses.

Answer: True
  TF   Moderate

13.60: Net income from operations plus other income minus other expenses equals net income.

Answer: True
TF Moderate

13.61: Gross profit minus cost of goods sold equals net sales.

Answer: False
TF Moderate

13.62: Administrative expenses are also called general expenses.

Answer: True
TF Easy

13.63: Nonoperating expenses are found in the other expense section of the income statement.

Answer: True
TF Moderate

13.64: A balance sheet where assets and liabilities are broken down into more detail is called a comprehensive balance sheet.

Answer: False
TF Easy

13.65: FICA Tax Payable would be classified as a current liability.

Answer: True
TF Easy

13.66: Store Equipment would normally be classified as a current asset.

Answer: False
TF Easy

13.67: Additional investments by the owner would be subtracted from beginning capital to compute ending capital.

Answer: False
TF Easy

13.68: Merchandise Inventory would be classified as a current asset.

Answer: True
TF Moderate

13.69: Prepaid Insurance would be classified as a current asset.

Answer: True
TF   Easy

13.70: The average time it takes to buy and sell merchandise and collect accounts receivable is the operating cycle for a business.

Answer: True
TF   Moderate

13.71: Some of the information used in preparing the statement of owner's equity comes from the income statement columns of the worksheet.

Answer: True
TF   Difficult

13.72: Land is a long-lived asset, and is never depreciated.

Answer: True
TF   Moderate

13.73: Long-lived assets would be listed according to how long the asset will last, with the longest life asset listed first.

Answer: False
TF   Difficult

13.74: The adjusting entry to record rental income that is earned would be a debit to Unearned Rent and a credit to Rental Income.

Answer: True
TF   Moderate

13.75: The entry to record the adjustment for depreciation on equipment would be a debit to Depreciation Expense, Equipment and a credit to Accumulated Depreciation, Equipment.

Answer: True
TF   Moderate

13.76: The periodic inventory system adds goods bought during the period to the Merchandise Inventory account.

Answer: False
TF   Difficult

13.77: The general ledger balances are used to prepare the post-closing trial balance.

Answer: True
TF Moderate

13.78: The post-closing trial balance would not include temporary accounts.

Answer: True
TF Moderate

13.79: Reversing entries help reduce potential errors and simplify the record-keeping process.

Answer: True
TF Moderate

13.80: Reversing entries are the opposite of adjusting entries.

Answer: True
TF Difficult

13.81: Not all adjusting entries are reversed.

Answer: True
TF Moderate

13.82: Reversing entries are recorded on the first day of the new accounting period.

Answer: True
TF Moderate

13.83: After the closing process, the permanent accounts are set back to zero.

Answer: False
TF Moderate

13.84: The owner's equity statement is the same for a service business as for a merchandise business.

Answer: True
TF Easy

13.85: Liquidity refers to how quickly an asset can be converted to cash.

Answer: True
TF Moderate

13.86: A goal of closing entries is to update capital.

Answer: True
      TF Easy

13.87: In closing entries, the Income Summary account is closed to
      the Capital account.

Answer: True
      TF Moderate

13.88: The following amounts are on the Mungh Company worksheet for the month ended September 30, 19xx.
Required: Calculate the following:
a. Net sales
b. Net purchases
c. Net cost of purchases
d. Goods available for sale
e. Cost of goods sold
f. Gross profit

ACCOUNT	INCOME STATEMENT	
	DEBIT	CREDIT
Sales		32
Sales Returns and Allowances	2	
Sales Discounts	1	
Income Summary	9	11
Purchases	20	
Purchases Discount		1
Purchases Returns and Allowances		2
Freight-In	1	

Answer:

MUNGH COMPANY
Partial Income Statement
For the Month Ended September 30, 19xx

Revenue:
Gross Sales $32
Less: Sales Ret. and Allow. $2
      Sales Discount 1   3

Net Sales .... (a) $29

Cost of Goods Sold:
Merchandise Inventory 9/1/xx .... $ 9
Purchases $20
Less: Purch. Discount $1
      Purch. Ret. and Allow. 2   3
                                 --   ---
Net Purchases .... $17 (b)
Add: Freight-In   1

Net Cost of Purchases .... 18 (c)

Cost of Goods Available for Sale .... $27 (d)
Less: Merchandise Inventory 9/30/xx 11

Cost of Goods Sold .... (e)   16

Gross Profit .... (f) $13
ES   Moderate

13.89: The following accounts are on the Balance Sheet section of Appleton Company worksheet for the month ended July 31, 19xx. Required: Prepare a classified balance sheet.

ACCOUNT	BALANCE SHEET	
	DEBIT	CREDIT
Cash	3	
Accounts Receivable	5	
Merchandise Inventory	7	
Store Equipment	15	
Accum. Depr., Store Equip.		3
Accounts Payable		7
Mortgage Payable		12
Appleton, Capital		4

Additional information: Withdrawals for the period are $2, and Net Income is $6.

Answer:

APPLETON COMPANY
Balance Sheet
July 31, 19xx

Assets

Current Assets:
Cash	$ 3	
Accounts Receivable	5	
Merchandise Inventory	7	
Total Current Assets		$15

Plant and Equipment:
Store Equipment	$15	
Less: Accumulated Depr.	3	12
Total Assets		$27
		===

Liabilities

Current Liabilities:
Accounts Payable	$ 7
Long-Term Liabilities	12
Total Liabilities	$19

Owner's Equity
Appleton, Capital, September 30, 19xx	8
Total Liabilities and Owner's Equity	$27
	===

ES   Moderate

13.90: Prepare the adjusting journal entries from the following items on the Smithson Company worksheet.

ADJUSTMENTS

	Debit	Credit
Interest Receivable	(a) 5	
Merchandise Inventory	(c) 4	(d) 7
Supplies on Hand		(b) 2
Interest Income		(a) 5
Supplies Expense	(b) 2	
Income Summary	(d) 7	(c) 4

Answer: (a)   Interest Receivable   5
              Interest Income   5

       (b)   Supplies Expense   2
              Supplies on Hand   2

       (c)   Merchandise Inventory   4
              Income Summary   4

       (d)   Income Summary   7
              Merchandise Inventory   7

       ES   Easy

13.91: Prepare <u>compound</u> closing entries from the following information on the Des Moines Storage Company worksheet income statement columns.

INCOME STATEMENT

	DEBIT	CREDIT
Sales		$34
Sales Ret. and Allow.	$ 2	
Income Summary	9	11
Purchases	22	
Pur. Ret. and Allow.		3
Sales Salaries Expense	5	
Office Salaries Expense	2	

Answer: Sales   34
        Purchases Ret. and Allow.3
           Income Summary   37

        Income Summary   31
           Sales Salaries Expense   5
           Office Salaries Expense   2
           Purchases   22
           Sales Returns and Allow.   2

        Income Summary   8
           Capital   8

        ES   Moderate

13.92: Adams Company's adjusting entries included the following
items:

Interest Expense	200	
Interest Payable		200
Depreciation Expense	50	
Accumulated Depreciation		50
Interest Receivable	90	
Interest Income		90

Required: Prepare the appropriate reversing entries.

Answer:

Interest Payable	200	
Interest Expense		200
Interest Income	90	
Interest Receivable		90

ES   Moderate

13.93: Bontel Bakery's reversing entries on December 1 included the following items:

Utilities Payable	300	
Utilities Expense		300
Rental Income	700	
Rent Receivable		700

Bontel's transactions the first week of December included:

Dec. 5 Paid utilities bill $400
7 Collected rent due $900

Required: a. Post the December 1 reversing entries and December transactions to T accounts.
b. Determine the utilities expense and rent income for December by footing the T accounts.

Answer:

```
    Utilities Expense              Utilities Payable
              |300  12/1                   12/1  300|
    12/5 400  |                                     |
    --------- |----------          -------- |--------
    Bal.  100 |                             |


    Rent Receivable               Rental Income
              |700  12/1                   12/1  700|
              |                                     |900  12/7
              |                            -------- |---------
              |                                     |200  Bal.


        Cash
    12/7 900 |400  12/5
             |
             |
```

ES Moderate

13.94: Give the category, classification, and the report(s) on which each of the following appear.

ITEM	CATEGORY	CLASSIFICATION	REPORT
0. Cash	Asset	Current Asset	Balance Sheet
a. Accts. Rec.			
b. Accts. Pay.			
c. Mortgage Pay.			
d. Office Equip.			
e. Prepaid Ins.			

Answer:

ITEM	CATEGORY	CLASSIFICATION	REPORT
0.	Asset	Current Asset	Balance Sheet
a.	Asset	Current Asset	Balance Sheet
b.	Liabilities	Current Liab.	Balance Sheet
c.	Liabilities	Long-term Liab.	Balance Sheet
d.	Asset	Plant and Equip.	Balance Sheet
e.	Asset	Current Asset	Balance Sheet

ES Moderate

13.95: Give the category and the report(s) on which each of the following appear.

Item	Category	Report
0. Sales	Revenue	Income Statement
a. Sales Salaries		
b. Office Salaries		
c. Interest Expense		
d. Miscellaneous Income		
e. Sales discounts		

Answer:

Item	Category	Report
0. Sales	Revenue	Inc. Stat.
a. Sales Salaries	Selling expense	Inc. Stat.
b. Office Salaries	Administrative expense	Inc. Stat.
c. Interest Expense	Other expense	Inc. Stat.
d. Miscellaneous Income	Other income	Inc. Stat.
e. Sales Discounts	Contra revenue	Inc. Stat.

ES   Moderate

13.96: Discuss the purpose of a detailed income statement. Briefly describe the major kinds of business activities covered on a detailed income statement.

Answer: A detailed income statement provides information as to how well the business has performed. It reports the company's net sales, merchandise returned by customers, the cost of goods sold versus the selling price, goods returned to suppliers, and cost of freight. It also breaks down expenses into those directly related to selling activities and those related to administrative or office activity. Income and expenses not directly related to the business's main activities are shown in a separate category.
ES   Moderate

13.97: Discuss the purpose of a classified balance sheet. Include
a description of the major balance sheet classifications
including: current assets, plant and equipment, current
liabilities, and long-term liabilities.

Answer: A classified balance sheet provides more detail about the
firm's assets and liabilities. The major categories
included for assets are current assets, and plant and
equipment assets. Current assets are cash and other assets
that will be converted into cash or used up during the
normal operating cycle, or one year, whichever is longer.
Plant and equipment assets are long-lived assets that are
used in the production or sale of goods or services.

The major categories included for liabilities are
current liabilities and long-term liabilities. Current
liabilities are debts or obligations that must be satisfied
within one year or one operating cycle, whichever is longer.
Long-term liabilities are debts that are not due for a
comparatively long period, usually for more than one year.
ES Moderate

14. Accounting for Bad Debts

14.1: The two approaches for estimating bad debt are:
   a) balance sheet and income statement methods.
   b) balance sheet and net realizable value methods.
   c) income statement and net realizable value methods.
   d) net realizable value method and direct write-off method.

Answer: (a)
   MC   Easy

14.2: What type of account is Allowance for Doubtful Accounts?
   a) Asset   b) Contra asset
   c) Revenue   d) Expense

Answer: (b)
   MC   Easy

14.3: Which financial statement reports Bad Debts Expense?
   a) Balance sheet
   b) Income statement
   c) Statement of owner's equity
   d) None of the above

Answer: (b)
   MC   Easy

14.4: What type of account is Bad Debts Expense?
   a) Asset   b) Contra asset
   c) Revenue   d) Expense

Answer: (d)
   MC   Easy

14.5: Which financial statement reports Allowance for Doubtful Accounts?
   a) Statement of owner's equity
   b) Income statement
   c) Balance sheet
   d) None of the above

Answer: (c)
   MC   Easy

14.6: The journal entry to record the estimate of uncollectible accounts includes:
   a) debit Sales, credit Allowance for Doubtful Accounts.
   b) debit Bad Debts Expense, credit Accounts Receivable.
   c) debit Accounts Receivable, credit Bad Debts Expense.
   d) debit Bad Debts Expense, credit Allowance for Doubtful Accounts.

Answer: (d)
   MC   Moderate

14.7: The journal entry to record Harry's Hats estimate that 1% of credit sales will be uncollectible would include:
   a) debit Bad Debts Expense, credit Allowance for Doubtful Accounts.
   b) debit Sales, credit Allowance for Doubtful Accounts.
   c) debit Bad Debts Expense, credit Accounts Receivable.
   d) debit Allowance for Doubtful Accounts, credit Accounts Receivable.

Answer: (a)
   MC   Moderate

14.8: The amount of accounts receivable a company estimates it will collect is the:
   a) gross accounts receivable.
   b) bad debts allowance.
   c) net realizable value.
   d) accounts receivable allowance.

Answer: (c)
   MC   Moderate

14.9: Net Realizable Value may be defined as:
   a) gross accounts receivable.
   b) future bad debts estimates.
   c) gross accounts receivable minus allowance for uncollectible accounts.
   d) past bad debts expense.

Answer: (c)
   MC   Easy

14.10: Abby's Antiques estimates it will collect $800 of the $1,000 owed by customers. The estimated collectible amount is the:
   a) bad debts allowance.
   b) net realizable value.
   c) allowance for doubtful accounts.
   d) gross accounts receivable.

Answer: (b)
   MC   Moderate

14.11: The amount <u>remaining</u> after Allowance for Doubtful Accounts is deducted from Accounts Receivable is:
   a) net realizable value.
   b) bad debts expense.
   c) bad debts allowance.
   d) gross accounts receivable.

Answer: (a)
   MC   Moderate

14.12: The journal entry to write off an account judged to be uncollectible under the allowance method is:
   a) debit Sales, credit Allowance for Doubtful Accounts.
   b) debit Accounts Receivable, credit Bad Debts Expense.
   c) debit Allowance for Doubtful Accounts, credit Accounts Receivable.
   d) debit Bad Debts Expense, credit Accounts Receivable.

Answer: (c)
   MC   Moderate

14.13: Vaughn Music Company learns the accounts receivable for customer Al Badnews is uncollectible. The journal entry under the allowance method would be:
   a) debit Allowance for Doubtful Accounts, credit Accounts Receivable.
   b) debit Sales, credit Allowance for Doubtful Accounts.
   c) debit Bad Debts Expense, credit Accounts Receivable.
   d) debit Allowance for Doubtful Accounts, credit Bad Debts Expense.

Answer: (a)
   MC   Moderate

14.14: What would be the basis for the following journal entry if it appears on a firm's records?
   Allowance for Doubtful Accounts   150
       Accounts Receivable   150

   a) The firm is estimating its uncollectible accounts.
   b) The firm is writing off an uncollectible account.
   c) The firm is making a collection of a previously written off account.
   d) It is a reversing entry.

Answer: (b)
   MC   Moderate

267

14.15: Which account is classified as a contra asset?
a) Bad Debts Expense
b) Accounts Receivable
c) Net Realizable Value
d) Allowance for Doubtful Accounts

Answer: (d)
MC   Easy

14.16: This account is a contra asset with a credit balance:
a) Bad Debts Expense.
b) Allowance for Doubtful Accounts.
c) Accounts Payable.
d) Bad Debts Recovered.

Answer: (b)
MC   Easy

14.17: Under the direct write-off method, the Bad Debts Expense account is recognized:
a) at the end of each accounting period.
b) when a customer's account is declared to be uncollectible.
c) within one year of granting credit to a customer.
d) each time a customer receives credit.

Answer: (b)
MC   Moderate

14.18: The Allowance for Doubtful Accounts is adjusted:
a) at the end of each accounting period.
b) each time a customer's debt is satisfied.
c) within one year of granting credit to a customer.
d) each time a customer is granted credit.

Answer: (a)
MC   Moderate

14.19: Which method uses a percentage of net credit sales to calculate the Bad Debts Expense?
a) Income statement approach
b) Balance sheet approach
c) Aging the accounts receivable
d) Direct write-off

Answer: (a)
MC   Easy

14.20: J & L Clothing Store estimates that approximately $1.50 out of every $100 of credit sales proves to be uncollectible. J & L calculates bad debts expense using:
a) aging method.   b) direct write-off method.
c) balance sheet method.   d) income statement method.

Answer: (d)
      MC   Moderate

14.21: The current balance of Allowance for Doubtful Accounts is considered when calculating the current period's bad debt expense under this method.
a) Balance Sheet method   b) Income Statement method
c) Direct Write-off method   d) All of the above

Answer: (a)
      MC   Moderate

14.22: Flora's Flowers estimates that approximately $150 of the $4,000 Accounts Receivable are uncollectible. Flora calculates bad debts expense using:
a) direct write-off method.   b) income statement method.
c) gross method.   d) balance sheet method.

Answer: (d)
      MC   Moderate

14.23: When customer Smith's account is written off under the allowance method:
a) net assets will be unchanged.
b) net income will decrease.
c) net income will increase.
d) total assets will increase.

Answer: (a)
      MC   Moderate

14.24: Dolly's Drug Store writes off a customer's account under the allowance method. This will cause:
a) net assets to decrease.
b) total assets to increase.
c) net income to increase.
d) no change in net assets.

Answer: (d)
      MC   Moderate

14.25: Patty's Painting Service is able to collect an amount
previously written off last year under the direct method.
The journal entry will:
a) decrease Bad Debts Expense.
b) increase Bad Debts Recovered.
c) decrease Accounts Receivable.
d) decrease Cash.

Answer: (b)
MC Moderate

14.26: A company writes off a specific account as uncollectible,
but later the customer pays. The journal entry to record
the reinstatement under the allowance method is:
a) decrease Cash.
b) increases Sales.
c) increase Allowance for Doubtful Accounts.
d) decrease Bad Debts Expense.

Answer: (c)
MC Difficult

14.27: When a year-end adjustment is made for estimated bad debts:
a) net income is unchanged.
b) liabilities increase.
c) net assets decrease.
d) total assets are unchanged.

Answer: (c)
MC Moderate

14.28: Bjay's Bakery increases Allowance for Doubtful Accounts $300
at year-end. As a result:
a) total assets are unchanged.
b) net income is unchanged.
c) net assets increase.
d) net assets decrease.

Answer: (d)
MC Moderate

14.29: A company is not able to reasonably estimate its Bad Debts
Expense. The method it may use is:
a) net realizable value method.
b) direct write-off method.
c) aging method.
d) income statement method.

Answer: (b)
MC Moderate

14.30: Fanny's Candies' losses from uncollectible accounts are very inconsistent. Fanny should record bad debts expense using:
   a) direct write-off method.
   b) income statement method.
   c) aging method.
   d) net realizable value method.

Answer: (a)
   MC   Moderate

14.31: What would be the basis for the following entry on a firm's records?

   Bad Debt Expense   150
      Accounts Receivable   150

   a) The firm is using the direct write-off method.
   b) The firm is writing off an uncollectible account.
   c) The firm is not using the allowance method for writing off accounts.
   d) All of the above.

Answer: (d)
   MC   Easy

14.32: A debit balance in Allowance for Doubtful Accounts means:
   a) a posting error has been made.
   b) bad debts losses have been overestimated.
   c) more losses have been written off than estimated.
   d) the balance sheet method is being used.

Answer: (c)
   MC   Easy

14.33: After posting all the write-offs for the year, Bjay's Bakery's Allowance for Doubtful Accounts has a debit balance. This means:
   a) more losses have been written off than estimated.
   b) the income statement method is being used.
   c) a posting error was made.
   d) the aging method is being used.

Answer: (a)
   MC   Easy

14.34: Ben's Boats has written off more accounts than its previous estimate provided for. This means:
   a) allowance for doubtful accounts has a debit balance.
   b) there was an error in posting.
   c) the aging method is being used.
   d) the income statement method is being used.

Answer: (a)
   MC   Moderate

14.35: Gross accounts receivable are $10,000. Allowance for Doubtful Accounts has a credit balance of $200. Net sales for the year are $150,000. In the past, 1% of sales had proved uncollectible, and an aging of the receivables indicates $1,200 is doubtful. Under the income statement method, bad debts expense for the year is:
   a) $1,000.   b) $1,500.   c) $1,200.   d) $900.

Answer: (b)
   MC   Difficult

14.36: Gross accounts receivable are $10,000. Allowance for Doubtful Accounts has a credit balance of $200. Net sales for the year are $150,000. In the past, 1% of sales had proved uncollectible, and an aging of the receivables indicates $1,200 is doubtful. Under the balance sheet method, bad debts expense for the year is:
   a) $1,000.   b) $1,500.   c) $1,200.   d) $900.

Answer: (a)
   MC   Difficult

14.37: Gross accounts receivable are $10,000. Allowance for Doubtful Accounts has a credit balance of $200. Net sales for the year are $150,000. In the past, 1% of sales had proved uncollectible, and an aging of the receivables indicated $1,200 as being uncollectible. What would be the adjusted balance of the allowance account under the income statement approach?
   a) $1,700   b) $1,200   c) $1,000   d) $900

Answer: (a)
   MC   Difficult

14.38: Gross accounts receivable are $10,000. Allowance for Doubtful Accounts has a credit balance of $200. Net sales for the year are $150,000. In the past, 1% of sales had proved uncollectible, and an aging of the receivables indicates $1,200 as being uncollectible. What would be the adjusted balance of the allowance account under the balance sheet approach?
   a) $1,700   b) $1,200   c) $1,000   d) $900

Answer: (b)
   MC   Difficult

14.39: Using the income statement method, the estimated bad debts expense for the year is $3,000. If the balance of Allowance for Doubtful Accounts is $900 debit before adjustment, what is the balance after adjustment?
   a) $3,000   b) $900   c) $3,900   d) $2,100

Answer: (d)
   MC   Moderate

272

14.40: Using the <u>balance sheet</u> method, estimated uncollectible accounts are $3,000. If the balance of Allowance for Doubtful Accounts is $900 credit before adjustment, what is the balance after adjustment?
   a) $900   b) $3,000   c) $2,100   d) $3,900

Answer: (b)
   MC   Moderate

14.41: Using the <u>aging</u> method, estimated uncollectible accounts are $3,000. If the balance of Allowance for Doubtful Accounts is $800 <u>debit</u> before adjustment, what is <u>bad debts expense</u> adjustment for the period?
   a) $3,000   b) $800   c) $2,200   d) $3,800

Answer: (d)
   MC   Moderate

14.42: Sharon's Sales balance of Accounts Receivable is $4,000. The balance of the allowance account is $600 credit. Sharon writes off a $150 uncollectible account. The effect on <u>net realizable value</u> (NRV) of the receivables:
   a) reduces NRV.
   b) increases NRV.
   c) cannot be determined from information given.
   d) is unchanged.

Answer: (d)
   MC   Difficult

14.43: Using the <u>aging</u> method, estimated uncollectible accounts are $2,700. If the balance of Allowance for Doubtful Accounts is $800 <u>credit</u> before adjustment, what is bad debts expense for the period?
   a) $2,700   b) $800   c) $1,900   d) $3,500

Answer: (c)
   MC   Moderate

14.44: The net realizable value of a company's accounts receivables is:
   a) unchanged at the time of a specific write-off.
   b) decreased at the time of a specific write-off.
   c) increased at the time of a specific write-off.
   d) the guaranteed amount the company will collect from its customers.

Answer: (a)
   MC   Moderate

14.45: At December 31, 19xx, King Company's unadjusted Allowance for Doubtful Accounts showed a <u>debit</u> balance of $432. An aging of the accounts receivable indicates probable uncollectible accounts of $390. The year end adjusting entry for bad debts expense:
a) includes a debit to the allowance account for $2.
b) includes a credit to the allowance account for $42.
c) includes a debit to the allowance account for $822.
d) includes a credit to the allowance account for $822.

Answer: (d)
MC   Moderate

14.46: Tampa Furniture's Allowance for Doubtful Accounts had an unadjusted <u>debit</u> balance of $300. The manager estimates that $700 of the accounts receivable is uncollectible. The year end adjusting entry for bad debts expense:
a) includes a debit to the allowance account for $1,000.
b) includes a debit to the expense account for $700.
c) includes a credit to the expense account for $1,000.
d) includes a debit to the expense account for $1,000.

Answer: (d)
MC   Moderate

14.47: In the direct write-off method, writing off an account causes:
a) an increase in liabilities.
b) an increase in accounts receivable.
c) a decrease in the allowance account.
d) an increase in expense.

Answer: (d)
MC   Moderate

14.48: Miami Company uses Allowance for Doubtful Accounts. When Miami writes off an uncollectible account, there is:
a) a decrease in accounts receivable.
b) an increase in expense.
c) a decrease in net income.
d) All of the above.

Answer: (a)
MC   Moderate

14.49: San Francisco Tours collected $90 on an account that had been <u>directly written off</u> the previous year. The journal entry to record the transaction would include:
a) a debit to the Allowance for Doubtful Accounts.
b) a debit to Bad Debts Recovered.
c) a credit to Bad Debts Expense.
d) a credit to Bad Debts Recovered.

Answer: (d)
MC   Moderate

14.50: For tax purposes, Bad Debts Expense is calculated using:
a) income statement method.
b) balance sheet method.
c) net realizable value method.
d) direct write-off method.

Answer: (d)
MC   Moderate

14.51: Gross accounts receivable are $10,000. Allowance for
Doubtful Accounts has a credit balance of $200. Net sales
for the year are $150,000. In the past, 1% of sales had
proved uncollectible, and an aging of the receivables
indicates $1,200 as being uncollectible. Actual accounts
written off during the year totaled $1,400. Bad Debts
Expense for income tax purposes is:
a) balance sheet method, $900.
b) income statement method, $1,500.
c) direct write-off method, $1,400.
d) None of the above.

Answer: (c)
MC   Moderate

14.52: Which of the following accounts are used under the direct
write-off method?
a) Bad Debts Recovered   b) Bad Debts Expense
c) Accounts Receivable   d) All of the above.

Answer: (d)
MC   Easy

14.53: Bad Debts Recovered is a(n):
a) asset account.   b) liability account.
c) revenue account.   d) expense account.

Answer: (c)
MC   Easy

14.54: If R. Hopes Law Firm uses a percentage of net fees in
computing the amount of bad debts expense:
a) no allowance account is required.
b) the relationship between revenues and expenses is
emphasized more than the receivables on the balance sheet
date.
c) the adjusted balance of the allowance account is equal
to the expected losses calculated using the aging method.
d) past-due accounts are listed separately on the balance
sheet.

Answer: (b)
MC   Moderate

14.55: Bad Debts Expense is recognized in the year the sale was earned when using income statement allowance method.

Answer: True
TF Moderate

14.56: The Allowance for Doubtful Accounts is shown on the income statement as an operating expense.

Answer: False
TF Moderate

14.57: The normal balance of the allowance account is a credit.

Answer: True
TF Easy

14.58: The normal balance of the Bad Debts Expense is a credit.

Answer: False
TF Easy

14.59: Bad Debts Expense would be reported on the balance sheet.

Answer: False
TF Easy

14.60: When the estimate for uncollectible accounts is made, the accounts that will be uncollectible are not known for sure.

Answer: True
TF Moderate

14.61: The subsidiary ledger for accounts receivable is affected when posting the entry to record a written-off account.

Answer: True
TF Moderate

14.62: The income statement approach estimates a percentage of accounts receivable that is uncollectible.

Answer: False
TF Difficult

14.63: The balance sheet approach estimates a percentage of sales that is uncollectible.

Answer: False
TF Difficult

14.64: Using the balance sheet method, the balance in the Allowance for Doubtful Accounts is ignored.

Answer: False
TF Moderate

14.65: Using the income statement method, the balance in the Allowance for Doubtful Accounts is ignored.

Answer: True
TF Moderate

14.66: The beginning balance in the Allowance for Doubtful Accounts represents potential bad debts from previous periods.

Answer: True
TF Moderate

14.67: The Aging of Accounts Receivable is an income statement method.

Answer: False
TF Easy

14.68: The direct write-off method does not estimate Bad Debts Expense but writes off accounts that are determined to be uncollectible.

Answer: True
TF Moderate

14.69: To record the estimate for Bad Debts Expense using the direct write-off method, Bad Debts would be debited and Allowance for Doubtful Accounts would be credited.

Answer: False
TF Moderate

14.70: The direct write-off method is acceptable for federal income tax purposes.

Answer: True
TF Easy

14.71: The net realizable value of accounts receivable is unchanged when an account is written off as uncollectible.

Answer: True
TF Moderate

14.72: Before recording the receipt of payment for an account that was previously written off as uncollectible under the allowance method, it is necessary to debit Accounts Receivable, customer name, and credit Allowance for Doubtful Accounts.

Answer: True
TF Moderate

14.73: When an accounts receivable is written off as uncollectible, it decreases the Bad Debts Expense.

Answer: False
TF Moderate

14.74: If an estimate is recorded for uncollectible accounts, it is still necessary to write off an account that is determined to be uncollectible.

Answer: True
TF Moderate

14.75: If Bad Debts Expense for the year is based on a percent of accounts receivable, the balance in the Allowance for Doubtful Accounts is taken into consideration when preparing the adjusting entry for Bad Debts Expense.

Answer: True
TF Difficult

14.76: If more than one customer is written off, a compound entry may be used.

Answer: True
TF Easy

14.77: Bad Debts Recovered is an expense account.

Answer: False
TF Moderate

14.78: If a recovery of a written off account is made in the same year as it was written off, the Bad Debts Recovered account would be used.

Answer: False
TF Difficult

14.79: The Allowance for Doubtful Accounts account is not used when the direct write-off method is in use.

Answer: True
        TF   Moderate

14.80: The Tax Reform Act of 1986 eliminates the Bad Debts Expense.

Answer: False
        TF   Easy

14.81: Businesses may keep two sets of books when meeting IRS regulations and following correct procedures for accrual accounting.

Answer: True
        TF   Moderate

14.82: The Allowance for Doubtful Accounts would be reported on the Income Statement.

Answer: False
        TF   Moderate

14.83: The Bad Debts Recovered account would be reported on the Balance Sheet.

Answer: False
        TF   Moderate

14.84: After an account is written off, two entries are required to indicate a collection of the previously written off account.

Answer: True
        TF   Moderate

14.85: Prepare the adjusting journal entry of Bad Debts Expense from the following information using the income statement approach.

        Net Sales for the year $150,000
        Balance in the allowance account   500 credit
        Estimated percentage of sales uncollectible   1%
        Estimated uncollectible accounts-aging   2,000

Answer: Bad Debts Expense   1,500
           Allowance for Doubtful Accounts   1,500

        ES   Moderate

14.86: Prepare the adjusting journal entry for Bad Debts Expense
from the following information using the balance sheet
approach.

Net Sales for the year	$150,000
Balance in the allowance account	500 Debit
Estimated percentage of sales uncollectible	1%
Estimated uncollectible accounts-aging	2,000

Answer: Bad Debts Expense   2,500
          Allowance for Doubtful Accounts   2,500
        ES   Moderate

14.87: a.   Calculate the estimated uncollectible accounts from the
            following aging analysis.
       b.   Prepare the adjusting journal entry. The unadjusted
            balance of the allowance account is $100 credit.

	GROSS REC.	ESTIMATED % LOSS	AMOUNT NEEDED IN ALLOW. ACCT.
Not yet due	$3,600	3	
Days past due			
1-30	2,000	4	
31-60	870	10	
61-90	200	20	
Over 90 days	330	50	
Total Accts. Rec.	======	Tot. required in allowance =============	

Answer: a.   Total Gross Receivables $7,000
             Amount needed in allowance account.
             $108
                80
                87
                40
               165

             $480

        b.   Bad Debts Expense   380
               Allowance for Doubtful Acct.   380

        ES   Moderate

14.88: a. Calculate the estimated uncollectible accounts from the following aging analysis.
b. Prepare the adjusting journal entry. The unadjusted balance of the allowance account is $200 <u>debit</u>.

	GROSS REC.	ESTIMATED % LOSS	AMOUNT NEEDED ALLOW. ACCOUNT
Not yet due	$4,000	2	
Days past due			
1-30	2,500	3	
31-60	900	12	
61-90	600	25	
Over 90 days	300	40	
Total Acct. Rec.	$ ======	Total required in allowance $	========

Answer: a. Total Accounts Receivable $8,300
Amount needed in allowance account
```
$ 80
  75
 108
 150
 120
 ----
$533
```

b. Bad Debts Expense   733
       Allowance for Doubtful Accts.   733
ES Moderate

14.89: Prepare a partial balance sheet for the Patben Company at December 31, 19xx, from the following information:
```
Cash                        $10,000
Petty Cash                      100
Accounts Receivable           6,000
Bad Debts Expense             1,400
Merchandise Inventory         1,800
Allowance for Doubtful Accts.   200
```

Answer:
```
                    PATBEN
                 BALANCE SHEET
               December 31, 19xx

        Assets
Cash                                    $10,000
Petty Cash                                  100
Accounts Receivable          $6,000
Less: Allow. for Doubtful Accts.   200    5,800
Merchandise Inventory        ------     1,800
                                        -------
   Current Assets                       $17,700
                                        =======
```

ES Moderate

14.90: Prepare general journal entries to record the following transactions for the Boulder Company. (The company uses the income statement approach for recording bad debts expense.)

```
19xx
Dec. 31  Record Bad Debts Expense, $1,000
19xx
Jan.  3  Wrote off B. Gruen's account as uncollectible, $50
Mar.  4  Wrote off A. Wolf's account as uncollectible, $75
Jul.  5  Recovered $40 from A. Wolf
Aug. 19  Wrote off M. Shep's account as uncollectible, $130
Nov.  7  Recovered $25 from B. Gruen
```

Answer:
```
19xx
Dec. 31 Bad Debts Expense                       1,000
            Allowance for Doubtful Accounts              1,000


19xx
Jan.  3 Allowance for Doubtful Accounts     50
            Accounts Receivable, B. Gruen                  50


Mar.  4 Allowance for Doubtful Accounts     75
            Accounts Receivable, A. Wolf                   75


Jul.  5 Accounts Receivable, A. Wolf        40
            Allowance for Doubtful Accounts                40

        Cash                                40
            Accounts Receivable, A. Wolf                   40


Aug. 19 Allowance for Doubtful Accounts    130
            Accounts Receivable, M. Shep                  130


Nov.  7 Accounts Receivable, B. Gruen       25
            Allowance for Doubtful Accounts                25

        Cash                                25
            Accounts Receivable, B. Gruen                  25
```

ES   Moderate

282

14.91: Wooden Rack Company uses the direct write-off method for recording bad debts. Journalize the following transactions for Wooden:

19xx
Mar. 13 Wrote off P. Pansy's account for $180
Apr. 17 Wrote off Cahun Soy's account for $75
Jul. 5 Recovered $50 from Cahun Soy

19xx
Jan. 9 Recovered $180 from P. Pansy

Answer: 19xx

Mar. 13	Bad Debts Expense	180	
	Accounts Receivable, P. Pansy		180
Apr. 17	Bad Debts Expense	75	
	Accounts Receivable, C. Soy		75
Jul. 5	Accounts Receivable, C. Soy	50	
	Bad Debts Expense		50
	Cash	50	
	Accounts Receivable, C. Soy		50

19xx

Jan 9	Accounts Receivable, P. Pansy	180	
	Bad Debts Recovered		180
	Cash	180	
	Accounts Receivable, P. Pansy		180

ES Moderate

283

14.92: Describe and contrast the procedures for estimating uncollectible accounts under the (a) income statement approach, (b) the balance sheet approach, and (c) the direct write-off approach.

Answer: (a)
Under the income statement approach, Bad Debts Expense is associated with the current year's sales. Based on the past several years, a company will calculate the average Bad Debts Expense as a percent of net credit sales. It will then apply this percentage to the current year's sales to estimate its future bad debt losses.

(b)
Under the balance sheet approach, the firm uses accounts receivable on the balance sheet as its basis to estimate bad debts expense. It is assumed the longer an account has been due and not paid, the more likely it is not going to be collected. The procedure includes preparing a schedule based on an analysis of Accounts Receivable according to how many days past due the accounts are. This is called aging the Accounts Receivable. A sliding scale of percents, based on previous experience, is applied to the total amount of receivables due in each time period. The calculation then serves as the basis for the total amount required in the Allowance for Doubtful Accounts account.

(c)
Under the direct write-off approach, an account that is determined to be uncollectible is directly written off to the current year's Bad Debts Expense account without regard to when the original sale was made.
ES Moderate

14.93: Evaluate the differences of the effect on the financial statements between the income statement approach and the balance sheet approach for estimating bad debts expense on the financial statement presentation.

Answer: The income statement approach places its major emphasis on the matching principle. This approach calculates the amount of bad debts expense for the year based on a percent of net credit sales. The balance in the Allowance for Doubtful Accounts is ignored. A carryover balance in the allowance account represents a carryover of potential bad debts from prior years.

The balance sheet approach places its major emphasis on values reported on the balance sheet and the principle of conservatism. It is assumed that the longer an account has been due and not paid, the more likely it is not going to be paid. The net realizable value of the receivables is estimated by an analysis of the accounts according to how many days they are past due and applying percentages based on previous experience.
ES Moderate

15. Notes Receivable and Notes Payable

15.1: When Art Smith makes a written promise to pay a certain sum of money to Thomas Able on July 5, 19xx, Art signs a:
   a) promissory accounts payable.
   b) promissory note payable.
   c) promissory accounts receivable.
   d) promissory note receivable.

Answer: (b)
   MC   Moderate

15.2: Barry Nelson borrowed $250 from Sharon Appley. Barry promised, in writing, that he would repay the money to Sharon on February 19, 19xx. At the time of the loan, Sharon records the transaction as a(n):
   a) accounts receivable.
   b) accounts payable.
   c) promissory note receivable.
   d) promissory note payable.

Answer: (c)
   MC   Moderate

15.3: An advantage of a promissory note receivable over an accounts receivable is to:
   a) establish formal proof against the borrower.
   b) put all the facts in writing.
   c) collect a fee for the use of one's money.
   d) All of the above.

Answer: (d)
   MC   Moderate

15.4: A reason to use a formal promissory note is to:
   a) guarantee payment of the loan.
   b) give additional time to settle past due accounts.
   c) simplify the recordkeeping.
   d) None of the above.

Answer: (b)
   MC   Moderate

15.5: The person or company that borrows money and signs a note payable is the:
   a) maker.   b) payee.
   c) drawee.   d) principle person.

Answer: (a)
   MC   Easy

15.6: Charlie Upton borrowed $100 from Downtown Bank and signed a promissory note. Charlie is the:

    a) payee.
    c) creditor.
    b) drawee.
    d) None of the above.

Answer: (d)
    MC   Moderate

15.7: Baker Company is borrowing $10,000 and issues a note payable. The $10,000 is the:

    a) proceeds.
    c) guaranteed amount.
    b) principal.
    d) net.

Answer: (b)
    MC   Easy

15.8: Charles borrows $2,000 from Victor and gives Victor a promissory note. Victor is the:

    a) drawer.   b) payee.   c) payor.   d) maker.

Answer: (b)
    MC   Easy

15.9: P. Holmes loaned $50 to S. Mitchell and received a promissory note. P. Holmes is the:

    a) maker.   b) drawee.   c) payee.   d) debtor.

Answer: (c)
    MC   Moderate

15.10: Rick promises to pay Ben $1,000 plus 12% interest to be repaid in 90 days. The interest rate is the:

    a) monthly rate.
    b) 90 day rate.
    c) annual rate.
    d) cannot be determined from information given.

Answer: (c)
    MC   Easy

15.11: The date a promissory note will come due is the:

    a) promise date.
    c) date of the note.
    b) end of loan date.
    d) maturity date.

Answer: (d)
    MC   Easy

15.12: Interest income is on a merchandise company's income statement under the heading:
   a) sales revenue.
   b) other income.
   c) fees earned.
   d) notes receivable.

Answer: (b)
   MC   Moderate

15.13: Interest expense is on a merchandise company's income statement under the heading:
   a) borrowing expense.
   b) operating expense.
   c) sales expense.
   d) other expenses.

Answer: (d)
   MC   Moderate

15.14: Slow Company needs additional time to pay its accounts payable to Lenn Company. Slow makes a written promise to pay Lenn the amount on a certain date. Lenn records this transaction as follows:
   a) debit Notes Receivable, credit Accounts Receivable.
   b) debit Cash, credit Accounts Receivable.
   c) debit Accounts Receivable, credit Notes Receivable.
   d) debit Notes Receivable, credit Cash.

Answer: (a)
   MC   Moderate

15.15: Lenn Company grants Slow Company additional time to pay its past due account. Slow makes a written promise to pay Lenn the amount on a certain date. Lenn records this transaction as follows:
   a) debit Notes Receivable, credit Accounts Receivable.
   b) debit Cash, credit Accounts Receivable.
   c) debit Accounts Receivable, credit Notes Receivable.
   d) debit Accounts Payable, credit Notes Payable.

Answer: (a)
   MC   Moderate

15.16: Broke Company issues a promissory note to Sale Company to get extended time on an account payable. Broke records this transaction as follows:
   a) debit Accounts Receivable, credit Notes Receivable.
   b) debit Notes Receivable, credit Accounts Receivable.
   c) debit Notes Payable, credit Accounts Payable.
   d) debit Accounts Payable, credit Notes Payable.

Answer: (d)
   MC   Moderate

15.17: Boost Buy needed more time to pay off its account to SANY TV Company. SANY accepted a promissory note from Boost. Boost records the transaction as follows:
   a) debit Notes Payable, credit Accounts Payable.
   b) debit Notes Receivable, credit Accounts Receivable.
   c) debit Accounts Payable, credit Notes Payable.
   d) debit Accounts Receivable, credit Notes Payable.

Answer: (c)
   MC   Moderate

15.18: The basic formula for calculating the interest on a note is:
   a) Interest = Principal * Rate - Time.
   b) Interest = Principal * Rate * Time.
   c) Interest = Principal * Time - Rate.
   d) Interest = Principal * Rate + Time.

Answer: (b)
   MC   Easy

15.19: In the basic formula for calculating interest, rate refers to:
   a) interest per day.   b) interest per month.
   c) percent per year.   d) monthly payment amount.

Answer: (c)
   MC   Easy

15.20: In the basic formula for calculating interest on a promissory note, principle refers to:
   a) the original amount borrowed.
   b) the amount to be repaid.
   c) the proceeds.
   d) maturity value.

Answer: (a)
   MC   Easy

15.21: Interest calculated for one year on a $1,000, 12% promissory note is:
   a) $12.   b) $1.20.   c) $120.   d) $1,200.

Answer: (c)
   MC   Moderate

15.22: Interest calculated for four months on a $3,000, 10% promissory note is:
   a) $1.   b) $100.   c) $30.   d) $300.

Answer: (b)
   MC   Moderate

15.23: Using a 360-day year, interest calculated for 60 days on a
       $4,000, 15% promissory note is:
       a) $600.   b) $60.   c) $10.   d) $100.

Answer: (d)
       MC   Moderate

15.24: Given a 360-day year, the interest expense on a $5,000, 12%,
       66-day promissory note payable is:
       a) $11.   b) $110.   c) $100.   d) $66.

Answer: (b)
       MC   Moderate

15.25: The maturity date for a 21-day note dated January 30 is:
       a) February 21.   b) February 22.
       c) February 20.   d) February 28.

Answer: (c)
       MC   Moderate

15.26: The maturity date for a 66-day note dated June 28 is:
       a) September 2.   b) September 1.
       c) August 28.   d) August 31.

Answer: (a)
       MC   Moderate

15.27: The maturity date for a three-month note dated January 31
       is:
       a) May 1.   b) April 30.   c) May 31.   d) April 29.

Answer: (b)
       MC   Moderate

15.28: Calculate the maturity value of a $3,000, 12%, one-year
       note.
       a) $360   b) $3,600   c) $3,000   d) $3,360

Answer: (d)
       MC   Moderate

15.29: Botton Equipment accepts a promissory note for $3,500 from a
       customer on August 1, to be repaid in seven months plus 18%
       interest. The maturity value of the note is:
       a) $3,867.50.   b) $4,130.
       c) $367.50.   d) None of the above.

Answer: (a)
       MC   Moderate

15.30: If Joan's Company fails to pay the maturity value on the due
date of its promissory note payable, the note is said to be:
   a) canceled.   b) grossed.
   c) dishonored.   d) displaced.

Answer: (c)
   MC Easy

15.31: On June 15, Sununu Company issued a 12%, 60-day, $11,000
promissory note to Wagmart Company. Sununu should record the
payment of the note on the maturity day as:
   a) debit Notes Payable $11,200, credit Cash $11,220.
   b) debit Notes Payable $11,000, debit Interest Payable
   $220, credit Cash $11,220.
   c) debit Notes Payable $11,000, debit Interest Expense
   $220, credit Cash $11,220.
   d) debit Notes Payable $11,000, credit Cash $11,000.

Answer: (c)
   MC Moderate

15.32: Olde Sales Company sold merchandise to Newton Company and
received a promissory note from Newton. Olde should record
the transaction as:
   a) debit Notes Receivable and credit Sales for the
   principal amount of the note.
   b) debit Notes Receivable and credit Sales for the maturity
   value of the note.
   c) debit Accounts Receivable and credit Sales for the
   maturity amount of the note.
   d) debit Accounts Receivable and credit Sales for the
   principal amount of the note.

Answer: (a)
   MC Moderate

15.33: Newton Company purchased merchandise from Olde Company and
issued a promissory note. Newton should record the
transaction as:
   a) debit Purchases and credit Notes Payable for the face
   amount of the note.
   b) debit Purchases and credit Notes Payable for the
   maturity value of the note.
   c) debit Purchases and credit Accounts Payable for the face
   amount of the note.
   d) debit Purchases and credit Accounts Payable for the
   maturity value of the note.

Answer: (a)
   MC Moderate

15.34: Trenton Enterprises was unable to collect a $1,000 note receivable plus $60 interest on the maturity date, but hoped to collect the amount in the future. Trenton should record this as:
a) debit Bad Debts Expense $1,000, credit Notes Receivable $1,000.
b) debit Allowance for Doubtful Accounts $1,060, credit Notes Receivable $1,060.
c) debit Accounts Receivable $1,060, credit Interest Income $60, credit Notes Receivable $1,000.
d) debit Accounts Receivable $1,000, debit Interest Income $60, credit Cash $1,060.

Answer: (c)
MC Difficult

15.35: Bully Company did not pay its promissory note payable of $1,500 plus $90 interest on the maturity date. Bully should record this on the maturity date as:
a) debit Notes Payable $1,500, debit Interest Expense $90, credit Accounts Payable $1,590.
b) debit Notes Payable $1,590, credit Accounts Payable $1,590.
c) debit Accounts Payable, $1,590, credit Notes Payable $1,500, credit Interest Expense $90.
d) debit Notes Payable $1,500, debit Interest Expense $90, credit Allowance for Doubtful Accounts $1,590.

Answer: (a)
MC Difficult

15.36: The proceeds from discounting a Notes Receivable are the:
a) maturity value minus principal.
b) principal minus discount.
c) principal plus discount.
d) maturity value minus discount.

Answer: (d)
MC Difficult

15.37: The discount period on a discounted note is:
a) the same as the original period of the note.
b) the original note period plus 10 days.
c) the time between the discount date and the maturity date.
d) the original note period minus 10 days.

Answer: (c)
MC Difficult

15.38: The amount the bank charges when it discounts a note is calculated as:
a) bank discount = note principal * bank discount rate * (discount period /360 days).
b) bank discount = maturity value * bank discount rate * (original note period /360 days).
c) bank discount = maturity value * bank discount rate + original interest rate * (discount period /360 days).
d) bank discount = maturity value * bank discount rate * (discount period /360 days).

Answer: (d)
MC   Difficult

15.39: On May 31, Blue Company discounts a customer's 16%, 90-day, $10,000 note dated May 1. The discount rate charged by the bank is 12%. The discount period is:
a) 90 days.   b) 30 days.   c) one year.   d) 60 days.

Answer: (d)
MC   Moderate

15.40: Round Tire Company endorses a customer's note dated June 1 to the bank on June 16. The interest rate on the note is 10% and the bank discount rate is 12%. The note matures on July 31. The discount period is:
a) 60 days.   b) 45 days.   c) 44 days.   d) 46 days.

Answer: (b)
MC   Moderate

15.41: May Company discounts a customer's 12%, $5,000, 60-day note dated August 1, on August 16. The discount period is 45 days and the bank discount rate is 15%. The maturity value of the note is $5,100. The bank discount is:
a) $93.75.   b) $95.63.   c) $76.50.   d) $125.

Answer: (b)
MC   Difficult

15.42: Broke Company discounts a customer's 12%, $6,000, 90-day note dated July 1, on August 15. The discount period is 45 days and the bank discount rate is 18%. The maturity value of the note is $6,180. The bank discount is $139. The proceeds of the note are:
a) $6,041.   b) $6,319.   c) $5,861.   d) $6,139.

Answer: (a)
MC   Difficult

15.43: Lucky Aces discounted a customer's $4,000 note at the bank and received proceeds of $3,930. Lucky would record the receipt of cash as:
 a) debit Cash $4,000, credit Notes Receivable $4,000.
 b) debit Cash $4,000, credit Interest Income $70, credit Notes Receivable $3,930.
 c) debit Cash $3,930, debit Interest Expense $70, credit Notes Receivable $4,000.
 d) debit Notes Receivable $4,000, credit Cash $3,930, credit Interest Income $70.

Answer: (c)
    MC Difficult

15.44: When Josette Sales endorsed customer Shorta Fund's note to Big Bank, Josette agreed to pay the note at maturity if Shorta failed to pay. Josette's liability is a(n):
 a) contra liability.   b) expense.
 c) liability.   d) contingent liability.

Answer: (d)
    MC Moderate

15.45: When Josette Sales endorsed customer Shorta Fund's $5,000 note to Big Bank, Josette agreed to pay the note at maturity if Shorta failed to pay. The bank notified Josette that Shorta defaulted on the note. Josetta paid the bank the $5,100 maturity value of the note plus a $25 protest fee. Josette should record the payment to the bank as:
 a) debit Accounts Receivable $5,125, credit Cash $5,125.
 b) debit Bad Debts Expense $5,125, credit Cash $5,125.
 c) debit Notes Receivable $5,000, debit Interest Expense $100, debit Protest Fee Expense $25, credit Cash $5,125.
 d) debit Notes Receivable $5,125, credit Cash $5,125.

Answer: (a)
    MC Moderate

15.46: The entry to record the cash received on a note discounted at less than face value is:
 a) debit Cash, credit Interest Income, credit Notes Receivable.
 b) debit Cash, debit Interest Expense, credit Notes Receivable.
 c) debit Cash, credit Interest Expense.
 d) debit Notes Receivable, credit Cash.

Answer: (b)
    MC Moderate

15.47: Smithson Enterprises discounts its own 90-day, 12%, $10,000
note payable at a bank. It records the proceeds as:
a) debit Cash $9,700, debit Discounts on Notes Payable
$300, credit Notes Payable $10,000.
b) debit Cash $10,000, credit Notes Payable $10,000.
c) debit Cash $8,800, debit Discount on Notes Payable
$1,200, credit Notes Payable $10,000.
d) debit Cash $9,700, credit Notes Payable $9,700.

Answer: (a)
MC Difficult

15.48: An adjustment that must be made for the interest on a note
payable that is incurred during the period but not paid or
recorded because payment is not due is called:
a) accrued interest expense.
b) accrued interest income.
c) notes payable.
d) discount payable liability.

Answer: (a)
MC Moderate

15.49: At December 31, the adjustment for interest income for a
$12,000, 60-day, 10% notes receivable dated December 16
would be:
a) debit Interest Expense $50, credit Interest Payable $50.
b) debit Interest Receivable $50, credit Interest Income
$50.
c) debit Interest Receivable $200, credit Interest Income
$200.
d) None of the above.

Answer: (b)
MC Difficult

15.50: The current liability on the balance sheet for $10,000 Notes
Payable that was discounted with a $150 discount will look
as follows:
a) Notes Payable $10,000.
b) Notes Payable $9,850.
c) Notes Payable $10,000
   Less: Dis. on Notes Pay.   150 $9,850.
                                 ----
d) Notes Payable $10,000
   Less: Dis. on Notes Pay.   150 $10,150.

Answer: (c)
MC Difficult

15.51: When paying a $10,000 notes payable with a $150 discount, the journal entry is:
  a) debit Discount on Notes Payable $150, debit Notes Payable $9,850, credit Cash $10,000.
  b) debit Notes Payable $9,850, credit Cash $9,850.
  c) debit Interest Expense $150, debit Notes Payable $10,000, credit Cash $10,000, credit Discount on Notes Payable $150.
  d) None of the above.

Answer: (c)
        MC   Moderate

15.52: S. Berg discounted her own $10,000, 60 day, 12% promissory note at NW Bank. The proceeds were $9,800. The effective interest rate charged by the bank was:
  a) 12.24%.
  b) 24%.
  c) 20%.
  d) cannot be determined from the above information.

Answer: (a)
        MC   Difficult

15.53: Bankers Bank discounted a customer's $5,000, 90 day, 10% note. The proceeds received by the customer amounted to $4,875. The effective interest rate the bank charged its customer was:
  a) 10.51%.   b) 10.33%.   c) 10.26%.   d) 10.20%.

Answer: (c)
        MC   Difficult

15.54: The formula for calculating interest on a note is principal * rate * time.

Answer: True
        TF   Moderate

15.55: A note payable is a formal promise to pay and an accounts payable is an informal promise to pay.

Answer: True
        TF   Easy

15.56: The company that receives notes would normally not keep a ledger for all the notes outstanding.

Answer: False
        TF   Moderate

15.57: Notes Receivable is a current asset on the balance sheet.

Answer: True
   TF   Easy

15.58: Notes Payable is a current liability on the income statement.

Answer: False
   TF   Moderate

15.59: A note that is paid on the maturity date is considered dishonored.

Answer: False
   TF   Easy

15.60: A dishonored note must be transferred back to Accounts Receivable on the seller's books.

Answer: True
   TF   Moderate

15.61: The maturity value of a note equals the principal minus interest.

Answer: False
   TF   Easy

15.62: The bank discount on its own customer's note equals principal times the interest rate.

Answer: True
   TF   Moderate

15.63: A contingent liability is avoided when a discounted note is endorsed without recourse.

Answer: True
   TF   Moderate

15.64: Accrued interest income is income that has been earned during the period but not received or recorded because payment is not due.

Answer: True
   TF   Moderate

15.65: Discount on Notes Payable is a contra liability account that records interest deducted in advance.

Answer: True
TF   Moderate

15.66: On the seller's books, the journal entry to record the payment of a discounted note at maturity is a debit to Notes Payable and Interest Expense, and a credit to Cash.

Answer: False
TF   Difficult

15.67: The bank discount is based on the maturity value of the note.

Answer: True
TF   Moderate

15.68: The payee is the person to whom the note is payable.

Answer: True
TF   Moderate

15.69: Interest can be calculated by moving the decimal two places to the left when the rate times the number of days equal 360.

Answer: True
TF   Moderate

15.70: The interest on $25,000 at 16% for 90 days would be $1,000.00.

Answer: True
TF   Difficult

15.71: The proceeds on a $20,000 note discounted at 12% for 60 days would be $19,500.

Answer: False
TF   Difficult

15.72: A company would receive $14,700 for a $15,000 note discounted at 8% for 90 days.

Answer: True
TF   Difficult

15.73: Accounts Receivable has a stronger legal claim than Notes Receivable.

Answer: False
TF   Easy

15.74: The payor is the party to whom the note is payable.

Answer: False
TF   Easy

15.75: The exact maturity date is easily calculated when the note is stated in months.

Answer: True
TF   Easy

15.76: Interest is normally stated as an annual rate.

Answer: True
TF   Easy

15.77: When an accounts receivable is exchanged for a notes receivable, a shift in assets occurs.

Answer: True
TF   Moderate

15.78: Proceeds are found by taking maturity value and adding the bank discount.

Answer: False
TF   Moderate

15.79: The proceeds can never be less than the face value.

Answer: False
TF   Moderate

15.80: $20,132.67 is the proceeds of a $20,000.00, 60-day, 6% note discounted at 12% with 10 days left before maturity.

Answer: True
TF   Difficult

15.81: A potential liability is called a contingent liability.

Answer: True
TF   Moderate

15.82: Discount on Notes Payable is when interest is deducted in advance.

Answer: True
TF Moderate

15.83: Discount on Notes Payable is eventually an expense for the business.

Answer: True
TF Moderate

15.84: Calculate the interest for the following:
a. $12,000   12%   1 year
b. $ 8,000   13%   7 months
c. $ 6,000   10%   80 days

Answer: a. $1,440.
b. $606.67
c. $133.33
ES Easy

15.85: Find the maturity dates for the following:
a. An 82-day note dated March 3.
b. A 4-month note dated January 31.
c. A one-year note dated February 1, 19x5.

Answer: a. May 24
b. May 31
c. Feb. 1, 19x6
ES Easy

15.86: Prepare the journal entries for Abilene Company for the following transactions.
a. Abilene sold $6,000 of merchandise to Baltimore Company on account.
b. Abilene received a 90-day, $6,000, 12% note for a time extension of past due account of Baltimore Company.
c. Collected the Baltimore note on the maturity date.

Answer: a. Accounts Rec., Baltimore Co.   6,000
            Sales   6,000

b. Notes Rec., Baltimore Co.   6,000
      Accounts Rec., Baltimore Co.   6,000

c. Cash   6,180
      Interest Income   180
      Notes Rec., Baltimore Co.   6,000
ES Moderate

15.87: Prepare the journal entries for the following transactions
for New Orleans Sales Company.
a. New Orleans sold $4,000 of merchandise to Salvadore
Imports Company on account.
b. New Orleans accepted a 60-day, 9% note from Salvadore in
settlement of its account.
c. Salvadore defaulted on its note on the maturity date.
d. Collected the previously defaulted Salvadore note plus
$25 additional interest.

Answer: a. Accounts Rec., Salvadore   4,000
               Sales   4,000

         b. Notes Rec., Salvadore   4,000
               Accounts Rec., Salvadore   4,000

         c. Accounts Rec., Salvadore   4,060
               Interest Income   60
               Notes Rec., Salvadore   4,000

         d. Cash   4,085
               Interest Income   25
               Accounts Rec., Salvadore   4,060
         ES Moderate

15.88: Prepare journal entries for the following transactions for
Salvadore Imports Company.
a. Purchased $4,000 of merchandise from New Orleans Sales
Company on account.
b. Gave New Orleans Sales Company a 60-day, 9% note
settlement of the accounts payable.
c. Salvadore defaulted on its note on the maturity date.
d. Salvadore paid the previously defaulted note plus $25
additional interest.

Answer: a. Purchases   4,000
               Accounts Pay., New Orleans   4,000

         b. Accounts Pay., New Orleans   4,000
               Notes Pay., New Orleans   4,000

         c. Notes Pay., New Orleans   4,000
             Interest Expense   60
               Accounts Pay., New Orleans   4,060

         d. Accounts Pay., New Orleans   4,060
             Interest Expense   25
               Cash   4,085
         ES Moderate

15.89: Prepare general journal entries for the San Diego Builders
       Company for the following transactions.

       Aug. 1 Received a $9,000, 60-day, 12% note from
                Rio Developers in settlement of its account.
             16 Discounted the note at Texas Bank, which charged
                a bank discount rate of 15%.
       Sep. 30 Rio defaulted on the note. The bank charged a
                $25 protest fee.
       Oct. 15 Collected the defaulted note plus $100 additional
                interest.

Answer: Aug. 1 Notes Rec., Rio   9,000
                   Accounts Rec., Rio   9,000

             16 Cash   9,007.88
                   Notes Rec., Rio   9,000
                   Interest Income   7.88

       Sep. 30 Accounts Rec., Rio   9,205
                   Cash   9,205

       Oct. 15 Cash   9,305
                   Accounts Rec., Rio   9,205
                   Interest Income   100
       ES Difficult

15.90: Prepare general journal entries for Maryland Enterprises for
       the following transactions.

       19x5
       Dec. 1 Discounted its own $10,000, 45-day, 12% note
                at Friendly Bank.
             31 Accrued the interest expense on the discounted note.

       19x6
       Jan. 15 Paid the discounted note.

Answer: 19x5
       Dec. 1 Cash   9,850
                 Discount on Notes Pay.   150
                   Notes Pay., Friendly   10,000

            31 Interest Expense   100
                   Discount on Notes Pay.   100

       19x6
       Jan. 15 Notes Pay., Friendly 10,000
                   Cash   10,000
                 Interest Expense   50
                   Discount on Notes Pay.   50
       ES Difficult

15.91: Judy McKay Company is considering accepting a $10,000, 60-day, 12% promissory note from C. Redd to extend additional time to settle a past due account. Discuss some of the reasons why McKay would accept a promissory note from Redd.

Answer:
a. To have a stronger legal claim for collecting the past due account. In this case the note acts as formal proof of the transaction.
b. To collect a fee for the use of McKay's money over a period of time. The interest on the note will be $200.
c. McKay has the option of discounting Redd's note at the bank for an earlier receipt of cash.

ES Moderate

15.92: Describe (a) the function of a promissory note and (b) explain its various parts and features.

Answer:
a. A promissory note is a written promise by a borrower to pay a certain sum of money to the lender at a fixed future date.

b.
1. The amount borrowed is called the principal.
2. The interest rate is the percentage of interest charged for the use of money. It is the annual rate.
3. The maturity date is the due date of the promissory note.
4. The maker is the one promising to pay the note. The maker must sign the note to make it valid.
5. The payee is the one to whom the note is payable.
6. The maturity value is the total amount payable, including interest, at the maturity date.
7. The note must state that the maker promises to pay a certain sum to the payee on a certain determinable date.

ES Moderate

15.93: Benny Hall negotiated a $10,000 bank loan for 120 days at a bank rate of 10%. The bank deducted the interest in advance.
Required (show your calculations):
(a) Calculate the amount of interest charged by the bank.
(b) Calculate the amount of cash Benny received from the bank.
(c) Calculate the effective interest rate charged by the bank.
(d) Prepare Benny's journal entry for the transaction.

Answer: (a) $10,000 * 0.10 * 120/360 = $333.33
(b) $10,000 - $333.33 = $9,666.67
(c) ($10,000 * 0.10)/$9,666.67 = 10.34 percent.
(d)

```
Cash                          9,666.67
Discount on Note Payable       333.33
        Notes Payable                      10,000
```

ES   Difficult

HOMEWORK QUIZZES

1. Introduction to Accounting Concepts and Procedures

1.1: The Income Statement is prepared first so the information
     can be used to prepare the Statement of Owner's Equity.

Answer: True
       TF   Moderate

1.2: The accounting functions involve: analyzing, recording,
     classifying, summarizing, and reporting information.

Answer: True
       TF   Moderate

1.3: If total liabilities are $8,000 and owner's equity is
     $10,000, the total assets must be:
     a) $20,000.   b) $18,000.   c) $14,000.   d) $2,000.

Answer: (b)
       MC   Moderate

1.4: Alice Cann's cash investment in her new business will:
     a) increase an asset and increase a liability.
     b) decrease an asset and increase a liability.
     c) increase an asset and increase an owner's equity.
     d) increase an asset and decrease an owner's equity.

Answer: (c)
       MC   Moderate

1.5: If Vegas Service collects $5,200 from customers on account:

     a) total assets are unchanged.
     b) owner's equity decreases.
     c) owner's equity increases.
     d) liabilities increase.

Answer: (a)
       MC   Moderate

1.6: Assets are equal to:
     a) liabilities + owner's equity.
     b) liabilities - owner's equity.
     c) liabilities - revenues.
     d) revenues - expenses.

Answer: (a)
       MC   Easy

1.7: Van Border purchased new equipment for his construction company. He pays $5,000 cash and agrees to pay the $15,000 remainder by the end of the year. The effect on the basic accounting equation will be:
a) decrease Cash $5,000 and increase Equipment $5,000.
b) decrease Cash $5,000, increase Equipment $20,000, and increase Accounts Payable $15,000.
c) decrease Cash $5,000, increase Equipment $15,000, and increase Accounts Payable $10,000.
d) decrease Cash $20,000 and increase Equipment $20,000.

Answer: (b)
MC   Moderate

1.8: A decrease in owner's equity that results from the business operations is:
a) an expense.   b) revenue.
c) liability.   d) an asset.

Answer: (a)
MC   Easy

1.9: A decrease in owner's equity resulting from the owner's use of cash or assets for personal use is:

a) an expense.   b) a liability.
c) an asset.   d) a withdrawal.

Answer: (d)
MC   Easy

1.10: Des Moines Services Company expenses were greater than its revenues during the accounting period:
a) assets will decrease more than liabilities.
b) owner's equity will decrease more than assets.
c) the business incurred a net loss.
d) the cash account will decrease.

Answer: (c)
MC   Moderate

2. Debits and Credits

2.1: A chart of accounts is a listing of the accounts and their ending balances.

Answer: False
    TF Easy

2.2: The left hand side of an account is called the credit side.

Answer: False
    TF Easy

2.3: A trial balance is a listing of all the accounts in the ledger and their ending balances.

Answer: True
    TF Easy

2.4: The Office Supplies account is:
    a) a revenue, and it has a normal debit balance.
    b) an expense, and it has a normal credit balance.
    c) an asset, and it has a normal debit balance.
    d) an asset, and it has a normal credit balance.

Answer: (c)
    MC Easy

2.5: Joe, the owner of Computer Sales, paid his personal VISA bill using a company check. The correct entry to record the transaction is:
    a) credit Cash, debit Withdrawals.
    b) credit Cash, debit Supplies Expense.
    c) credit Cash, debit Capital.
    d) credit Cash, debit Accounts Receivable.

Answer: (a)
    MC Moderate

2.6: The Accounts Receivable account has total debit postings of $2,300 and credit postings of $1,800. The balance of the account is:
    a) $4,100 debit.   b) $500 debit.
    c) $500 credit.   d) $4,100 credit.

Answer: (b)
    MC Moderate

2.7: Every transaction affects at least _____ T account(s).
　　a) one　　　　　　　　　　　b) two
　　c) three　　　　　　　　　　d) unlimited.

Answer: (b)
　　MC　Easy

2.8: The Accounts Payable account has total debit postings of
　　$600 and credit postings of $900.　The balance is:
　　a) $1,500 debit.　　　　　　　b) $1,500 credit.
　　c) $300 credit.　　　　　　　d) $300 debit.

Answer: (c)
　　MC　Moderate

2.9: The beginning balance in Cash was $400.　Additional cash of
　　$800 was received.　Checks were written for $700.　The cash
　　balance is:
　　a) $900.　　　b) $500.　　　c) $700.　　　d) $800.

Answer: (b)
　　MC　Moderate

2.10: The Tiger Company's books show total Service Fees of
　　$12,000, total expenses of $7,000, and total cash received
　　from customers of $2,000.　The company's net income was:
　　a) $6,000.　　　b) $2,000.　　　c) $5,000.　　　d) $12,000.

Answer: (c)
　　MC　Difficult

3. Beginning the Accounting Cycle

3.1: Recording transactions in the journal is called journalizing.

Answer: True
TF   Easy

3.2: An accounting period that runs for any 12 consecutive months is called the calender year.

Answer: False
TF   Moderate

3.3: Transferring information from the journal to the ledger is called posting.

Answer: True
TF   Easy

3.4: The first step of the accounting cycle is:
   a) recording journal entries.
   b) posting to the ledger.
   c) preparing a trial balance.
   d) analyzing business transactions.

Answer: (d)
MC   Moderate

3.5: A journal entry affecting more than two accounts is called a:
   a) multi-level entry.   b) multi-step entry.
   c) compound entry.   d) simple entry.

Answer: (c)
MC   Easy

3.6: In the month of July, John's Company paid three months' rent in advance. The journal entry to record this transaction is:
   a) Prepaid Rent   b) Rent Expense
         Cash   Cash

   c) Cash   d) Cash
         Prepaid Rent   Rent Expense

Answer: (a)
MC   Moderate

3.7: The entry to record Roman Comapny's payment of $300 for repairs to equipment it owns would include:
   a) debit Cash, $300; credit Repairs Expense, $300.
   b) debit Cash, $300; credit Accounts Payable, $300.
   c) debit Repair Expense, $300; credit Cash, $300.
   d) debit Repairs Expense, $300; credit Accounts Payable, $300.

Answer: (c)
   MC   Moderate

3.8: Brim Company's total assets and total liabilities increased $800. The transaction could have been:
   a) purchase of supplies for cash, $800.
   b) purchase of supplies for $1,000 with a down payment of $200.
   c) payment of rent for the month, $800.
   d) None of the above.

Answer: (b)
   MC   Moderate

3.9: Which of the following transactions would cause the trial balance to be out of balance?
   a) A debit to Cash and a debit to Equipment for $400
   b) A credit to Cash and a debit to Supplies for the same amount
   c) A debit to Accounts Receivable and a credit to Accounting Fees for $300
   d) All of the above.

Answer: (a)
   MC   Moderate

3.10: In preparing the trial balance of the Computer Store, the withdrawal account was listed as a credit for $150. What will be the difference between the debit and credit side of the trial balance?
   a) $150   b) $200   c) $300   d) $600

Answer: (c)
   MC   Difficult

4. The Accounting Cycle Continued

4.1: Supplies and prepaid rent are assumed to have a longer life than equipment.

Answer: False
   TF Moderate

4.2: The original cost of an asset is referred to as the historical cost.

Answer: True
   TF Easy

4.3: To allocate or spread the cost of an asset over its useful life is called depreciation.

Answer: True
   TF Moderate

4.4: Peabody Company's estimated depreciation for office equipment is $100. The adjusting entry would include:
   a) a credit to Accumulated Depreciation for $100.
   b) a credit to Depreciation Expense for $100.
   c) a debit to Accumulated Depreciation for $100.
   d) a credit to Office Equipment for $100.

Answer: (a)
   MC Moderate

4.5: Sam's Shoe Store showed store supplies available, $400. A count of the supplies left on hand as of May 31 is $150. The adjusting entry for Store Supplies would include:
   a) a debit to Store Supplies Expense for $250.
   b) a credit to Store Supplies Expense for $250.
   c) a debit to Store Supplies for $150.
   d) a credit to Store Supplies Expense for $150.

Answer: (a)
   MC Moderate

4.6: The two columns for figures on financial statements are used for:
   a) indicating debits and credits.
   b) balancing accounts.
   c) subtotaling and totaling.
   d) None of the above.

Answer: (c)
   MC Easy

4.7: The ending figure for capital is:
   a) extended to the balance sheet columns.
   b) revealed by the net income.
   c) indicated in the trial balance.
   d) not on the worksheet.

Answer: (d)
   MC   Moderate

4.8: Gerald Company's accrued wages are $300. Which of the
   following is the required adjusting entry?
   a) Debit Salaries Expense, $300; debit Salaries Payable,
   $300
   b) Debit Salaries Expense, $300; credit Salaries Payable,
   $300
   c) Debit Salaries Payable, $300; credit Salaries Expense,
   $300
   d) Debit Salaries Payable, $300; credit Cash, $300

Answer: (b)
   MC   Moderate

4.9: On September 1, Crumm Company paid in advance $7,000 for
   seven months' rent. The September 30 adjusting entry for
   rent expense should include:
   a) debit Rent Expense, $2,500.
   b) credit Prepaid Rent, $3,500.
   c) debit Rent Expense, $2,000.
   d) debit Rent Expense, $1,000.

Answer: (d)
   MC   Moderate

4.10: Clarion Newspaper received its electric bill for December on
   December 31, but did not pay or record it. This resulted
   in:
   a) understated assets.
   b) overstated new income.
   c) overstated liabilities.
   d) understated owner's equity.

Answer: (b)
   MC   Difficult

5. The Accounting Cycle Completed

5.1: Entries in the journal to update revenue accounts are called closing entries.

Answer: False
TF   Easy

5.2: Entries in the journal to clear temporary accounts and to update the capital account are called adjusting entries.

Answer: False
TF   Moderate

5.3: The last step of the accounting cycle is the preparation of the post-closing trial balance.

Answer: True
TF   Moderate

5.4: The adjusting entries are journalized:
a) before preparing financial reports.
b) after preparing financial reports.
c) at the beginning of the accounting period.
d) whenever time permits.

Answer: (b)
MC   Moderate

5.5: After posting the closing entries, which of the following accounts is most likely not to have a zero balance?
a) Prepaid Insurance   b) Advertising Expense
c) G. Smith, Withdrawals   d) Medical Fees

Answer: (a)
MC   Moderate

5.6: Which of the following accounts would be considered a temporary account?
a) Revenue   b) Assets
c) Liabilities   d) Owner's equity

Answer: (a)
MC   Easy

5.7: The balance in the A. Gray, Withdrawals account was $6,600. The entry to close the account would include:
   a) debit to Income Summary, 46,600.
   b) credit to Income Summary, $6,600.
   c) credit to A. Gray, Capital, $6,600.
   d) credit to A. Gray, Withdrawals, $6,600.

Answer: (d)
   MC   Moderate

5.8: The Income Summary account shows debits of $20,000 and credits of $18,000. This is a result of:
   a) net income of $2,000.   b) net loss of $2,000.
   c) net income of $38,000.   d) net loss of $38,000.

Answer: (b)
   MC   Moderate

5.9: Accounts in which the balances are carried over from one accounting period to another are called.
   a) real accounts.   b) nominal accounts.
   c) temporary accounts.   d) zero accounts.

Answer: (a)
   MC   Moderate

5.10: After the closing process is complete, the accounting equation is:
   a) assets = liabilities + beginning capital.
   b) assets = liabilities + ending capital.
   c) assets = liabilities + owner's equity + revenue - expenses.
   d) reduced to the owner's equity.

Answer: (b)
   MC   Moderate

6. Banking Procedures and Control of Cash

6.1: A signature card is kept in the bank files so that possible forgeries could be spotted.

Answer: True
TF   Easy

6.2: A restrictive endorsement limits further use of a check.

Answer: True
TF   Moderate

6.3: External control includes control over the assets as well as ways of monitoring the company's operations.

Answer: False
TF   Moderate

6.4: Bank statements show all the following except:
a) deposits received and checks paid.
b) the beginning and ending balances shown on the bank's records.
c) the beginning and ending balances shown on the depositor's general ledger.
d) items debited and credited to the checking account.

Answer: (c)
MC   Moderate

6.5: A blank endorsement on a check:
a) can be further endorsed by someone else.
b) cannot be further endorsed by someone else.
c) is the safest type of endorsement.
d) only permits the original endorser to get the money.

Answer: (a)
MC   Moderate

6.6: Checks that have been processed by the bank and are no longer negotiable are:
a) outstanding checks.
b) cancelled checks.
c) checks in process.
d) All of the above are negotiable.

Answer: (b)
MC   Moderate

6.7: Deposits not yet added into the bank balance are called:
    a) deposits in transit.   b) late deposits.
    c) deposits on hold.   d) outstanding deposits.

Answer: (a)
    MC Easy

6.8: The journal entry to adjust the records from Candy Cane
Confectionary's bank reconciliation would include:
    a) the total of outstanding checks.
    b) deposits in transit.
    c) correction of any errors on the bank statement.
    d) correction of any errors or omissions in the company
cash account.

Answer: (d)
    MC Moderate

6.9: The entry to replenish a $50 petty cash fund which has cash
of $10 and valid receipts for $38 would include:
    a) a credit to Cash for $38.
    b) a debit to Cash for $38.
    c) a credit to Cash for $40.
    d) a credit to Petty Cash for $40.

Answer: (c)
    MC Moderate

6.10: Southern Cooking Restaurant's journal entry to establish a
$100 petty cash fund for the office would include a:
    a) credit to Cash for $100.
    b) credit to Petty Cash for $100.
    c) debit to Cash for $100.
    d) debit to Office Expense for $100.

Answer: (a)
    MC Easy

7. Payroll Concepts and Procedures: Employee Taxes

7.1: Net pay and gross pay have the same meaning.

Answer: False
TF   Easy

7.2: Regular earnings are equal to total earnings less deductions.

Answer: False
TF   Moderate

7.3: The payroll information for a pay period is found in the payroll register.

Answer: True
TF   Moderate

7.4: Which of the following would not typically be an employee payroll withholding?
a) Union dues
b) Purchases of savings bonds
c) Federal income tax
d) Unemployment taxes

Answer: (d)
MC   Moderate

7.5: Joan works 48 hours as a waitress in a restaurant. Compute her weekly pay. Her hourly rate of pay is $4.00 per hour. Remember that overtime is over 44 hours.
a) $192   b) $200   c) $210   d) $230

Answer: (b)
MC   Moderate

7.6: If Andy Cox's cumulative earnings prior to this pay period are $60,000 and his gross pay for the week is $1,000, what is his FICA--Social Security tax when the tax rate is: 6.2 percent on $60,600.
a) $37.20   b) $30.00   c) $0   d) $62.00

Answer: (a)
MC   Moderate

7.7: The amount of FICA-Social Security and FICA-Medicare taxes
an employer must pay is:
   a) less than the amount withheld from the employee.
   b) does not depend on the amount withheld from the
   employee.
   c) equal to the amount withheld from the employee.
   d) greater than the amount withheld from the employee.

Answer: (c)
   MC   Moderate

7.8: Which of the following is an optional payroll deduction?
   a) Union dues   b) Federal income taxes
   c) FICA   d) State income taxes.

Answer: (a)
   MC   Moderate

7.9: Compute employee FICA taxes for the year on earnings of
$42,000 at 6.2 percent Social Security and 1.45 percent
Medicare.
   a) $3,213.00   b) $32,130.00
   c) $32,130.30   d) $321.30

Answer: (a)
   MC   Moderate

7.10: The Office Salaries Expense account would be used to record:
   a) net earnings for the office workers.
   b) a credit to the amount owed to the office workers.
   c) gross earnings for the office workers.
   d) a debit for the amount net pay owed to the office
   workers.

Answer: (c)
   MC   Moderate

8. The Employers's Tax Responsibilities: Principles...

8.1: A deposit must be made when filing the W-2 form.

Answer: False
       TF   Easy

8.2: An employer can reduce the state unemployment tax rate by providing steady employment for the employees.

Answer: True
       TF   Moderate

8.3: Employers are responsible for deducting FUTA tax from the employee's earnings.

Answer: False
       TF   Moderate

8.4: Federal tax deposits are:
     a) paid to an authorized commerical depository.
     b) paid to a Federal Reserve Bank.
     c) not paid directly to the IRS.
     d) All of the above.

Answer: (d)
       MC   Moderate

8.5: A merit-rating plan:
     a) creates ideal employee evaluation plans.
     b) raises unemployment rates substantially.
     c) is for responsible employees.
     d) reduces the employer's state unemployment tax rate if low unemployment is maintained.

Answer: (d)
       MC   Moderate

8.6: The general journal entry to record the monthly payroll tax would include:
     a) a debit to Salaries Expense.
     b) a credit to Salaries Payable.
     c) a debit to Salaries Payable.
     d) a debit to Payroll Tax Expense.

Answer: (d)
       MC   Moderate

8.7: The employer's total FICA, SUTA, and FUTA tax is recorded
     as:
      a) a debit to Payroll Tax Expense.
      b) a credit to Payroll Tax Expense.
      c) a credit to Payroll Tax Payable.
      d) a debit to Payroll Tax Payable.

Answer: (a)
     MC   Moderate

8.8: The entry to record the payroll would include:
      a) a debit to Salaries Expense for the gross payroll.
      b) a debit to State Unemployment Taxes Payable.
      c) a debit to Salaries Payable.
      d) a debit to Salaries Expense for the net pay.

Answer: (a)
     MC   Moderate

8.9: John Grey's cumulative earnings before this pay period was
     $6,900; gross pay for the week is $300. How much of this
     week's pay is subject to taxes for FUTA and SUTA?
      a) $300   b) $100   c) $0   d) $6,900

Answer: (b)
     MC   Moderate

8.10: Russell Bear's cumulative earnings before this pay period
      was $6,700; gross for the week is $500. How much of this
      week's pay is subject to taxes for SUTA and FUTA? The rates
      are SUTA, 5.4 percent and FUTA, .8 percent with a base of
      $7,000.
       a) $300   b) $500   c) $6,700   d) $0

Answer: (a)
     MC   Moderate

9. Special Journals: Sales and Cash Receipts

9.1: A special ledger for the controlling account in the general ledger would be called a subsidiary ledger.

Answer: True
TF   Easy

9.2: When merchandise is sold on account, the transaction is recorded in the cash receipts journal.

Answer: False
TF   Moderate

9.3: Recording to the accounts receivable ledger should be performed at the end of the month.

Answer: False
TF   Moderate

9.4: Sam Able returned $100 of merchandise to Buy Company. His original purchase was $400, with terms 2/10, n/30. If Sam pays the balance of his account within the discount period, how much should he pay?
   a) $294   b) $292   c) $300   d) $306

Answer: (a)
MC   Moderate

9.5: The total of all cash and credit sales equals:
   a) gross sales.   b) net sales.
   c) net income.   d) gross profit.

Answer: (a)
MC   Easy

9.6: Generally, the revenue account for a merchandising firm is:
   a) Gross Profit.   b) Gross Sales.
   c) Net Sales.   d) Sales.

Answer: (d)
MC   Easy

9.7: Barbara's Bakery reports net sales of $15,000. If Sales Returns and Allowances are $1,500 and Sales Discounts are $150, what are gross sales?
   a) $13,000   b) $13,350   c) $16,650   d) $13,500

Answer: (c)
MC   Moderate

9.8: A listing of customers and their ending balances is called:
   a) a list of the receivables.
   b) a schedule of accounts receivable.
   c) a customer list.
   d) a chart of customers.

Answer: (b)
   MC   Easy

9.9: Gina's Flower Shop received payment in full for goods sold within the discount period on a $1,000 sales invoice, terms 1/10, n/30. Which entry records this transaction?
   a) Debit Accounts Receivable, credit Flower Sales for $1,000
   b) Debit Cash, credit Accounts Receivable for $990
   c) Debit Cash for $990, debit Sales Discount for $10, and credit Accounts Receivable for $1,000
   d) Debit Cash for $990, debit Sales Discount for $10, and credit Flower Sales for $1,000

Answer: (c)
   MC   Moderate

9.10: Sales Discounts would appear as a debit in the:
   a) cash receipts jouranl.   b) general journal.
   c) sales journal.   d) some other journal.

Answer: (a)
   MC   Moderate

10. Special Journals: Purchases and Cash Payments

10.1: Supplies are debited to the Purchase account.

Answer: False
        TF Moderate

10.2: Shipping costs are sometimes prepaid by the seller and the cost is added to the sales invoice.

Answer: True
        TF Easy

10.3: The Purchases Returns and Allowances account normally has a debit balance.

Answer: False
        TF Easy

10.4: Which special journal is used to record merchandise or other items bought on account?
      a) Sales journal   b) Cash receipts journal
      c) Purchases journal   d) Cash payments journal

Answer: (c)
        MC Moderate

10.5: A form completed at the time the shipment arrives is the:
      a) purchase invoice.   b) sales invoice.
      c) purchase order.   d) receiving report.

Answer: (d)
        MC Moderate

10.6: At the end of the month, the Sundry column total is posted to:
      a) Sundry account in the general ledger.
      b) a miscellaneous account in the general ledger.
      c) each asset account.
      d) is not posted.

Answer: (d)
        MC Moderate

10.7: When a debit memorandum for returned merchandise for Beams Co. is recorded and posted the entry is:
a) debit Purchases Returns & Allowances, credit Accounts Payable in the general ledger.
b) debit Accounts Payable, credit Purchases.
c) debit Beams Co. in the accounts payable ledger, debit Accounts Payable in the general ledger, credit Purchases Returns & Allowances.
d) debit Purchases, credit Accounts Pyable.

Answer: (c)
MC   Moderate

10.8: The main source for preparing the schedule of accounts payable is the:
a) purchase journal.
b) accounts payable general ledger account.
c) trial balance.
d) accounts payable subsidiary ledger.

Answer: (d)
MC   Moderate

10.9: Discounts which reduce the price for customers who buy items for resale or to produce other goods are:
a) purchase discounts.
b) purchases returns and allowances.
c) trade discounts.
d) cash discounts.

Answer: (c)
MC   Moderate

10.10: Lynn, Inc. made payment in full within the discount period on a $2,000 invoice, terms 2/10, n/30. The entry to record this transaction includes a:
a) debit to Accounts Payable, $1,960, credit to Purchases Discount, $40, and credit to Cash, $2,000.
b) debit to Accounts Payable, $2,000, credit to Purchases Discount, $40, and credit to Cash $1,960.
c) debit to Accounts Payable, $2,000, credit to Cash, $2,000.
d) debit to Cash, $2,000, credit to Accounts Payable, $2,000.

Answer: (b)
MC   Moderate

11. The Combined Journal

11.1: The cash basis of accounting occurs when revenue is recorded upon receipt and expenses are recorded upon payment.

Answer: True
    TF Easy

11.2: A special journal that replaces the general journal is called the combined journal.

Answer: True
    TF Moderate

11.3: An "X" in the posting reference column means posting is made to the Sundry account.

Answer: False
    TF Moderate

11.4: The cash basis method may be used because:
    a) it is simple.
    b) it applies the matching principles concept.
    c) it is required for companies with inventory.
    d) it does not require an understanding of business.

Answer: (a)
    MC Moderate

11.5: The method that records expenses when paid, and revenue when cash is received, with adjustments for long-term assets, is:
    a) cash method.
    b) modified cash-basis method.
    c) accrual method.
    d) None of the above.

Answer: (b)
    MC Moderate

11.6: What type of business would not use a modified cash-basis method of accounting?
    a) Professional services   b) Accounting services
    c) Department store   d) Architects

Answer: (c)
    MC Moderate

11.7: Which of the following accounts are treated the same under the modified cash-basis and the accrual basis?
  a) Equipment b) Accounts Receivable
  c) Professional Fees d) Inventory

Answer: (a)
  MC Moderate

11.8: Net income using the cash basis method equals:
  a) revenue (earned) plus expenses (incurred).
  b) revenue (cash received) plus expenses (paid).
  c) revenue (cash received) minus expenses (paid).
  d) revenue (earned) minus expenses (incurred).

Answer: (c)
  MC Moderate

11.9: How is a combined journal proved?
  a) By comparing total cash paid out with the total cash received
  b) By comparing the total debits with the total credits
  c) By comparing the Sundry column with the Cash column
  d) By comparing the total debits with the cash received

Answer: (b)
  MC Moderate

11.10: Adjusting and closing entries for a company using a combined journal are:
  a) not required.
  b) recorded in the general journal.
  c) recorded in special columns.
  d) recorded in the Sundry columns of the combined journal.

Answer: (d)
  MC Moderate

12. Preparing a Worksheet for a Merchandise Company

12.1: The inventory method that continually updates the inventory is called perpetual.

Answer: True
TF   Easy

12.2: The inventory method that is updated at the end of the period is called periodic.

Answer: True
TF   Easy

12.3: When an adjustment is made, the beginning inventory is transferred to Capital.

Answer: False
TF   Moderate

12.4: Merchandise inventory is:
   a) goods a company plans to sell to its customers.
   b) a current asset on the balance sheet.
   c) an important item on a merchandise company's financial statements.
   d) All the above.

Answer: (d)
MC   Moderate

12.5: The perpetual inventory system is used when the company has:
   a) high volume and low unit prices.
   b) a high variety of merchandise and high unit prices.
   c) low volume and high unit prices.
   d) low variety and low unit prices.

Answer: (c)
MC   Moderate

12.6: Beginning Inventory is $65, Net Purchases are $1,000, and Sales Returns and Allowances are $200. Goods Available for Sales is:
   a) $1,065.   b) $865.
   c) $1,000.   d) None of the above.

Answer: (a)
MC   Moderate

12.7: An account used in a periodic inventory method to record
buying of merchandise for resale is called:
a) sales.   b) purchases.
c) supplies.   d) beginning inventory.

Answer: (b)
MC   Moderate

12.8: What type of account is Unearned Rent?
a) Asset   b) Liability
c) Revenue   d) Expense

Answer: (b)
MC   Moderate

12.9: Which inventory appears in the balance sheet column of the
worksheet?
a) Beginning inventory
b) Ending inventory
c) Combination of beginning and ending inventories
d) Inventory does not appear on the balance sheet

Answer: (b)
MC   Moderate

12.10: What financial report shows the amount for Freight-In?
a) Income Statement
b) Balance Sheet
c) Statement of Owner's Equity
d) Trial Balance.

Answer: (a)
MC   Moderate

13. Completion of Accounting Cycle for a Merchandise Co.

13.1: The ending capital on the Statement of Owner's Equity also appears on the Balance Sheet.

Answer: True
TF Moderate

13.2: Assets that are long-lived are called Prepaid Expenses.

Answer: False
TF Moderate

13.3: Liabilities that are not due and payable for more than a year are called Long-Term Liabilities.

Answer: True
TF Moderate

13.4: The correct worksheet columns to use for preparing the income statement are the:
a) adjustments columns.
b) income statement columns.
c) adjusted trial balance columns.
d) trial balnce columns.

Answer: (b)
MC Moderate

13.5: To calculate gross profit:
a) subtract Freight-In from net purchases.
b) subtract ending inventory from cost of goods available for sale.
c) subtract cost of goods sold from net sales.
d) add freight to net purchases.

Answer: (c)
MC Moderate

13.6: Net Sales + Sales Discounts + Sales Returns and Allowances determines:
a) net income.
b) net income from operations.
c) gross profit.
d) gross sales.

Answer: (d)
MC Moderate

13.7: Which of the following is not an operating expense?
   a) Cost of goods sold   b) Advertising expense
   c) Freight-out   d) General office expenses

Answer: (a)
   MC   Moderate

13.8: Paper used to wrap customers' purchases is a(n):
   a) selling expense.   b) administrative expense.
   c) cost of goods sold.   d) other expenses.

Answer: (a)
   MC   Moderate

13.9: A landlord collected six months rent in advance from a
tenant. This would be classified as a(n):
   a) current asset.   b) other income.
   c) revenue.   d) current liability.

Answer: (d)
   MC   Moderate

13.10: After closing entries have been posted:
   a) the temporary accounts are zeroed out.
   b) the capital account includes the current net profit or
   loss.
   c) the post-closing trial balance is prepared.
   d) All the above.

Answer: (d)
   MC   Moderate

14. Accounting for Bad Debts

14.1: Allowance for Doubtful Accounts is an example of a contra-asset account.

Answer: True
TF   Easy

14.2: Net Realizable Value is the amount that is left after subtracting the Allowance for Doubtful Accounts from Accounts Payable.

Answer: False
TF   Difficult

14.3: The income statement approach determines the bad debts expense by multiplying a percentage of net credit sales.

Answer: True
TF   Moderate

14.4: Which financial statement reports Allowances for Doubtful Accounts?
    a) Statement of owner's equity
    b) Income statement
    c) Balance sheet
    d) None of the above.

Answer: (c)
MC   Moderate

14.5: Abby's Antiques estimates it will collect $800 of the $1,000 owed by customers. The estimated collectible amount is the:
    a) bad debts allowances.
    b) net realizable value.
    c) allowance for doubtful accounts.
    d) gross accounts receivable.

Answer: (b)
MC   Moderate

14.6: What would the basis for the following journal entry if it appears on a firm's records?
        Allowance for Doubtful Accounts   150
            Accounts Receivable   150
    a) The firm is estimating its uncollectible accounts.
    b) The firm is writing off an uncollectible account.
    c) The firm is making a collection of a previously written off account.
    d) It is a reversing entry.

Answer: (b)
MC   Moderate

14.7: The journal entry to write off an account judged to be uncollectible under the allowance method is:
   a) debit Sales, credit Allowance for Doubtful Accounts.
   b) debit Accounts Receivable, credit Bad Debts Expense.
   c) debit Allowance for Doubtful Accounts, credit Accounts Receivable.
   d) debit Bad Debts Expense, credit Accounts Receivable.

Answer: (c)
   MC   Moderate

14.8: Gross accounts receivable are $10,000. Allowance for Doubtful Accounts has a credit balance of $200. Net sales for the year are $150,000. In the past, 1 percent of sales had proved uncollectible, and an aging of the receivables indicates $1,000 is doubtful. Under the income statment mentod, bad debts expense for the year is:
   a) $1,000.   b) $1,500.   c) $1,200.   d) $900.

Answer: (b)
   MC   Difficult

14.9: Gross accounts receivable are $10,000. Allowance for Doubtful Accounts has a credit balance of $200. Net sales for the year are $150,000. In the past, 1 percent of sales had proved uncollectile, and an aging of the receivable indicates $1,200 as being uncollectible. What would be the adjusted balance of the allowance account under the balance sheet approach?
   a) $1,700   b) $1,200   c) $1,000   d) $900

Answer: (b)
   MC   Difficult

14.10: Bad Debts Recovered is a(n):
   a) asset account.   b) liability account.
   c) revenue account.   d) expense account.

Answer: (c)
   MC   Moderate

15. Notes Receivable and Notes Payable

15.1: A written promise by a borrower to pay in the future is called a notes payable.

Answer: True
TF   Easy

15.2: The amount borrowed on a note is called the principal.

Answer: True
TF   Moderate

15.3: The one who promises to pay is called the payee.

Answer: False
TF   Moderate

15.4: An advantage of a promissory note receivable over an accounts receivable is to:
a) establish a stronger legal claim against the borrower.
b) put all the facts in writing.
c) collect a fee for the use of one's money.
d) All of the above.

Answer: (d)
MC   Moderate

15.5: The person or company that borrows money and signs a note payable is the:
a) maker.   b) payee.
c) drawee.   d) principle person.

Answer: (a)
MC   Moderate

15.6: Rick promises to pay Joe $1,000 plus 12 percent interest to be repaid in 90 days. The interest rate is the:
a) monthly rate.
b) 90 day rate.
c) annual rate.
d) cannot be determined from the information given.

Answer: (c)
MC   Moderate

15.7: Broke Company issues a promissory note to Sale Company to obtain extended time on an account payable. Broke records this transaction as follows:
   a) debit Accounts Receivable, credit Notes Receivable.
   b) debit Notes Receivable, credit Accounts Receivable.
   c) debit Notes Payable, credit Accounts Payable.
   d) debit Accounts Payable, credit Notes Payable.

Answer: (d)
   MC   Moderate

15.8: Interest income is on a merchandise company's income statement under the heading:
   a) sales revenue.   b) other income.
   c) fees earned.   d) notes receivable.

Answer: (b)
   MC   Moderate

15.9: Interest calculated for four months on a $3,000, 10 percent promissory note is:
   a) $1.   b) $100.   c) $30.   d) $300.

Answer: (b)
   MC   Moderate

15.10: The proceeds from discounting a Notes Receivable are the:
   a) maturity value minus principal.
   b) principal minus discount.
   c) principal plus discount.
   d) maturity value minus discount.

Answer: (d)
   MC   Moderate

ACHIEVEMENT TESTS with SOLUTIONS

SLATER COLLEGE ACCOUNTING
Sixth Edition
Achievement Test 1A
Chapters 1 and 2

Part	Perfect Score	Student's Score
I	20	
II	30	
III	15	
IV	15	
V	20	
Total	100	

NAME_____

Class_____ Date_____

PART I MATCHING

Match the following terms with the definitions or statements listed below. Indicate your answers in the spaces provided. (Two points per term)

a. Assets
b. Balance sheet
c. Capital
d. Partnership
e. Corporation

f. Debit
g. Expenses
h. Income statement
i. Net income
j. Sole proprietorship
k. Revenue

Answer

_____ 1. A business owned by stockholders.
_____ 2. Costs incurred in running a business.
_____ 3. When revenue is larger than expenses.
_____ 4. The left-hand side of an account.
_____ 5. Properties of value owned by a business.
_____ 6. A report as of a particular date that shows the amount of assets, liabilities, and capital.
_____ 7. A business with two or more co-owners.
_____ 8. A report that details the performance of a firm for a specific period of time.
_____ 9. An amount earned by performing services for customers or selling goods to customers.
_____ 10. A business with one owner.

PART II TABLE COMPLETION

For each account listed identify the category it belongs to, the normal balance (debit or credit), and the financial report the account appears. (Two points per item)

Account	Category	Normal Balance	Financial Report
0. Cash	Asset	Debit	Balance Sheet
1. Rent Expense			
2. Accounts Payable			
3. J. Ray, Withdrawal			
4. Equipment			
5. Rental Fees Earned			

PART III FINANCIAL STATEMENTS

Use the following information to prepare an (1) Income Statement and
(2) Statement of Owner's Equity for the month ended March 31, 19xx
for J. Brown Company. (Fifteen points total)

J. Brown, Capital	$1,350
Service Fees Earned	800
Utilities Expense	100
Advertising Expense	200
J. Brown, Withdrawals	150

J. Brown Company
Income Statement

_____

J. Brown Company
Statement of Owner's Equity

_____

PART IV TRIAL BALANCE

The following is a list of accounts and their balances for Bally Company for the month ended April 30. Prepare a trial balance in good form. (Fifteen points total)

Cash	$1,000	L. Bally, Withdrawals	$ 100
Accounts Payable	500	Accounts Receivable	700
Office Equipment	2,000	Services Fees	1,000
L. Bally, Capital	2,500	Rent Expense	200

Bally Company
Trial Balance
April 30, 19xx

	Debit	Credit

PART V PROBLEM

Using the chart of accounts below, indicate for each transaction the accounts that should be debited and credited by inserting the proper account number in the space provided. (One point per item)

111	Cash	312	R. Holmes, Withdrawals
112	Accounts Receivable	411	Delivery Fees Earned
121	Delivery Equipment	511	Salaries Expense
211	Accounts Payable	512	Rent Expense
311	R. Holmes, Capital	513	Advertising Expense

Debit	Credit		Transaction
=====	======		============
_____	_____	1.	Invested cash in the business.
_____	_____	2.	Received cash for delivery services performed.
_____	_____	3.	Billed a customer for services performed.
_____	_____	4.	Paid accounts payable.
_____	_____	5.	Collected accounts receivable.
_____	_____	6.	Withdrew cash for personal use.
_____	_____	7.	Paid advertising expense.
_____	_____	8.	Paid rent expense for the month.
_____	_____	9.	Purchased delivery equipment on account.
_____	_____	10.	Paid salaries for the week.

SLATER COLLEGE ACCOUNTING

Sixth Edition

Achievement Test 2A

Chapters 3 and 4

Name_____

Class_____Date_____

Part	Perfect Score	Student Score
I	18	
II	20	
III	24	
IV	38	
Total	100	

PART I JOURNAL ENTRIES

Randy Babbit started a cleaning service in June, 19xx. Journalize the following June transactions. (Three points per entry)

June 2 R. Babbit invested $7,000 cash and $1,200 equipment he already owned into his new business.

10 Paid rent expense, $200.

15 Billed customers for services performed, $1,000.

16 Purchased supplies on account, $500.

20 Received one-half amount due from June billings, $500.

25 Hired a helper and paid her salary, $150.

GENERAL JOURNAL

Date		Account Titles and Description	PR	Debit	Credit

PART II MATCHING

Match the following terms with the definitions or statements listed below. Indicate your answers in the spaces provided. (Two points for each correct answer.)

a. Worksheet
b. Accounting period
c. Accumulated depreciation
d. Book value
e. Cross-referencing
f. General journal

g. Normal balance
h. Posting
i. Slide
j. Transposition
k. Trial balance
l. Accounting cycle

Answer

_____ 1. A multi-column form used by accountants as an aid in gathering data to complete the accounting cycle.

_____ 2. An informal listing of the ledger accounts and their balances that aids in proving the equality of debits and credits.

_____ 3. A form used to record business transactions in chronological order.

_____ 4. The period of time for which an income statement is prepared.

_____ 5. The side of an account that increases according to the rules of debit and credit.

_____ 6. The error that results in adding or deleting zeros in the writing of a number.

_____ 7. The transferring of information to a ledger.

_____ 8. A contra asset account that summarizes the amount of depreciation that has been taken on an asset.

_____ 9. Cost of equipment less accumulated depreciation.

_____ 10. Adding account numbers to the PR columns in the ledger and the journal to indicate the source and destination of each transaction, respectively.

PART III PREPARING FINANCIAL STATEMENTS

Prepare the following for Brad Consulting Service, for the month ended June 30, 19xx.

(1) Complete the following partial worksheet (Six points)
(2) Income Statement (Six points)
(3) Statement of Owner's Equity (Six points)
(4) Balance Sheet (Six points)

Account Title	Income Statement		Balance Sheet	
	DR	CR	DR	CR
Cash			4	
Accounts Rec.			6	
Supplies			2	
Accounts Pay.				9
F. Brad, Cap.				6
F. Brad, Wthdr.			2	
Service Rev.		8		
Salaries Exp.	4			
Rent Exp.	3			
Supplies Exp.	2			
Sub Totals	9	8	14	15
Profit (Loss)				
Totals				

Brad Consulting Service
Income Statement
For the Month Ended June 30, 19xx

Brad Consulting Service
Statement of Owner's Equity
June 30, 19xx

Brad Consulting Service
Balance Sheet
June 30, 19xx

PART IV WORKSHEET

Using the information given below, complete the Worksheet for Benpat Company for the year ended December 31, 19xx. (Two points per adjustment, one point per item in the Adjusted Trial Balance, Income Statement, and Balance Sheet columns)

Adjustments:

Depreciation Expense for the period:	$5.
Supplies on hand at the end of the period:	$5.
Wages owed, but not paid:	$3.

BENPAT COMPANY
Worksheet
For the Year Ended December 31, 19xx

Account Title	Trial Balance DR	CR	Adjustmnts DR	CR	Adjusted Trial Bal. DR	CR	Income Statement DR	CR	Balance Sheet DR	CR
Cash	5									
Accts. Rec.	12									
Supplies	7									
Ppd. Rent	9									
Store Eqt.	32									
Accm. Depr.		18								
Accts. Pay.		7								
Benpat,Cap.		25								
Benpat,Wthdr.	5									
Fees Rev.		45								
Wages Exp.	15									
Utlty Exp.	5									
Misc. Exp.	5									

SLATER COLLEGE ACCOUNTING
Sixth Edition
Achievement Test 3A
Chapters 5 and 6

Name_____

Class_____Date_____

Part	Perfect Score	Student Score
I	20	
II	16	
III	20	
IV	29	
V	15	
Total	100	

PART I MATCHING
Match the following terms with the definitions or statements listed below. Indicate your answers in the spaces provided. (Two points per term)

a. Adjusting entries
b. Check truncation
c. Closing entries
d. Credit memorandum
e. Debit memorandum

f. Income summary
g. Outstanding checks
h. Payee
i. Petty cash
j. Post-closing trial balance

Answer

_____ 1. The person or company to whom the check is payable.

_____ 2. Increase to the depositor's balance shown on the bank statement.

_____ 3. A fund that allows payment of small amounts without the writing of checks.

_____ 4. Entries that are prepared to (a) reduce or clear all temporary accounts to a zero balance, and (b) update capital to a new balance.

_____ 5. A temporary account in the ledger that summarizes revenue and expenses and transfers its balance (net income or net loss) to capital.

_____ 6. Decrease to the depositor's balance shown on the bank statement.

_____ 7. Procedure whereby checks are not returned to the drawer with the bank statement, but are kept by the bank for a period of time.

_____ 8. Checks written by the company that were not processed by the bank prior to preparation of the bank statement.

_____ 9. The final step in the accounting cycle that lists only permanent accounts and their balances.

_____10. Journal entries needed to update accounts at the end of an accounting period to match revenues and expenses.

PART II TABLE COMPLETION

In the first space below, indicate whether each account is a real or nominal account using (R) Real Account and (N) Nominal Account. In the second space below, indicate by an (X) if the account should be closed. (Two points per line)

_N_	_X_	0.	_Advertising Expense_
_____	_____	1.	Accounts Receivable
_____	_____	2.	Rental Fees
_____	_____	3.	Depreciation Expense
_____	_____	4.	Accumulated Depreciation
_____	_____	5.	Salaries Payable
_____	_____	6.	Prepaid Rent
_____	_____	7.	Income Summary
_____	_____	8.	Insurance Expense

PART III JOURNAL ENTRIES

From the T accounts below, journalize the necessary closing entries in good form.   (Five points per entry)

```
Insurance Expense          Wages Expense          Depreciation Expense
    500      |               1,500    |                1,000    |
             |                        |                         |

T. Rogers, Capital          Income Summary          Accounting Fees
         | 15,000                     |                         | 5,000
         |                            |                         |

T. Rogers, Withdrawals
  1,200    |
           |
```

GENERAL JOURNAL

Date		Account Title and Description	PR	Debit	Credit

PART IV BANK RECONCILIATION AND JOURNAL ENTRIES

Use the information below to (1) construct a bank reconciliation
for Mahr Company as of April 30, 19xx, and (2) prepare the
necessary journal entries to update the general ledger accounts.
(Twenty points for the bank reconciliation and nine points for
the journal entries)

Balance per bank statement	$5,300
Deposit in transit	3,000
Checkbook balance	6,500
Checks outstanding	1,709
NSF check (debit memo) customer ck.	200
Error on check. Amount on the check was $87, the amount on the check stub was $78 in payment for office supplies	9
The bank collected a note receivable for Mahr	300

MAHR COMPANY

Checkbook Balance _____ Balance per Bank _____

_____

_____

_____

_____

_____

_____

_____

_____

_____

_____

GENERAL JOURNAL

Date		Account Title and Description	PR	Debit	Credit

PART V PETTY CASH JOURNAL ENTRIES

Prepare journal entries for the following petty cash fund transactions. (Five points for each journal entry)

Jul 1 Established an $85 petty cash fund.
     9 Increased the petty cash fund to $100.
     31 Replenished the petty cash fund. Currency and coins $20, $12 donation expense, $21 postage expense, $37 office supplies expense and $15 miscellaneous expense.

GENERAL JOURNAL

Date		Account Title and Description	PR	Debit	Credit

SLATER COLLEGE ACCOUNTING

Sixth Edition
Achievement Test 4A
Chapters 7 and 8

Name_____

Class_____Date_____

`Part	Perfect Score	Student Score
I	20	
II	20	
III	12	
IV	36	
V	12	
Total	100	

PART I MATCHING

Match the following terms with the definitions or statements listed below. Indicate your answers in the spaces provided. (Two points per term)

a. Employer identification no.
b. Federal unemployment tax
c. Merit rating plan
d. Office salaries expense
e. Payroll register

f. State unemployment tax
g. Taxable earnings
h. Workers' compensation insurance
i. Form 941
j. Form W-2

Answer

_____ 1. An account used to record gross earnings for office salaries for the period.

_____ 2. A report to be completed for each quarter indicating total FICA (Social Security and Medicare) owed plus federal income tax withheld for the quarter.

_____ 3. A tax usually paid by employers to the state.

_____ 4. A form completed by the employer at the end of the calendar year to provide a summary of gross earnings and deductions to each employee.

_____ 5. Employers' insurance requirement protecting their employees against losses due to injury or death incurred while on the job.

_____ 6. Shows amount of earnings subject to a tax.

_____ 7. A percentage rate assigned to a business by the state in calculating state unemployment tax.

_____ 8. Identification number for reporting and paying taxes.

_____ 9. A multi-column form that can be used to record payroll data and is used to journalize the payroll entry.

_____10. An unemployment tax paid by employers to the federal government.

PART II TRUE OR FALSE

Indicate if the following questions are TRUE or FALSE in the spaces provided. (Two points per question)

Answer

_____ 1. The more allowances a person claims, the less FICA tax paid.

_____ 2. The payroll information for a pay period is found in the payroll register.

_____ 3. Net pay and gross pay mean the same thing.

_____ 4. The Federal Unemployment Tax Act was established to allow the federal government to monitor state unemployment programs.

_____ 5. Someone who is paid on a semi-monthly basis is paid 26 times during the year.

_____ 6. The employer is required to pay for medical insurance for the employee for non-job-related accidents.

_____ 7. The Fair Labor Standards Act is also called the Wages and Hours Law.

_____ 8. Maximum tax credit allowed against FUTA is 6.2%.

_____ 9. Payroll Tax Expense is the account the employer uses for the employer's payroll taxes (FICA, FUTA, and SUTA).

_____ 10. The cost of workers' compensation insurance must be estimated and paid in advance by the employer.

PART III PROBLEM

From the following information, please complete the chart for gross earnings for the week. Assume an overtime rate of time and a half over 40 hours. (Four points per employee)

	Hourly Rate	No. of Hours Worked	Gross Earnings
Jane Holmes	$7	42	_____
Jerry Dodds	8	35	_____
Jessica Dagget	10	43	_____

PART IV PROBLEM A

Prepare a general journal payroll entry for Lincoln Market using the following information. (Twenty points for entry)

	Cumulative Earnings Before Payroll	Weekly Salary	Dept.
Sharon Small	$40,000	$ 500	Office
Marianne Kelly	35,000	800	Sales
Jay Jones	60,000	1,000	Office

Assume the following:
a.   FICA: Social Security, 6.2% on $60,600; Medicare, 1.45%.
b.   Federal income tax is 15% of gross pay.
c.   Each employee pays $10 per week for medical insurance.

GENERAL JOURNAL

Date		Account Title and Description	PR	Debit	Credit

PART IV PROBLEM B

Using the information below, determine the amount of the payroll tax expense for Clare's Company. In your answer list the amounts for FICA: (Social Security and Medicare), SUTA, and FUTA. (Four points per answer)

Employee	Gross pay
E. Stewart	$1,500
J. Moore	500
K. Jones	600

Assume: FICA tax rates are Social Security 6.2%, and Medicare 1.45%; state unemployment tax rate is 5.0%; and federal unemployment tax rate is 0.8%. All employees have earned less than $7,000.

FICA-Social Security   _____

FICA-Medicare   _____

SUTA   _____

FUTA   _____

PART V JOURNAL ENTRIES

Estimate the annual advance premium and prepare the general journal entry using the following data. (Twelve points for journal entry)

Type of Work	Estimated Payroll	Rate Per $100
Sales	$20,000	$ .50
Office	5,000	.25
Nursing Staff	80,000	2.00

GENERAL JOURNAL

Date		Account Title and Description	PR	Debit	Credit

SLATER COLLEGE ACCOUNTING
Sixth Edition
Achievement Test 5A
Chapters 9 and 10

Name_____

Class_____Date_____

Part	Perfect Score	Student Score
I	20	
II	20	
III	22	
IV	14	
V	24	
Total	100	

PART I TRUE OR FALSE
Indicate if the following questions are TRUE or FALSE in the spaces provided. (Two points per question)

Answers

_____1.   Payment for merchandise should not be made until approval is given.

_____2.   Shipping costs are sometimes prepaid by the seller and the cost is added to the sales invoice.

_____3.   Purchases Discount is a contra revenue account.

_____4.   The accounts payable column total in the Purchase Journal is posted to the accounts payable general ledger account at the end of the month.

_____5.   Trade discounts are recorded in the journal.

_____6.   Sales Tax Payable is an owner's equity account with a credit balance.

_____7.   All receipts of cash should be recorded in the Cash Receipts Journal.

_____8.   A special ledger supporting the controlling account in the general ledger would be called a subsidiary ledger.

_____9.   Firms that use special journals can eliminate the general journal.

____10.   Net Sales is computed by adding Gross Sales, Sales Discount and Sales Returns and Allowances.

PART II PROBLEM

On May 6, R. Alexander purchased merchandise for his jewelry store. The invoice was for $80,000 plus freight, $1,500, terms 1/15, n/30. On May 10, R. Alexander returned merchandise for $15,000 credit. On May 19, R. Alexander paid the amount owed. Answer the following questions. (Five points per question)

    a.   The credit to Accounts Payable on May 6 is _____.

    b.   The debit to Accounts Payable on May 10 is _____.

    c.   The credit to Purchases Discount on May 19 is _____.

    d.   The credit to Cash on May 19 is _____.

PART III PROBLEMS

Purple Furniture Company sold K. Daniels a bedroom set for $2,500 plus sales tax of 6%. Terms of the sale are 1/10, n/30. Date of the sale was May 22, date of the payment was June 5.

Required: Determine the amount K. Daniels should pay Purple Furniture on June 5. (Eleven points)

$_____

Use the following information to answer the questions below. (Eleven points)

Sales Returns and Allowances	$ 500
Gross Profit	1,800
Net Income	800
Sales Discount	500
Sales	3,000

The Net Sales are _____.

PART IV PROBLEM

Indicate the journal in which each of the following transactions should be recorded by placing the letters representing the appropriate journal in the space provided. (Two points per question)

Choice of journals:
- S Sales Journal
- CR Cash Receipts
- P Purchase
- CP Cash Payments
- GJ General Journal

a. _____ Purchased merchandise on account.

b. _____ Issued a credit memo to a customer for returned merchandise.

c. _____ Sold merchandise on account.

d. _____ Received credit on account for an allowance.

e. _____ Sold merchandise for cash.

f. _____ Purchased merchandise for cash.

g. _____ Owner withdrew cash from the business.

PART V PROBLEM

The following are transactions for M. Thomas for the month of March. Journalize the transactions in the appropriate journals. (One and one-half points per entry. Post transactions properly. (One and one-half points per account.)

Mar 1   M. Thomas invested an additional $10,000 in his business.

Mar 3   Sold $1,500 of merchandise on account to Tom Miller, sales invoice No. 12, terms 1/10, n/30.

Mar 5   Sold $800 of merchandise on account to Greg Pound, sales invoice No. 13, terms 2/10, n/30.

Mar 13 Received cash from T. Miller in payment for Mar 3 transaction, less the discount.

Mar 14 Issued credit memorandum No. 1 to G. Pound for $100 for merchandise returned from Mar 5 sale on account.

Mar 15 Received cash from G. Pound for the amount due, less the discount.

Mar 23 Sold equipment at cost for cash, $7,000.

SALES JOURNAL

Date		Account Debited	Terms	Inv. No.	PR	Dr. A/R Cr. Sales

GENERAL JOURNAL

Date		Account Titles and Description	PR	Debit	Credit

CASH RECEIPTS JOURNAL

Date	Cash Dr.	Sales Dis. Dr.	Acct. Rec. Cr.	Sales Cr.	Sundry Acct.	Post Ref.	Amount Cr.

GENERAL LEDGER

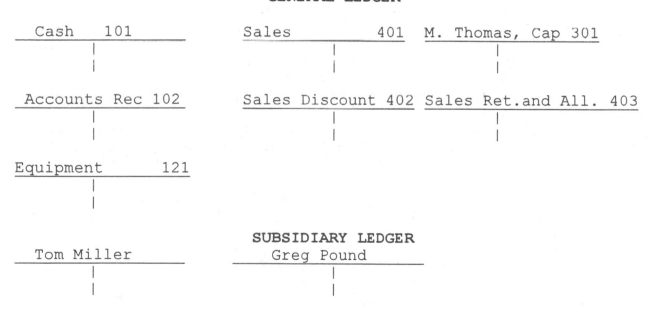

Cash   101

Sales   401

M. Thomas, Cap 301

Accounts Rec 102

Sales Discount 402

Sales Ret.and All. 403

Equipment   121

SUBSIDIARY LEDGER

Tom Miller

Greg Pound

355

SLATER COLLEGE ACCOUNTING
Sixth Edition
Achievement Test 6A
Chapters 11 and 12

Name_____

Class_____Date_____

Part	Perfect Score	Student Score
I	20	
II	20	
III	18	
IV	16	
V	26	
Total	100	

PART I MATCHING

Match the following terms with the definitions or statements listed below. Indicate your answers in the spaces provided. (Two points per term)

a. Ending merchandise inventory
b. Modified cash-basis
c. Accrual accounting
d. Cash-basis
e. Combined journal
f. Perpetual inventory
g. Unearned revenue
h. Mortgage payable
i. Payroll tax expense
j. Periodic inventory

Answer

_____ 1. The goods that remain unsold at the end of the accounting period. It is an asset on the new balance sheet.

_____ 2. An inventory system that, at the end of each accounting period, calculates the cost of the unsold goods on hand.

_____ 3. An inventory system that keeps continual track of each type of inventory by recording units on hand at the beginning, units sold, and the current balance after each sale or purchase.

_____ 4. A combination of cash-basis and accrual basis systems.

_____ 5. An accounting system whereby the revenues are recorded when earned and expenses when incurred to earn that revenue.

_____ 6. An accounting system whereby revenue is recorded when cash is received, and expenses are recorded when they are paid.

_____ 7. The employer's share of payroll taxes.

_____ 8. A liability account for recording receipt of an advance payment for goods or services.

_____ 9. A liability account showing amount owed on a mortgage.

_____ 10. A special journal that could replace the general journal under cash-basis and modified cash-basis.

PART II TABLE COMPLETION

The combined journal for Charlie's Garden Service has the following headings with appropriate columns for indicating debits and credits: Cash, Explanation, Sundry, Fees, Salary Expense, FICA Payable, and FIT Payable.

The following is a partial chart of accounts for Charlie's Garden Service:

111	Cash	513	Salaries Expense
211	FICA Tax Payable	514	Payroll Tax Expense
212	Federal Income Tax Payable	520	Mowing Expense
411	Mowing Fees	525	Rental Expense

Indicate, in the format below, the account numbers and the debit and credit amounts for the following transactions under the modified cash-basis. (Four points per transaction)

Debit		Credit			
Account	Amount	Account	Amount		
111	$7	411	8	0.	Received cash from customer $8
				a.	Paid for mowing supplies $2
				b.	Paid three months' rental for tractor $6
				c.	Received a refund for supplies $1
				d.	Paid the payroll. Gross pay $8, FICA $1, FIT $2
				e.	Paid the FICA and FIT from d. above. Don't forget the employer's share of FICA

PART III NORMAL BALANCES

Indicate the normal balance of each of the following accounts. Place a (DR) for debit and a (CR) for credit. (Two points per answer)

Answer

_____ 1. Sales Discount
_____ 2. FICA Tax Payable
_____ 3. Unearned Revenue
_____ 4. Mortgage Payable
_____ 5. Purchases Returns and Allowances
_____ 6. Merchandise Inventory (beginning of the period)
_____ 7. Freight-In
_____ 8. Payroll Tax Expense
_____ 9. Purchases Discount

PART IV PROBLEM

Use the following information to answer the questions below. (Four points per question)

Sales	$3,200	Beginning Inventory	$ 75
Sales Discount	40	Net Purchases	2,320
Sales Returns		Ending Inventory	51
and Allowance	35	Operating Expenses	360

a. The Net Sales are _____.
b. The Cost of Goods Sold are _____.
c. The Gross Profit is _____.
d. The Net Income is _____.

PART V WORKSHEET

Use the following information to complete the partial worksheet for Bertie Company. Record the appropriate adjusting entries using the data below and extend the balances over to the adjusted trial balance. (Four points per adjustment and one point for each item properly brought over to the adjusted trial balance columns)

Merchandise Inventory—ending	$14
Store supplies on hand	6
Depreciation on store equipment	2
Accrued salaries	3

Bertie Company Partial Worksheet For the Year Ended December 31, 19xx						
Account Titles	Trial Balance		Adjustments		Adjusted Trial Balance	
	Debit	Credit	Debit	Credit	Debit	Credit
Merchandise Inv.	11					
Store Supplies	10					
Store Equipment	20					
Accumulated Depn.		6				
Store Equipment						
Salaries Payable						
Income Summary						
Salary Expense	10					
Depreciation Expense						
Store Supplies Exp.						

SLATER COLLEGE ACCOUNTING
Sixth Edition
Achievement Test 7A
Chapters 13 and 14

Name_____

Class_____Date_____

Part	Perfect Score	Student Score
I	.30	
II	15	
III	12	
IV	20	
V	23	
Total	100	

PART I MATCHING

Match the following terms with the definitions or statements listed below. Indicate your answers in the spaces provided. (Three points per term)

a. Direct write-off
b. Net realizable value
c. Bad debts expense
d. Classified balance sheet
e. Current liabilities

f. Administrative expenses
g. Aging the receivables
h. Operating cycle
i. Other income
j. Reversing entries

Answer

_____ 1. Year-end optional bookkeeping technique in which certain adjusting entries are reversed or switched on the first day of the new accounting period.

_____ 2. The operating expense account that estimates the amount of credit sales that will probably not be collectible in a given accounting period.

_____ 3. The amount (Accounts Receivable - Allowance for Doubtful Accounts) that is expected to be collected.

_____ 4. Obligations that will come due within one year or within the operating cycle, whichever is longer.

_____ 5. Average time it takes to buy and sell merchandise and then collect accounts receivable.

_____ 6. The procedure of classifying accounts receivable by the number of days elapsed from due date.

_____ 7. The method of writing off uncollectibles when they occur and thus not using the Allowance for Doubtful Accounts.

_____ 8. A financial report that categorizes assets as current or plant and equipment, and groups liabilities as current or long term.

_____ 9. Any revenue other than revenue from sales and that appears in a separate section on the income statement.

_____ 10. Expenses such as general office expenses incurred indirectly in the selling of goods.

PART II CLOSING ENTRIES

Prepare <u>compound</u> closing entries from the following information on the Des Moines Storage Company Worksheet Income Statement columns. (Five points per entry)

	INCOME STATEMENT	
	Debit	Credit
Sales		40
Sales Returns and Allowances	3	
Purchases	20	
Purchases Returns and Allowances		3
Sales Salaries Expense	4	
Office Salaries Expense	2	

GENERAL JOURNAL					
Date		Account Titles and Descriptions	PR	Debit	Credit

PART III REVERSING ENTRIES

Baker Company adjusting entries included the following items. Prepare the appropriate reversing entries. (Four points each)

GENERAL JOURNAL

Date		Account Titles and Description	PR	Debit	Credit
1994		Adjusting Entries			
Dec	31	Salaries Expense		600	
		Salaries Payable			600
	31	Depreciation Expense		50	
		Accumulated Depreciation			50
	31	Accounts Receivable		100	
		Fees Income			100
		Reversing Entries			

PART IV PROBLEM

Using the following information:

a.   Calculate the estimated uncollectible accounts from the following aging analysis. (Fourteen points possible)

b.   Journalize the adjusting journal entry required. The unadjusted balance of the allowance account is $100 <u>credit</u>. (Six points for entry)

Time Period	Total Receivables	Estimated % Loss	Amount needed in Allowance Acct.
Not yet due	3,600	3	
Days past due			
1-30	2,000	4	
31-60	870	10	
61-90	200	20	
Over 90 days	330	50	
Total Accts. Rec			

GENERAL JOURNAL					
Date		Account Titles and Description	PR	Debit	Credit

PART V PROBLEMS PART A

Prepare general journal entries to record the following transactions for the Boulder Company. (The company uses the income statement approach for recording bad debts expense.) (Three points per entry)

19x4

Dec 31   Credit sales for the period were $100,000. The balance of Accounts Receivable was $10,000. Estimated bad debts average 1% of credit sales.

19x5

Jan 3   Wrote off B. Gruen's account as uncollectible, $50
Mar 4   Wrote off A. Wolf's account as uncollectible, $75
Jul 5   Recovered $40 from A. Wolf

Date		Account Titles	PR	Debit	Credit

PART V PROBLEMS PART B

Prepare a partial classified balance sheet for Patben Company at December 31, 19xx from the following information. (Eleven points total)

Cash	$10,000
Petty Cash	100
Accounts Receivable	6,000
Delivery Equipment	15,000
Bad Debts Expense	1,400
Merchandise Inventory	1,800
Allow. for Doubtful Accts.	200
Accumulated Depreciation	3,000
Depreciation Expense	700

Patben
Balance Sheet
December 31, 19xx

SLATER COLLEGE ACCOUNTING
Sixth Edition
Achievement Test 8A
Chapter 15

Name_____

Class_____Date_____

Part	Perfect Score	Student Score
I	20	
II	20	
III	18	
IV	12	
V	30	
Total	100	

PART I MATCHING
Match the following terms with the definitions or statements listed below. Indicate your answers in the spaces provided. (Two points per term)

a. Bank discount
b. Contingent liability
c. Default
d. Dishonored note
e. Discount period

f. Maker
g. Maturity value
h. Note proceeds
i. Payee
j. Principal

Answer

_____ 1. The amount of time the bank holds a discounted note until the maturity date.
_____ 2. One to whom the note is payable.
_____ 3. Maturity value of a note less bank discount.
_____ 4. One promising to pay a note.
_____ 5. The face amount of the note.
_____ 6. Liability on the part of one who discounts a note if the maker of the note defaults at maturity date.
_____ 7. Failure of maker to pay the maturity value of a note when due.
_____ 8. A note not paid at maturity by the maker.
_____ 9. The amount of the note that is due on the date of maturity, including interest.
_____ 10. The amount the bank charges to hold a discounted note until maturity.

PART II TRUE OR FALSE
Indicate if the following questions are TRUE or FALSE in the spaces provided. (Two points per question)

Answer

_____ 1. The bank discount on discounted notes receivable equals principal times the bank discount rate.
_____ 2. A note payable is a formal written promise to pay.
_____ 3. A dishonored note must be transferred back to Accounts Receivable on the payee's books.
_____ 4. The formula for calculating interest on a note is interest * rate * time.
_____ 5. A contingent liability is avoided when a discounted note is endorsed without recourse.

_____

_____ 6. Accrued interest income is revenue that has been earned during the period but not received or recorded because payment is not due.

_____ 7. Discount on Notes Payable is a contra liability account that records interest deducted in advance.

_____ 8. The proceeds can never be less than the face value.

_____ 9. Accounts Receivable has a stronger legal claim than Notes Receivable.

_____ 10. One promising to pay the note is the maker.

PART III INTEREST AND MATURITY DATE CALCULATIONS

Calculate the interest for the following. (Three points per calculation)

a. $12,000   12%   1 year   _____

b.   8,000   13%   7 months _____

c.   6,000   10%   80 days   _____

Calculate the maturity date for the following. (Three points per calculation)

a. A 90-day note dated March 3. _____

b. A 4-month note dated May 31. _____

c. A one-year note dated February 1, 19x5. _____

PART IV JOURNAL ENTRIES

Prepare the journal entries for Abilene Company for the following transactions. (Four points per entry)

a. Quinn sold $6,000 of merchandise on account to Baltimore Company.

b. Quinn received a 90-day, $6,000, 12% note for a time extension of past due account of Baltimore Company.

c. Collected the Baltimore note on the maturity date.

GENERAL JOURNAL

Date		Account Titles and Description	PR	Debit	Credit

PART V JOURNAL ENTRIES PART A

Prepare journal entries for the following transactions for Ross Imports Company. (Four points per entry)

a. Purchased $4,000 of merchandise from New Orleans Sales Company on account.

b. Gave New Orleans Sales Company a 60-day, 9% note settlement of the accounts payable.

c. Ross Imports paid the note plus interest.

GENERAL JOURNAL

Date		Account Titles and Description	PR	Debit	Credit

PART V JOURNAL ENTRIES PART B

Prepare general journal entries for Maryland Enterprises for the following transactions. (Four points per entry)

19x5

Nov 1 Discounted its own $10,000, 45-day, 12% note at Friendly Bank.

Dec 16 Paid the discounted note.

GENERAL JOURNAL

Date		Account Titles and Description	PR	Debit	Credit

PART V JOURNAL ENTRIES PART C

On May 15, 19x6 Major Co. gave Minor Co. a 180-day, $9,000,
8% note. On July 21, Minor Co. discounted the note at 9%.(Five points
per entry)
a. Journalize the entry for Minor to record the proceeds.
b. Record the entry for Minor if Major fails to pay at maturity.

GENERAL JOURNAL

Date		Account Titles and Description	PR	Debit	Credit

SLATER COLLEGE ACCOUNTING

Sixth Edition
Achievement Test 9A
Chapters 15 and 16

Name_____

Class_____Date_____

Part	Perfect Score	Student Score
I	27	
II	20	
III	20	
IV	18	
V	15	
Total	100	

PART I MULTIPLE CHOICE
Indicate your answers to the questions below in the spaces provided.
(Three points per question)

Answer

_____ 1. In the basic formula for calculating interest, <u>rate</u> refers to:
   a.   interest per day.
   b.   interest per month.
   c.   percent per year.
   d.   monthly payment amount.

_____ 2. In a perpetual inventory system:
   a.   the merchandise inventory account is increased every time inventory is purchased.
   b.   the cost of goods sold account is decreased every time inventory is sold.
   c.   purchases, freight, and purchases returns and allowances accounts are updated periodically.
   d.   All of the above.

_____ 3. J. Japes sold tires on account for $50. The tires had a cost of $30. The journal entry to record the sale under the perpetual system includes:
   a.   debit to Merchandise Inventory for $30.
   b.   debit to Cost of Goods Sold for $50.
   c.   debit to Cost of Goods Sold for $30.
   d.   debit to Merchandise Inventory for $50.

_____ 4. On May 31, Blue Company discounts a customer's 16%, 90-day, $10,000 note dated May 1. The discount rate charged by the bank is 12%. The discount period is:
   a.   90 days.
   b.   30 days.
   c.   one year.
   d.   60 days.

_____ 5. Lucky Aces discounted a customer's $4,000 note at the bank and received proceeds of $3,930. Lucky would record the receipt of cash as:
   a.   debit Cash $4,000, credit Notes Receivable $4,000.
   b.   debit Cash $4,000, credit Interest Income $70, credit Notes Receivable $3,930.
   c.   debit Cash $3,930, debit Interest Expense $70, credit Notes Receivable $4,000.
   d.   debit Notes Receivable $4,000, credit Cash $3,930, credit Interest Income $70.

_____ 6. The basic formula for calculating the interest on a note is:
   a.   Interest = Principle * rate - Time.
   b.   Interest = Principle * Rate * Time.
   c.   Interest = Principle * Time - Rate.
   d.   Interest = Principle * Rate + Time.

_____ 7. The specific invoice method has the advantage of:
   a.   an equal cost is assigned to each unit, thus net income does not fluctuate as much as with other methods.
   b.   flow of goods and flow of costs are the same.
   c.   it matches old selling prices and current costs.
   d.   ending inventory is valued at very old costs.

_____ 8. The inventory method where the cost flows follow the physical flows is:
   a.   FIFO.
   b.   LIFO.
   c.   weighted-average.
   d.   specific invoice.

_____ 9. The inventory method which produces the lowest income tax during a period of inflation is:
   a.   LIFO.
   b.   FIFO.
   c.   weighted-average.
   d.   specific invoice.

PART II MATCHING

Match the following terms with the definitions and the statements listed below. Indicate your answers in the spaces provided. (Two points per term)

   a.   Maturity value
   b.   Proceeds
   c.   Contingent liability
   d.   Discount period
   e.   Maker
   f.   Maturity date
   g.   Payee
   h.   Principal
   i.   Weighted-average method
   j.   Discount on notes payable
   k.   Retail method
   l.   Gross profit method
   m.   Consignee
   n.   FIFO method
   o.   LIFO method

_____ 1. Valuing of inventory where each item is assigned the same unit cost.

_____ 2. One to whom the note is payable.

_____ 3. One promising to pay a note.

_____ 4. Company or person to whom goods are shipped but who does not have ownership.

_____ 5. A method for estimating the value of ending inventory based on a cost ratio times the ending inventory at retail.

_____ 6. A method for estimating the value of inventory based on the assumption that the gross profit percent remains approximately the same from period to period.

_____ 7. Valuing of inventory with the assumption the last goods received in the store are the first to be sold.

_____ 8. The value of the note that is due on the date of maturity (principal + interest).

_____ 9. A contra liability account.

_____ 10. The face amount of the note.

PART III TRUE OR FALSE

Indicate if the following statements are TRUE or FALSE in the spaces provided. (Two points per question)

Answer

_____ 1. The gross profit method requires a physical inventory.

_____ 2. If a mistake is made in calculating ending inventory, it will take two accounting periods to be self correcting.

_____ 3. Discount on Notes Payable is a contra liability account used for recording interest deducted in advance.

_____ 4. The method used to assign costs to ending inventory will have a direct effect on cost of goods sold and profit.

_____ 5. Under the FIFO method, the assumption is that the newest goods are sold first.

_____ 6. In a perpetual inventory system, accounts for Purchases, Freight-In, and Purchases Returns and Allowances accounts are not used.

_____ 7. Accrued interest income is revenue has been earned during the period but not received or recorded because payment is not due.

_____ 8. Accounts Receivable has a stronger legal claim than Notes Receivable.

_____ 9. A dishonored note must be transferred back to Accounts Receivable on the payee's books.

_____ 10. A contingent liability is avoided when a discounted note is endorsed without recourse.

PART IV PROBLEM A

Drake's Supply has a beginning inventory and purchases of computer parts as follows:

	Quantity	Price Each
Beginning inventory	9	$8.00
First purchase	12	$8.50
Second purchase	17	$9.00

Required: Determine the cost of the 6 computer parts in the remaining inventory under each of the following assumptions: **(Three points per question)**

a. LIFO _____

b. FIFO _____

c. Weighted-average _____

PART IV PROBLEM B

Northwest Clothes uses the retail method to estimate cost of ending inventory. From the following facts, estimate the ending inventory at cost at August 31. **(Six points possible)**

	Cost	Retail
August 1 inventory	$ 1,500	$ 2,500
August net purchases	10,000	14,000
August net sales		13,500

Estimated ending inventory $_____

PART V INTEREST AND MATURITY DATE CALCULATIONS

Complete the following problems in the spaces provided. Show your calculations. **(Three points per calculation)**

Calculate the interest on the following:

Face Amount	Interest	Period
a. $ 7,000	14%	1 year
b. $ 6,000	9%	90 days
c. $10,000	11%	6 months

Determine the maturity dates for the following:

d. An 80-day note dated June 1. _____

e. A 5-month note dated December 31. _____

f. A one-year note dated June 1, 1995 _____

370

SOLUTIONS

ACHIEVEMENT TEST 1A
Chapters 1 and 2

PART I
MATCHING

1.	e	6.	b
2.	g	7.	d
3.	i	8.	h
4.	f	9.	k
5.	a	10.	j

PART II
TABLE COMPLETION

	Category	Normal Balance	Financial Report
1.	Expense	Debit	Income Statement
2.	Liability	Credit	Balance Sheet
3.	Withdrawal	Debit	Statement of Owner's Equity
4.	Asset	Debit	Balance Sheet
5.	Revenue	Credit	Income Statement

PART III
FINANCIAL STATEMENTS

J. Brown Company
Income Statement
For the month ended March 31, 19xx

Revenue		
Services Fees Earned		$800
Operating Expenses		
Advertising Expense	$200	
Utilities Expense	100	
Total Operating Expenses		300
Net Income		$500
		====

J. Brown Company
Statement of Owner's Equity
For the month ended March 31, 19xx

J. Brown Capital, March 1		$1,350
Net Income	$500	
Less Withdrawals	150	
Increase in Capital		350
J. Brown Capital, March 31		$1,700
		======

PART IV
TRIAL BALANCE

Bally Company
Trial Balance
April 30, 19xx

	Debit	Credit
Cash	1,000	
Accounts Receivable	700	
Office Equipment	2,000	
Accounts Payable		500
L. Bally, Capital		2,500
L. Bally, Withdrawals	100	
Service Fees		1,000
Rent Expense	200	
Totals	4,000	4,000

PART V
PROBLEM

	Debit	Credit
1.	111	311
2.	111	411
3.	112	411
4.	211	111
5.	111	112
6.	312	111
7.	513	111
8.	512	111
9.	121	211
10.	511	111

SOLUTIONS

ACHIEVEMENT TEST 2A
Chapters 3 and 4

PART I JOURNAL ENTRIES

June	2	Cash	7,000	
		Equipment	1,200	
		R. Babbit, Capital		8,200
	10	Rent Expense	200	
		Cash		200
	15	Accounts Receivable	1,000	
		Service Fees		1,000
	16	Supplies	500	
		Accounts Payable		500
	20	Cash	500	
		Accounts Receivable		1,000
	25	Salaries Expense	150	
		Cash		150

PART II MATCHING

1.	a		6.	i
2.	k		7.	h
3.	f		8.	c
4.	b		9.	d
5.	g		10.	e

PART III PREPARING FINANCIAL STATEMENTS

Account Title	Income Statement		Balance Sheet	
	DR	CR	DR	CR
Cash			4	
Accounts Rec.			6	
Supplies			2	
Accounts Pay.				9
F. Brad, Cap.				6
F. Brad, Wthdr.			2	
Service Rev.		8		
Salaries Exp.	4			
Rent Exp.	3			
Supplies Exp.	2			
Sub Totals	9	8	14	15
Profit (Loss)		1	1	
Totals	9	9	15	15

Brad Consulting Service
Income Statement
For the Month Ended June 30, 19xx

Revenue:		
Service Revenue		$8
Operating Expense		
Salaries Expense	$4	
Rent Expense	3	
Supplies Expense	2	
Total Operating Expenses		9
Net Loss		1

Brad Consulting Service
Statement of Owner's Equity
For the Month Ended June 30, 19xx

F. Brad, Capital, June 1, 19xx		$6
Less: Net Loss for June	$1	
Withdrawals for June	2	
Change in Capital for June		3
F. Brad, Capital, June 30, 19xx		$3

Brad Consulting Service
Balance Sheet
June 30, 19xx

Assets		Liabilities	
Cash	$4	Accounts Payable	$9
Accounts Receivable	6		
Supplies	2	Owner's Equity	
		F Brad, Capital,	
		June 30, 19xx	3
		Total Liabilities and	
Total Assets	$12	Owner's Equity	$12

PART IV WORKSHEET

BENPAT COMPANY
Worksheet
For the Year Ended December 31, 19xx

Account Title	Trial Balance		Adjust-ments		Adjusted Trial Balance		Income Statement		Balance Sheet	
	DR	CR	DR	CR	DR	CR	DR	CR	DR	CR
Cash	5				5				5	
Accts. Rec.	12				12				12	
Supplies	7			2	5				5	
Ppd. Rent	9				9				9	
Store Eqt.	32				32				32	
Accm. Depr.		18		5		23				23
Accts. Pay.		7				7				7
Benpat, Cap.		25				25				25
Benpat, Wthdr.	5				5				5	
Fees Rev.		45				45		45		
Wages Exp.	15		3		18		18			
Utlty. Exp.	5				5		5			
Misc. Exp.	5				5		5			
Totals	95	95								
Depn. Exp.			5		5		5			
Supl. Exp.			2		2		2			
Wages Pay.				3		3				3
Totals			10	10	103	103	35	45	68	58
Net Inc.							10			10
							45	45	68	68

375

SOLUTIONS

ACHIEVEMENT TEST 3A
Chapters 5 and 6

PART I MATCHING

1. h   2. d
3. i   4. c
5. f   6. e
7. b   8. g
9. j   10. a

PART II TABLE COMPLETION

1. R   2. N, X
3. N,X   4. R
5. R   6. R
7. N,X   8. N,X

PART III JOURNAL ENTRIES

Accounting Fees	5,000	
Income Summary		5,000
Income Summary	3,000	
Wages Expense		1,500
Depreciation Expense		1,000
Insurance Expense		500
Income Summary	2,000	
T. Rogers, Capital		2,000
T. Rogers, Capital	1,200	
T. Rogers, Withdrawal		1,200

PART IV BANK RECONCILIATION AND JOURNAL ENTRIES

Checkbook Balance	$6,500	Bal. per Bank	$5,300
Add:		Add:	
Note collected	300	Deposit in Transit	3,000
	$6,800		$8,300
Deduct:		Deduct:	
NSF Check	200	Outstanding Checks	1,709
Error	9		
Balance	$6,591		$6,591

```
April 30   Cash                    300
             Notes Receivable            300

           Accounts Receivable 200
             Cash                       200

           Office Supplies          9
             Cash                         9
```

PART V PETTY CASH JOURNAL ENTRIES

```
Jul 1      Petty Cash              85
             Cash                        85

Jul 9      Petty Cash              15
             Cash                        15

Jul 31     Donation Expense        12
           Postage Expense         21
           Office Supplies Exp.    37
           Miscellaneous Exp.      15
             Cash Short and Over          5
             Cash                        80
```

SOLUTIONS

ACHIEVEMENT TEST 4A
Chapters 7 and 8

PART I MATCHING

1.	d	2.	i
3.	f	4.	j
5.	h	6.	g
7.	c	8.	a
9.	e	10.	b

PART II TRUE OR FALSE

1.	F	2.	T
3.	F	4.	T
5.	F	6.	F
7.	T	8.	F
9.	T	10.	T

PART III PROBLEM

Jane Holmes	$301
Jerry Dodds	$280
Jessica Dagget	$445

PART IV PROBLEM A

Salaries Expense	2,300	
FICA-Social Security Pay		117.80
FICA-Medicare Pay		33.35
Federal Income Tax Pay		345.00
Medical Insurance		30.00
Salaries Pay		1,773.85

PART IV PROBLEM B

FICA-Social Security	$161.20
FICA-Medicare	37.70
SUTA	130.00
FUTA	20.80

PART V JOURNAL ENTRIES

Prepaid Workers' Compensation Ins.	1,712.50	
Cash		1,712.50

PART I MATCHING

1.	T	2.	T
3.	F	4.	T
5.	F	6.	F
7.	T	8.	T
9.	F	10.	F

PART II PROBLEM

a. $81,500
b.   15,000
c.   650
d.   65,850

PART III PROBLEMS

K. Daniels should pay Purple $2,650

Net Sales are $2,000

PART IV PROBLEM

a.	P	b.	GJ
c.	S	d.	GJ
e.	CR	f.	CP
g.	CP		

PART V PROBLEM

SALES JOURNAL

Date		Account Debited	Terms	Inv No	PR	Dr A/R Cr Sales
Mar	3	T. Miller	1/10,n/30	12	✓	1,500
	5	G. Pound	2/10,n/30	13	✓	800
	31					2,300
						=======
						(102) (401)

GENERAL JOURNAL

Date		Account Tiles and Description	PR	Debit	Credit
Mar	14	Sales Returns and Allow.	403	100	
		Acct. Rec./ G. Pound	102/✓		100

CASH RECEIPTS JOURNAL

Date	Cash Dr.	Sales Dis.Dr.	Acct. Rec.Cr.	Sales Cr.	Sundry Acct.	Post Ref.	Amount Cr.
Mar 1	10,000				Thomas, Cap.	301	10,000
13	1,485	15	1,500		T. Miller	✓	
15	686	14	700		G. Pound	✓	
23	7,000				Equipment	121	7,000
31	19,171	29	2,200				17,000
	======	======	=====				======
	(101)	(402)	(102)				(x)

GENERAL LEDGER

```
   Cash      101              Sales      401          Thomas, Cap.   301
19,171 |                          |2,300                   |10,000
       |                          |                        |

Accounts Rec. 102          Sales Discount 402      Sales Ret. and All. 403
2,200  |2,200                 29  |                   100  |
       |                          |                        |

  Equipment  121
       |7,000
       |
```

SUBSIDIARY LEDGER

```
  Tom Miller                  G. Pound
1,500|1,500                 800    | 100
                                   | 700
```

SOLUTIONS

ACHIEVEMENT TEST 6A
Chapters 11 and 12

PART I MATCHING

1.	a	6.	d
2	j	7.	i
3	f	8.	g
4.	b	9.	h
5.	c	10.	e

PART II   TABLE COMPLETION

Debit		Credit			
Account	Amount	Account	Amount		
111	$8	411	$8	0.	Received cash from customer $8
520	$2	111	$2	a.	Paid for mowing supplies $2
525	$6	111	$6	b.	Paid three months' rental for tractor $6
111	$1	520	$1	c.	Received a refund for supplies $1
513	$8	211 212 111	1 2 5	d.	Paid the payroll. Gross pay $8, FICA $1, FIT $2
211 212 514	1 2 1	111	4		Paid the FICA and FIT from d. above. Don't forget the employer's share of FICA

PART III   NORMAL BALANCES

1.	DR	6.	DR
2.	CR	7.	DR
3.	CR	8.	DR
4.	CR	9.	CR
5.	CR		

PART IV   PROBLEM

a. $3,125
b. $2,344
c. $781
d. $421

PART V WORKSHEET

Account Titles	Trial Balance		Adjustments		Adjusted Trial Balance	
	Debit	Credit	Debit	Credit	Debit	Credit
Merchandise Inv.	11		14	11	14	
Store Supplies	10			4	6	
Store Equipment	20				20	
Accumulated Depn. Store Equipment		6		2		8
Salaries Payable				3		3
Income Summary			11	14	11	14
Salary Expense	10		3		13	
Depreciation Expense			2		2	
Store Supplies Exp.			4		4	

Bertie Company
Partial Worksheet
For the Year Ended December 31, 19xx

SOLUTIONS

ACHIEVEMENT TEST 7A
Chapters 13 and 14

PART I MATCHING

1.	j	6.	g
2.	c	7.	a
3.	b	8.	d
4.	e	9.	i
5.	h	10.	f

PART II CLOSING ENTRIES

Sales	40	
Purchases Returns and Allow.	3	
Income Summary.		43
Income Summary	29	
Sales Salaries Expense		4
Office Salaries Expense		2
Purchases		20
Sales Returns and Allowances		3
Income Summary	14	
Capital		14

PART III REVERSING ENTRIES

Salaries Payable	600	
Salaries Expense		600
Fees Income	100	
Accounts Receivable		100

PART IV PROBLEM

Time period	Amount needed in allowance account
Not yet due	108
Days past due	
1-30	80
31-60	87
61-90	40
Over 90 days	165
Total amount needed	480

General journal entry:

Bad Debts Expense	380	
Allowance for Doubtful Accounts		380

PART V   PROBLEMS PART A

```
19x4
Dec 31    Bad Debts Expense                            1,000
              Allowance for Doubtful Accounts                  1,000
19x5
Jan 3     Allowance for Doubtful Accounts                50
              Accounts Receivable, B. Gruen                       50
Mar 4     Allowance for Doubtful Accounts                75
              Accounts Receivable, A. Wolf                        75
Jul 5     Accounts Receivable, A. Wolf                   40
              Allowance for Doubtful Accts.                       40
    5     Cash                                           40
              Accounts Receivable, A. Wolf                        40
```

PART V PROBLEMS PART B

PATBEN
Balance Sheet
December 31, 19xx

ASSETS

```
Current Assets
    Cash                                          $10,000
    Petty Cash                                        100
    Accounts Receivable              $6,000
    Less:Allowance for Doubtful Accounts  200     5,800
    Merchandise Inventory                         1,800
        Total Current Assets                    $17,700

Plant and Equipment
    Delivery Equipment              $15,000
    Less:  Accumulated Depreciation   3,000
        Total Plant and Equipment                12,000
Total Assets                                    $29,700
```

SOLUTIONS

ACHIEVEMENT TEST 8A
Chapter 15

PART I MATCHING

1.	e	2.	i
3.	h	4.	f
5.	j	6.	b
7.	c	8.	d
9.	g	10.	a

PART II TRUE OR FALSE

1.	F	2.	T
3.	T	4.	F
5.	T	6.	T
7.	T	8.	F
9.	F	10.	T

PART III INTEREST AND MATURITY DATE CALCULATIONS

a. $1,440.00

b.   606.67

c.   133.33

a.   June 1

b.   September 30

c.   February 1, 19x6

PART IV JOURNAL ENTRIES

Accounts Receivable/Baltimore	6,000	
Sales		6,000
Notes Receivable	6,000	
Accounts Receivable/Baltimore		6,000
Cash	6,180	
Interest Income		180
Notes Receivable		6,000

PART V JOURNAL ENTRIES PART A

Purchases	4,000	
Accounts Payable/New Orleans		4,000
Accounts Payable/New Orleans	4,000	
Notes Payable		4,000
Notes Payable	4,000	
Interest Expense	60	
Cash		4,060

PART V JOURNAL ENTRIES PART B

Nov 1	Cash	9,850	
	Discount on Notes Pay.	150	
	Notes Payable		10,000
Dec 16	Notes Payable	10,000	
	Cash		10,000
16	Interest Expense	150	
	Discount on Notes Pay		150

PART V JOURNAL ENTRIES PART C

May 15	Cash	9,095.58	
	Interest Income		95.58
	Notes Receivable		9,000.00
Nov 27	Accounts Rec./Major	9,360.00	
	Cash		9,360.00

SOLUTIONS

Achievement Test 9A
Chapters 15 and 16

PART I MULTIPLE CHOICE				PART II MATCHING			
1.	c	6.	b	1.	i	6.	l
2.	a	7.	b	2.	g	7.	o
3.	c	8.	d	3.	e	8.	a
4.	d	9.	a	4.	m	9.	j
5.	c			5.	k	10.	h

PART III TRUE OR FALSE

1.	F	6.	T
2.	T	7.	T
3.	T	8.	F
4.	T	9.	T
5.	F	10.	T

PART IV   PROBLEM A

a. 6 * 8 = <u>$48</u>
b. 6 * 9 = <u>$54</u>
c. 6 * $8.605 = <u>$51.63</u>

PART IV   PROBLEM B

		COST	RETAIL
Aug. 1	Inventory	1,500	2,500
Aug.	Net Purchases	10,000	14,000
	Goods Available	11,500	16,500

Cost to retail ratio:
$11,500/$16,500 = 0.697

Aug	Sales		13,500
	Inventory at retail		$3,000

Inventory at estimated cost:
0.697 x $3,000 =   <u>$2,091</u>

PART V   INTEREST AND MATURITY DATE CALCULATIONS

a.	$980	d.	Aug. 20
b.	$135	e.	May 31
c.	$550	f.	June 1, 1996

SLATER COLLEGE ACCOUNTING
Sixth Edition
Achievement Test 1B
Chapters 1 and 2

Name_____

Class_____ Date_____

Part	Perfect Score	Student Score
I	20	
II	15	
III	30	
IV	20	
V	15	
Total	100	

PART I MATCHING

Match the following terms with the definitions or statements listed below. Indicate your answers in the spaces provided. (Two points per term)

a. Accounts receivable
b. Balance sheet
c. Chart of accounts
d. Capital
e. Credit

f. Debit
g. Expenses
h. Income statement
i. Ledger
j. Sole proprietorship
k. Withdrawals

Answer

_____ 1. The right side of any account.
_____ 2. Costs incurred in running a business.
_____ 3. The group of accounts to which data is posted.
_____ 4. A list of account titles and account numbers to be used by a company.
_____ 5. An asset that indicates amounts owed by customers.
_____ 6. A report as of a particular date that includes the amount of assets, liabilities and owner's equity.
_____ 7. An account that records owner's equity.
_____ 8. A report that details the performance of a firm for a specific period of time.
_____ 9. Money or other assets an owner withdraws from a business for personal use.
_____ 10. A business that has one owner.

PART II TRIAL BALANCE

The following is a list of accounts and their balances for S. Mamie Company for the month ended June 30. Prepare a trial balance in good form. (Fifteen points total)

Cash	$1,300	S. Mamie, Withdrawals	$ 700
Accounts Payable	800	Accounts Receivable	1,500
Office Supplies	1,200	Management Fees	1,600
S. Mamie, Capital	2,500	Utilities Expense	200

S. Mamie Company
Trial Balance
June 30, 19xx

	Debit	Credit

PART III TABLE COMPLETION

For each account listed, identify the category it belongs to, the normal balance (debit or credit), and the financial report in which the account appears. (Two points per item)

Account	Category	Normal Balance	Financial Report
0. Cash	Asset	Debit	Balance Sheet
1. Gray, Beg. Cap.			
2. Utilities Exp.			
3. Cleaning Equip.			
4. Accts. Rec.			
5. Cleaning Fees			

PART IV PROBLEM

Using the chart of accounts below, indicate for each transaction the accounts that should be debited and credited by inserting the proper account number in the space provided. (One point per item)

111 Cash
112 Accounts Receivable
121 Delivery Equipment
211 Accounts Payable
311 H. Russell, Capital

312 H. Russell, Withdrawals
411 Delivery Fees Earned
511 Salaries Expense
512 Rent Expense
513 Advertising Expense

Debit	Credit		Transaction
_____	_____	1.	Purchased delivery equipment on account.
_____	_____	2.	Paid salaries for the week.
_____	_____	3.	Invested additional cash in the business.
_____	_____	4.	Received cash for services performed.
_____	_____	5.	Billed a client on account for services performed.
_____	_____	6.	Paid accounts payable.
_____	_____	7.	Collected accounts receivable.
_____	_____	8.	Withdrew cash for personal use.
_____	_____	9.	Paid advertising expense.
_____	_____	10.	Paid rent expense for the month.

PART V FINANCIAL STATEMENTS

Use the following information to prepare an (1) Income Statement and (2) Statement of Owner's Equity for the month ended September 30, 19xx for Monroe's Bike Repair Company. (Fifteen points total)

J. Monroe, Capital	$1,400
Repair Fees Earned	1,300
Utilities Expense	300
Advertising Expense	150
J. Monroe, Withdrawals	350

Monroe's Bike Repair Company
Income Statement

Monroe's Bike Repair Company
Statement of Owner's Equity

SLATER COLLEGE ACCOUNTING

Sixth Edition

Achievement Test 2B

Chapters 3 and 4

Name_____

Class_____Date_____

Part	Perfect Score	Student Score
I	20	
II	18	
III	38	
IV	24	
Total	100	

PART I MATCHING

Match the following terms with the definitions or statements listed below. Indicate your answers in the spaces provided. (Two points per term)

a. Accounting cycle   g. Normal balance
b. Accounting period   h. Posting
c. Accumulated depreciation i. Slide
d. Book value   j. Transposition
e. Cross-referencing   k. Trial balance
f. General journal   l. Worksheet

Answer

_____ 1. A multi-column form used by accountants as an aid in gathering data to complete the accounting cycle.

_____ 2. An informal listing of the ledger accounts and their balances that aids in proving the equality of debits and credits.

_____ 3. A form used to record business transactions in chronological order.

_____ 4. The period of time for which an income statement is prepared.

_____ 5. The side of an account that increases according to the rules of debit and credit.

_____ 6. The error that results by adding or deleting zeros in the writing of a number.

_____ 7. The transferring of information from a journal to a ledger.

_____ 8. A contra asset account that summarizes the amount of depreciation that has been taken on an asset.

_____ 9. Cost of equipment less accumulated depreciation.

_____ 10. Inserting the account number in the PR column of the ledger and the journal to indicate the source and the destination of the transaction, respectively.

PART II JOURNAL ENTRIES

Bobby Short started a bookkeeping business in June, 19xx. Journalize the following June transactions. (Three points per entry)

June 2   B. Short invested $9,000 cash and $1,500 equipment she already owned into her new business.

10   Paid rent expense, $300.

15   Billed customers for services performed, $2,000.

16   Purchased supplies on account, $500.

20   Received one-half amount due from June billings, $1,000.

25   Hired a junior clerk and paid his salary, $175.

GENERAL JOURNAL

Date		Account Titles and Description	PR	Debit	Credit

PART III WORKSHEET

Using the information given below, complete the Worksheet for Carol Company for the year ended December 31, 19xx. (Two points per adjustment, one point per item in the Adjusted Trial Balance, Income Statement, and Balance Sheet columns)

Adjustments:
- Depreciation Expense for the period: $5.
- Supplies on hand at the end of the period: $5.
- Wages owed, but not paid: $3.

CAROL COMPANY
Worksheet
For the Year Ended December 31, 19xx

Account Title	Trial Balance		Adjust-ments		Adjusted Trial Balance		Income Statement		Balance Sheet	
	DR	CR	DR	CR	DR	CR	DR	CR	DR	CR
Cash	5									
Accts. Rec.	12									
Supplies	7									
Ppd. Rent	9									
Store Eqpt.	32									
Accm Depr.		18								
Accts Pay.		7								
Carol, Cap.		25								
Carol, Wthdr.	5									
Fees Rev.		45								
Wages Exp.	15									
Utlty. Exp.	5									
Misc. Exp.	5									

PART IV PREPARING FINANCIAL STATEMENTS

Prepare the following for Rodney Enterprises, for the month ended June 30, 19xx.
(1) Complete the following partial worksheet (Six points)
(2) Income Statement (Six points)
(3) Statement of Owner's Equity (Six points)
(4) Balance Sheet (Six points)

Account Title	Income Statement		Balance Sheet	
	DR	CR	DR	CR
Cash			3	
Accounts Rec.			5	
Supplies			1	
Accounts Pay.				4
C. Rodney, Cap.				5
C. Rodney, Wthdr.			1	
Service Rev.		7		
Salaries Exp.	3			
Rent Exp.	2			
Supplies Exp.	1			
Sub Totals	6	7	10	9
Profit (Loss)				
Totals				

Rodney Enterprises
Income Statement
For the Month Ended June 30, 19xx

Rodney Enterprises
Statement of Owner's Equity
For the Month Ended June 30, 19xx

Rodney Enterprises
Balance Sheet
For the Month Ended June 30, 19xx

SLATER COLLEGE ACCOUNTING

Sixth Edition
Achievement Test 3B
Chapters 5 and 6

Name_____

Class_____Date_____

Part	Perfect Score	Student Score
I	20	
II	20	
III	16	
IV	29	
V	15	
Total	100	

PART I MATCHING

Match the following terms with the definitions or statements listed below. Indicate your answers in the spaces provided. (Two points per term)

a.	Bank reconciliation	f.	Internal control
b.	Cash short and over	g.	Permanent account
c.	Change fund	h.	Payee
d.	Deposit in transit	i.	Petty cash voucher
e.	Income summary	j.	Temporary accounts

Answer:

_____ 1. Fund that is used to make change for customers.

_____ 2. Process of reconciling the checkbook balance with the bank balance.

_____ 3. A form to complete when money is disbursed from petty cash.

_____ 4. Deposit made but not processed by the bank before the bank statement was issued.

_____ 5. A temporary account in the ledger that summarizes revenue and expenses. Its balance (net income or net loss) is transferred to capital.

_____ 6. The person or company to whom a check is payable.

_____ 7. Accounts whose balances are carried over to the next accounting period. Examples: assets, liabilities, capital.

_____ 8. Accounts whose balances at the end of an accounting period are not carried over to the next accounting period. Examples: revenue, expenses, withdrawals.

_____ 9. A system of procedures and methods to control a firm's assets as well as monitor its operations.

_____ 10. The account that records cash shortages.

PART II JOURNAL ENTRIES

From the T accounts below, journalize the necessary closing entries in good form. (Five points per entry)

Advertising Expense	Insurance Expense	Depreciation Expense
2,500 |	500 |	900 |
|	|	|

P. Kline, Capital	Income Summary	Decorating Fees
| 12,000	|	| 2,000
|	|	|

P. Kline, Withdrawals
|200
|

GENERAL JOURNAL

Date		Account Title and Description	PR	Debit	Credit

PART III TABLE COMPLETION

In the first space below, indicate whether each account is a real or nominal account using (R) Real Account and (N) Nominal Account. In the second space below, indicate by an (X) if the account should be closed. (Two points per line)

_N_	_X_	0.	_Advertising Expense_
___	___	1.	Salaries Payable
___	___	2.	Service Fees
___	___	3.	Accounts Payable
___	___	4.	Accumulated Depreciation
___	___	5.	Withdrawals
___	___	6.	Prepaid Rent
___	___	7.	Income Summary
___	___	8.	Salaries Expense

PART IV BANK RECONCILIATION AND JOURNAL ENTRIES

Use the information below to (1) construct a bank reconciliation for Wallace Company on November 30, 19xx, and (2) prepare the necessary journal entries to update the general ledger accounts. (Twenty points for the bank reconciliation and nine points for the journal entries)

Ending checkbook balance	$470
Ending bank statement balance	380
Deposits in transit	180
Outstanding checks	75
Bank service charge	15
NSF check (debit memo) customer ck.	20
The bank collected a note receivable	
for Wallace Co.	50

Wallace Company

_____

Checkbook Balance   Balance per Bank
_____
_____
_____
_____
_____
_____
_____
_____
_____
_____

GENERAL JOURNAL

Date		Account Title and Description	PR	Debit	Credit

PART V PETTY CASH JOURNAL ENTRIES

Prepare journal entries for the following petty cash fund transactions.
(Five points for each journal entry)

Jul   1   Established a $700 petty cash fund.
         9   Increased the petty cash fund $50.
     31   Replenished the petty cash fund. Currency and coins
             remaining were $60. Approved paid vouchers were:
             $450 donation expense, $100 postage expense,
             $135 office supplies expense and $15 miscellaneous
             expense.

GENERAL JOURNAL

Date		Account Title and Description	PR	Debit	Credit

SLATER COLLEGE ACCOUNTING

Sixth Edition
Achievement Test 4B
Chapters 7 and 8

Name_____

Class_____Date_____

Part	Perfect Score	Student Score
I	20	
II	20	
III	12	
IV	12	
V	36	
Total	100	

PART I MATCHING
Match the following terms with the definitions or statements listed below. Indicate your answers in the spaces provided. (Two points per term)

a. Employees earnings record
b. FICA-Social Security
c. Federal unemployment tax
d. Gross earnings
e. Net pay

f. State unemployment tax
g. Salaries Payable
h. Workers' compensation insurance
i. Form 941
j. Form W-4

Answer

_____ 1. A form filled out by employees to supply the employer with needed information about the number of allowances claimed, and marital status.

_____ 2. A report to be completed for each quarter indicating total FICA (Social Security and Medicare) owed plus federal income tax withheld for the quarter.

_____ 3. A tax usually paid by employers to the state.

_____ 4. A liability account that shows net pay.

_____ 5. Employer's insurance requirement protecting their employees against losses due to injury or death incurred while on the job.

_____ 6. A tax levied on both the employer and the employee up to a certain salary level.

_____ 7. Amount of pay received before any deductions.

_____ 8. A record that summarizes the total amount of wages paid and the deductions for the calendar year for an employee.

_____ 9. Gross pay less deductions. The amount the worker takes home.

_____ 10. An unemployment tax paid by employers to the federal government.

PART II TRUE OR FALSE

Indicate if the following questions are TRUE or FALSE in the spaces provided. (Two points per question)

Answer

_____ 1. Employers are responsible for deducting FUTA tax from the employees' earnings.

_____ 2. The two parts of FICA are Social Security (Old Age Survivors and Disability Insurance) and Medicare (hospital insurance).

_____ 3. The employer is required to pay for medical insurance for the employee for non-job-related accidents.

_____ 4. The Federal Unemployment Tax Act was established to allow the federal government to monitor state unemployment programs.

_____ 5. When an employee's earnings are greater than the FICA-Social Security base rate during the calendar year, no more FICA-Social Security tax is deducted from earnings.

_____ 6. The Payroll Tax Expense is recorded at the time the payroll is recorded.

_____ 7. The Fair Labor Standards Act is also called the Wages and Hours Law.

_____ 8. The payroll information for a pay period is found in the payroll register.

_____ 9. Payroll Tax Expense is the account the employer uses for the employer's payroll taxes (FICA, FUTA, and SUTA).

_____ 10. The cost of workers' compensation insurance must be estimated and paid in advance by the employer.

PART III JOURNAL ENTRIES

Estimate the annual advance premium and prepare the general journal entry using the following data. (Twelve points for journal entry)

Type of Work	Estimated Payroll	Rate Per $100
Sales	$30,000	$1.00
Office	40,000	.18
Factory	60,000	1.60

GENERAL JOURNAL

Date		Account Title and Description	PR	Debit	Credit

PART IV PROBLEM

From the following information, please complete the chart for gross earnings for the week. Assume an overtime rate of time and a half over 40 hours. (Four points per employee)

	Hourly Rate	No. of Hours Worked	Gross Earnings
Jack Ponds	$ 8	43	_____
Kate Zimmerman	10	35	_____
Joy Ford	9	45	_____

PART V PROBLEM A

Compute the net pay for each employee and prepare the journal entry for the payroll. FICA tax rate is: Social Security 6.2% on $60,600 and Medicare 1.45%; federal income tax is 15%; and medical insurance is $10 per employee. (Ten points for the computations and ten points for the entry)

	Cumulative Earnings Before Payroll	Weekly Salary	Dept.
Employee A	$35,000	$1,000	Office
Employee B	59,500	1,500	Sales

Employee A net pay _____

Employee B net pay _____

GENERAL JOURNAL

Date		Account Title and Description	PR	Debit	Credit

PART V PROBLEM B

Using the information below, determine the amount of the payroll tax expense for Lane's Archery. In your answer list the amounts for FICA: (Social Security and Medicare), SUTA, and FUTA. (Four points per answer)

Employee	Gross pay
S. Mitchell	$3,000
H. Gerber	500
V. Krame	1,500

Assume: FICA tax rates are Social Security 6.2%, and Medicare 1.45%; state unemployment tax rate is 5.0%; and federal unemployment tax rate is 0.8%. All employees have earned less than $7,000.

FICA-Social Security   _____

FICA-Medicare   _____

SUTA   _____

FUTA   _____

SLATER COLLEGE ACCOUNTING
Sixth Edition
Achievement Test 5B
Chapters 9 and 10

Name_____

Class_____Date_____

Part	Perfect Score	Student Score
I	20	
II	20	
III	22	
IV	14	
V	24	
Total	100	

PART I TRUE OR FALSE
Indicate if the following questions are TRUE or FALSE in the spaces provided. (Two points per question)

Answers

_____ 1. A purchase requisition is sent to the supplier when ordering merchandise.

_____ 2. Payment of cash is recorded in the cash receipts journal.

_____ 3. A list showing the ending balances owed to individual creditors is called a Schedule of Accounts Payable.

_____ 4. The accounts payable column total in the Purchase Journal is posted to the accounts payable general ledger account at the end of the month.

_____ 5. A credit memo is prepared by the seller for credit on returned merchandise.

_____ 6. Sales Tax Payable is an owner's equity account with a credit balance.

_____ 7. A sales invoice is prepared by the buyer of goods.

_____ 8. A special ledger supporting the controlling account would be called a subsidiary ledger.

_____ 9. Firms that use special journals can eliminate the general journal.

_____ 10. Gross Sales can be computed by adding Net Sales, Sales Discount and Sales Returns and Allowances.

PART II PROBLEM

On June 6, Joyce Jewelry Store purchased merchandise. The invoice was for $80,000 plus freight, $1,500, terms 1/15, n/30. On June 10, Joyce Jewelry returned merchandise for $10,000 credit. On June 15, Joyce Jewelry paid the amount owed. Answer the following questions. (Five points per question)

a.   The credit to Accounts Payable on June 6 is _____.

b.   The debit to Accounts Payable on June 10 is _____.

c.   The credit to Purchases Discount on June 15 is _____.

d.   The credit to Cash on June 15 is _____.

PART III PROBLEMS

Joyce Jewelry Store sold R. Alexander a diamond engagement ring for $2,500 plus sales tax of 5%. Terms of the sale are 1/10, n/30. Date of the sale was May 22, date of the payment was June 2.

Required: Determine the amount R. Alexander should pay Joyce Jewelry on June 2. (Eleven points)

$_____

Use the following information to answer the questions below.
(Eleven points)

Sales	$20,000
Gross Profit	1,800
Net Income	800
Sales Discount	500
Sales Returns and Allow.	3,000

The Net Sales are _____.

PART IV PROBLEM

Indicate the journal in which each of the following transactions should be recorded by placing the letters representing the appropriate journal in the space provided. (Two points per transaction)

Choice of journals: S   Sales Journal
                      CR Cash Receipts
                      P   Purchase
                      CP Cash Payments
                      GJ General Journal

a. _____   Sold merchandise on account.

b. _____   Prepared a debit memo for returned merchandise.

c. _____   Purchased merchandise on account.

d. _____   Purchased equipment, paid cash.

e. _____   Sold merchandise for cash.

f. _____   Paid the amount owed on account.

g. _____   Owner withdrew cash from the business.

PART V PROBLEM

The following are transactions for M. Thomas for the month of March. Journalize the transactions in the appropriate journals. (One and one-half points per entry) Post the information from the journal to the ledger properly. (One and one-half points per account)

Mar 1   J. Trieff invested an additional $13,000 in his business.

Mar 3   Sold $2,500 of merchandise on account to Gary Paine, sales invoice No. 10, terms 1/10, n/30.

Mar 5   Sold $800 of merchandise on account to Brad Edwards, sales invoice No. 11, terms 2/10, n/30.

Mar 13 Received cash from G. Paine for payment of Mar 3 transaction, less the discount.

Mar 14 Issued credit memorandum No. 1 to B. Edwards for $200 for merchandise returned from Mar 5 sale on account.

Mar 15 Received cash from B. Edwards for the amount due, less the discount.

Mar 23 Sold equipment at cost for cash, $7,000.

SALES JOURNAL

Date		Account Debited	Terms	Inv. No.	PR	Dr. A/R Cr. Sales

GENERAL JOURNAL

Date		Account Tiles and Description	PR	Debit	Credit

CASH RECEIPTS JOURNAL

Date	Cash Dr.	Sales Dis. Dr.	Acct. Rec. Cr.	Sales Cr.	Sundry Acct.	Post Ref.	Amount Cr.

GENERAL LEDGER

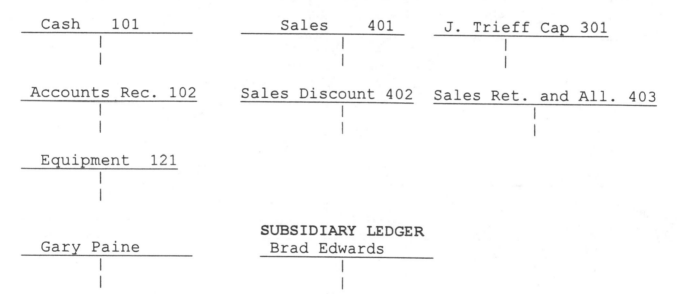

Cash   101

Sales   401

J. Trieff Cap 301

Accounts Rec. 102

Sales Discount 402

Sales Ret. and All. 403

Equipment   121

SUBSIDIARY LEDGER

Gary Paine

Brad Edwards

SLATER COLLEGE ACCOUNTING
Sixth Edition
Achievement Test 6B
Chapters 11 and 12

Name_____

Class_____Date_____

Part	Perfect Score	Student Score
I	26	
II	16	
III	20	
1V	20	
IV	18	
Total	100	

PART I WORKSHEET

Use the following information to complete the partial worksheet for Bertie Company. Record the appropriate adjusting entries using the data below and extend the balances over to the adjusted trial balance. (Four points per adjustment and one point for each item properly brought over to the adjusted trial balance columns)

Merchandise Inventory—ending	$15
Store supplies on hand	2
Depreciation on store equipment	1
Accrued salaries	3

Bertie Company
Partial Worksheet
For the Year Ended December 31, 19xx

Account Titles	Trial Balance Debit	Trial Balance Credit	Adjustments Debit	Adjustments Credit	Adjusted Trial Balance Debit	Adjusted Trial Balance Credit
Merchandise Inv.	11					
Store Supplies	10					
Store Equipment	20					
Accumulated Depn. Store Equipment		6				
Salaries Payable						
Income Summary						
Salary Expense	10					
Depreciation Expense						
Store Supplies Exp.						

PART II PROBLEM

Use the following information to answer the questions below. (Four points per question)

Sales	$4,200	Beginning Inventory	$ 100
Sales Discount	24	Net Purchases	2,000
Sales Returns and Allowances	30	Ending Inventory	50
		Operating Expenses	400

a. The Net Sales are _____.
b. The Cost of Goods Sold are _____.
c. The Gross Profit is _____.
d. The Net Income is _____.

PART III MATCHING

Match the following terms with the definitions or statements listed below. Indicate your answers in the spaces provided. (Two points per term)

a. Combined journal
b. Ending merchandise inventory
c. Modified cash-basis
d. Accrual accounting
e. Cash-basis

f. Periodic inventory
g. Perpetual inventory
h. Unearned revenue
i. Mortgage payable
j. Payroll tax expense

Answer

_____ 1. An inventory system that keeps continual track of each type of inventory by recording units on hand at beginning, units sold, and the current balance after each sale or purchase.

_____ 2. A combination of cash-basis and accrual basis systems.

_____ 3. The goods that remain unsold at the end of the accounting period. They are an asset on the new balance sheet.

_____ 4. An inventory system that, at the end of each accounting period, calculates the cost of the unsold goods on hand.

_____ 5. An accounting system whereby the revenues are recorded when earned and expenses when incurred to earn that revenue.

_____ 6. An accounting system whereby revenue is recorded when cash is received, and expenses are recorded when they are paid.

_____ 7. The employer's share of payroll taxes.

_____ 8. A liability account for recording an advance payment received for goods or services.

_____ 9. A liability account showing amount owed on a mortgage.

_____ 10. A special journal that could replace the general journal under cash-basis and modified cash-basis.

PART IV TABLE COMPLETION

The combined journal for Charlie's Garden Service has the following headings with appropriate columns for indicating debits and credits: Cash, Explanation, Sundry, Fees, Salary Expense, FICA Payable, and FIT Payable.

The following is a partial chart of accounts for Charlie's Garden Service:

111 Cash	513 Salaries Expense
211 FICA Tax Payable	514 Payroll Tax Expense
212 Federal Income Tax Payable	520 Mowing Expense
411 Mowing Fees	525 Rental Expense

Indicate, in the format below, the account numbers and the debit and credit amounts for the following transactions under the modified cash-basis. (Four points per transaction)

Debit Account	Debit Amount	Credit Account	Credit Amount		
111	$9	411	$9	0.	Received cash from customer $9
				a.	Paid for mowing supplies $3
				b.	Paid three months' rental for tractor $3
				c.	Received a refund for mowing supplies $2
				d.	Paid the payroll. Gross pay $10, FICA $1, FIT $2
				e.	Paid the FICA and FIT from d. above. Don't forget the employer's share of FICA

PART V NORMAL BALANCES

Indicate the normal balance of each of the following accounts. Place a (DR) for debit and a (CR) for credit. (Two points per answer)

Answer

_____ 1. Purchases Returns and Allowances
_____ 2. Merchandise Inventory (beginning of the period)
_____ 3. Freight-In
_____ 4. Sales Discount
_____ 5. FICA Taxes Payable
_____ 6. Unearned Revenue
_____ 7. Mortgage Payable
_____ 8. Payroll Tax Expense
_____ 9. Purchases Discount

SLATER COLLEGE ACCOUNTING
Sixth Edition
Achievement Test 7B
Chapters 13 and 14

Name_____

Class_____Date_____

Part	Perfect Score	Student Score
I	23	
II	30	
III	12	
IV	15	
V	20	
Total	100	

PART I PROBLEMS PART A

Prepare general journal entries to record the following transactions for the Boulder Company. (The company uses the income statement approach for recording bad debts expense.) (Three points per entry)

19x4

Dec 31 Credit sales for the period were $50,000. The balance of Accounts Receivable was $5,000. Estimated bad debts average 1% of credit sales.

19x5

Jan 3 Wrote off G. Acres' account as uncollectible, $40
Mar 4 Wrote off B. Good's account as uncollectible, $70
Jul 5 Recovered $35 from B. Good

Date		Account Titles and Description	PR	Debit	Credit

PART I PROBLEMS PART B

Prepare a partial classified balance sheet for Patben Company at December 31, 19xx from the following information. All the accounts have normal balances. (Eleven points total)

Cash	$15,000
Petty Cash	200
Accounts Receivable	9,000
Delivery Equipment	20,000
Bad Debts Expense	1,400
Merchandise Inventory	2,800
Allow. for Doubtful Accts.	200
Allowance for Depreciation	4,000
Depreciation Expense	800

<table>
<tr><td colspan="2" align="center">Patben
Balance Sheet
December 31, 19xx</td></tr>
<tr><td> </td><td> </td></tr>
<tr><td> </td><td> </td></tr>
<tr><td> </td><td> </td></tr>
<tr><td> </td><td> </td></tr>
<tr><td> </td><td> </td></tr>
<tr><td> </td><td> </td></tr>
<tr><td> </td><td> </td></tr>
<tr><td> </td><td> </td></tr>
<tr><td> </td><td> </td></tr>
<tr><td> </td><td> </td></tr>
<tr><td> </td><td> </td></tr>
<tr><td> </td><td> </td></tr>
<tr><td> </td><td> </td></tr>
</table>

PART II MATCHING

Match the following terms with the definitions or statements listed below. Indicate your answers in the spaces provided. (Three points per term)

a. Administrative expenses
b. Net realizable value
c. Operating cycle
d. Other income
e. Reversing entries

f. Direct write-off
g. Aging method
h. Bad debts expense
i. Classified balance sheet
j. Current liabilities

Answer

_____ 1. The amount (Accounts Receivable - Allowance for Doubtful Accounts) that is expected to be collected.

_____ 2. Obligations that will come due within one year or within the operating cycle, whichever is longer.

_____ 3. Year-end optional bookkeeping technique in which certain adjusting entries are reversed or switched on the first day of the new accounting period.

_____ 4. The operating expense account that estimates the amount of credit sales that will probably not be collectible in a given accounting period.

_____ 5. Average time it takes to buy and sell merchandise and then collect accounts receivable.

_____ 6. The procedure of classifying accounts receivable by the number of days elapsed from due date.

_____ 7. The method of writing off uncollectibles when they occur and thus <u>not</u> using the Allowance for Doubtful Accounts.

_____ 8. A financial report that categorizes assets as current or plant and equipment, and groups liabilities as current or long-term.

_____ 9. Any revenue other than revenue from sales and that appears in a separate section on the income statement.

_____ 10. Expenses such as general office expenses incurred indirectly in the selling of goods.

PART III REVERSING ENTRIES

Baker Company adjusting entries included the following items. Prepare the appropriate reversing entries. (Four points each)

Date			Account Titles and Description	PR	Debit	Credit
1994			**Adjusting Entries**			
Dec	31		Rent Expense		300	
			Rent Payable			300
	31		Bad Debts Expense		70	
			Allowance for Doubtful Accts.			70
	31		Accounts Receivable		200	
			Fees Income			200
			Reversing Entries			

PART IV CLOSING ENTRIES

Prepare <u>compound</u> closing entries from the following information on the Des Moines Storage Company Worksheet Income Statement columns. (Five points per entry)

	Income Statement	
	DEBIT	CREDIT
Sales		50
Sales Returns and Allowances	2	
Purchases	30	
Purchases Returns and Allowances		4
Sales Salaries Expense	5	
Office Salaries Expense	2	

Date		Account Titles	PR	Debit	Credit

PART V PROBLEM

Using the following information:
a. Calculate the estimated uncollectible accounts from the following analysis. (Fourteen points possible)
b. Journalize the adjusting journal entry required. The unadjusted balance of the allowance account is $100 credit (Six points for the entry)

Time Period	Total Receivables	Estimated % Loss	Amount needed in Allowance Acct.
Not yet due	4,600	3	
Days past due			
1-30	3,000	4	
31-60	970	10	
61-90	300	20	
Over 90 days	430	50	
Total Accts. Rec.			

Date		Account Titles	PR	Debit	Credit

SLATER COLLEGE ACCOUNTING
Sixth Edition
Achievement Test 8B
Chapter 15

Name_____

Class_____Date_____

`Part	Perfect Score	Student Score
I	20	
II	18	
III	24	
IV	9	
V	29	
Total	100	

PART I MATCHING
Match the following terms with the definitions or statements listed below. Indicate your answers in the spaces provided. (Three points per term)

a. Contingent liability
b. Discounting a note
c. Dishonored note
d. Discount period
e. Maker

f. Maturity date
g. Maturity value
h. Proceeds
i. Payee
j. Principal

Answer

_____ 1. The amount of time the bank holds a discounted note until the maturity date.
_____ 2. The individual/company to whom the note is payable.
_____ 3. Maturity value of a note less bank discount.
_____ 4. One promising to pay a note.
_____ 5. The face amount of the note.
_____ 6. The process or act of transferring the note to a bank before the maturity date.
_____ 7. Due date of the promissory note.
_____ 8. A note not paid at maturity by the maker.
_____ 9. The value of the note that is due on the date of maturity, including interest.
_____ 10. Potential liability if the maker of the note defaults.

PART II TRUE OR FALSE
Indicate if the following questions are TRUE or FALSE in the spaces provided. (Two points per question)

Answer
_____ 1. Effective rate of interest is lower than the stated rate on a discounted note.
_____ 2. The interest on $10,000 at 6% for 90 days would be $600.00.
_____ 3. The bank discount is based on the maturity value of the note.

415

_____ 4. Discount on Notes Payable is a contra liability account that records interest deducted in advance.

_____ 5. Proceeds are found by taking maturity value and adding the bank discount.

_____ 6. The payor is the individual/firm to whom the note is payable.

_____ 7. Accounts Receivable has a stronger legal claim than Notes Receivable.

_____ 8. A formal written promise by a borrower to pay a certain sum at a fixed future date is a promissory note.

_____ 9. The proceeds can never be less than the face value.

PART III INTEREST AND MATURITY DATE CALCULATIONS
Calculate the interest for the following. (Four points per calculation)

a. $10,000   8%   6 months   _____

b. 7,000   9%   1 year   _____

c. 6,000   10%   90 days   _____

Calculate the maturity date for the following. (Four points per calculation)

a. A 90-day note dated June 5. _____

b. A 4-month note dated December 31. _____

c. A one-year note dated March 1, 19x6. _____

PART IV JOURNAL ENTRIES

Prepare the journal entries for Jason Company for the following transactions. (Three points per entry)
  a. Jason sold $6,000 of merchandise to Gray Company.
  b. Jason received a 60-day, $6,000, 12% note for a time extension of past due account of Gray Company.
  c. Collected the Gray note on the maturity date.

GENERAL JOURNAL

Date		Account Titles and Description	PR	Debit	Credit

PART V JOURNAL ENTRIES PART A

Prepare journal entries for the following transactions for Greenbay Company. (Five points per entry)
  a. Purchased $3,000 of merchandise from Carlsen's Food Supply on account.
  b. Gave Carlsen's Food Supply a 60-day, 9% note in settlement of the accounts payable.
  c. Greenbay defaulted on its note on the maturity date.
  d. Greenbay paid the previously defaulted note plus $25 additional interest.

GENERAL JOURNAL

Date		Account Titles and Description	PR	Debit	Credit

PART V JOURNAL ENTRIES PART B

Prepare general journal entries for Holmes Enterprises for the
following transactions. (Four and one-half points per entry)

```
19x5
Nov  1    Discounted its own $10,000, 90-day, 9% note
          at First Bank.

Dec 16    Paid the discounted note.
```

GENERAL JOURNAL

Date		Account Titles and Description	PR	Debit	Credit

SLATER COLLEGE ACCOUNTING

Sixth Edition
Achievement Test 9B
Chapters 15 and 16

Name _____

Class _____ Date _____

Part	Perfect Score	Student Score
I	20	
II	20	
III	27	
IV	18	
V	15	
Total	100	

PART I TRUE OR FALSE

Indicate if the following statements are TRUE or FALSE in the spaces provided. (Two points per question)

Answer

_____ 1. Discount on Notes Payable is a contra liability account used for recording interest deducted in advance.

_____ 2. The method used to assign costs to ending inventory will have a direct effect on cost of goods sold and profit.

_____ 3. Under the FIFO method, the assumption is that the newest goods are sold first.

_____ 4. The gross profit method requires a physical inventory.

_____ 5. If a mistake is made in calculating ending inventory, it will take two accounting periods to be self correcting.

_____ 6. In a perpetual inventory system, accounts for Purchases, Freight-In, and Purchases Returns and Allowances accounts are not used.

_____ 7. A dishonored note must be transferred back to Accounts Receivable on the payee's books.

_____ 8. A contingent liability is avoided when a discounted note is endorsed without recourse.

_____ 9. Accrued interest income is revenue that has been earned during the period but not received or recorded because payment is not due.

_____ 10. Accounts Receivable has a stronger legal claim than Notes Receivable.

PART II MATCHING

Match the following terms with the definitions and the statements listed below. Indicate your answers in the spaces provided. (Two points per term)

a. Maturity value
b. Proceeds
c. Contingent liability
d. Discount period
e. Maker
f. Maturity date
g. Payee
h. Principal

i. Weighted-average method
j. Discount on notes payable
k. Retail method
l. Gross profit method
m. Consignee
n. FIFO method
o. LIFO method

_____ 1. A method for estimating the value of inventory based on the assumption that the gross profit percent remains approximately the same from period to period.

_____ 2. One promising to pay a note.

_____ 3. Company or person to whom goods are shipped but who does not have ownership.

_____ 4. A method for estimating the value of ending inventory based on a cost ratio times the ending inventory at retail.

_____ 5. Valuing of inventory with the assumption the last goods received in the store are the first to be sold.

_____ 6. The value of the note that is due on the date of maturity (principal + interest).

_____ 7. A contra liability account.

_____ 8. The face amount of the note.

_____ 9. Valuing of inventory where each item is assigned the same unit cost.

_____ 10. One to whom the note is payable.

PART III MULTIPLE CHOICE

Indicate your answers to the questions below in the spaces provided. (Three points per question)

Answer:

_____ 1. In the basic formula for calculating interest, <u>rate</u> refers to:
   a. interest per day.
   b. interest per month.
   c. percent per year.
   d. monthly payment amount.

_____ 2. In a perpetual inventory system:
   a. the merchandise inventory account is increased every time inventory is purchased.
   b. the cost of goods sold account is decreased every time inventory is sold.
   c. purchases, freight, and purchases returns and allowances accounts are updated periodically.
   d. All of the above.

_____ 3. J. Japes sold tires on account for $50. The tires had a cost of $30. The journal entry to record the sale under the perpetual system includes:
   a. debit to Merchandise Inventory for $30.
   b. debit to Cost of Goods Sold for $50.
   c. debit to Cost of Goods Sold for $30.
   d. debit to Merchandise Inventory for $50.

_____ 4. On May 31, Blue Company discounts a customer's 16%, 90-day, $10,000 note dated May 1. The discount rate charged by the bank is 12%. The discount period is:
    a.   90 days.
    b.   30 days.
    c.   one year.
    d.   60 days.

_____ 5. Lucky Aces discounted a customer's $4,000 note at the bank and received proceeds of $3,930. Lucky would record the receipt of cash as:
    a.   debit Cash $4,000, credit Notes Receivable $4,000.
    b.   debit Cash $4,000, credit Interest Income $70, credit Notes Receivable $3,930.
    c.   debit Cash $3,930, debit Interest Expense $70, credit Notes Receivable $4,000.
    d.   debit Notes Receivable $4,000, credit Cash $3,930, credit Interest Income $70.

_____ 6. The basic formula for calculating the interest on a note is:
    a.   Interest = Principle * Rate - Time.
    b.   Interest = Principle * Rate * Time.
    c.   Interest = Principle * Time - Rate.
    d.   Interest = Principle * Rate + Time.

_____ 7. The specific invoice method has the advantage of:
    a.   an equal cost is assigned to each unit; thus net income does not fluctuate as much as with other methods.
    b.   flow of goods and flow of costs are the same.
    c.   it matches old selling prices and current costs.
    d.   ending inventory is valued at very old costs.

_____ 8. The inventory method where the cost flows follow the physical flows is:
    a.   FIFO.
    b.   LIFO.
    c.   weighted-average.
    d.   specific invoice.

_____ 9. The inventory method which produces the lowest income tax during a period of inflation is:
    a.   LIFO.
    b.   FIFO.
    c.   weighted-average.
    d.   specific invoice.

PART IV INTEREST AND MATURITY DATE CALCULATIONS

Complete the following problems in the spaces provided. Show your calculations. (Three points per calculation)

Calculate the interest on the following:

Face Amount	Interest	Period
a. $ 7,000	13%	1 year
b. $ 6,000	10%	90 days
c. $10,000	12%	6 months

Determine the maturity dates for the following:

d.   An 82-day note dated June 1.   _____

e.   A 4-month note dated December 31.   _____

f.   A one-year note dated March 1, 1995   _____

PART V PROBLEM A

Drake's Supply has a beginning inventory and purchases of computer parts as follows:

	Quantity	Price Each
Beginning inventory	8	$8
First purchase	11	$8.50
Second purchase	16	$9.00

Required: Determine the cost of the 6 computer parts in the remaining inventory under each of the following assumptions:
(Three points per question)

a.   LIFO   _____
b.   FIFO   _____
c.   Weighted-average _____

PART V PROBLEM B

Northwest Clothes uses the retail method to estimate cost of ending inventory. From the following facts, estimate the ending inventory at cost at August 31. (Six points possible)

	Cost	Retail
August 1 inventory	$ 1,000	$ 1,500
August net purchases	10,000	14,000
August net sales		13,500

Estimated ending inventory $_____

SOLUTIONS

ACHIEVEMENT TEST 1B
Chapters 1 and 2

PART I
MATCHING

1.	e	6.	b	
2.	g	7.	d	
3.	i	8.	h	
4.	c	9.	k	
5.	a	10.	j	

PART II
TRIAL BALANCE

S. Mamie Company
Trial Balance
June 30, 19xx

	Debit	Credit
Cash	1,300	
Accounts Receivable	1,500	
Office Supplies	1,200	
Accounts Payable		800
S. Mamie, Capital		2,500
S. Mamie, Withdrawals	700	
Management Fees		1,600
Utilities Expense	200	
Totals	4,900	4,900

PART III
TABLE COMPLETION

	Category	Normal Balance	Financial Report
0.	Asset	Debit	Balance Sheet
1.	Capital	Credit	Statement of Owner's Equity
2.	Expense	Debit	Income Statement
3.	Asset	Debit	Balance Sheet
4.	Asset	Debit	Balance Sheet
5.	Revenue	Credit	Income Statement

PART IV PROBLEM

	Debit	Credit
1.	121	211
2.	511	111
3.	111	311
4.	111	411
5.	112	411
6.	211	111
7.	111	112
8.	312	111
9.	513	111
10.	512	111

PART V
FINANCIAL STATEMENTS

Monroe's Bike Repair Company
Income Statement
For the month ended September 30, 19xx

Revenue		
Repair Fees Earned		$1,300
Operating Expenses		
Advertising Expense	$150	
Utilities Expense	300	
Total Operating Expenses		450
Net Income		$850

Monroe's Bike Repair Company
Statement of Owner's Equity
For the month ended September 30, 19xx

J. Monroe Capital, September 1,		$1,400
Net Income	$850	
Less Withdrawals	350	
Increase in Capital		500
J. Monroe Capital, September 30		$1,900

SOLUTIONS

ACHIEVEMENT TEST 2B
Chapters 3 and 4

PART I MATCHING

1.	l	6.	i
2.	k	7.	h
3.	f	8.	c
4.	b	9.	d
5.	g	10.	e

PART II JOURNAL ENTRIES

June	2	Cash	9,000	
		Equipment	1,500	
		B. Short, Capital		10,500
	10	Rent Expense	300	
		Cash		300
	15	Accounts Receivable	2,000	
		Service Fees		2,000
	16	Supplies	500	
		Accounts Payable		500
	20	Cash	1,000	
		Accounts Receivable		1,000
	25	Salaries Expense	175	
		Cash		175

PART III WORKSHEET

Account Title	Trial Balance DR	Trial Balance CR	Adjust- ments DR	Adjust- ments CR	Adjusted Trial Balance DR	Adjusted Trial Balance CR	Income Statement DR	Income Statement CR	Balance Sheet DR	Balance Sheet CR

CAROL COMPANY
Worksheet
For the Year Ended December 31, 19xx

Account Title	Trial Balance		Adjust-ments		Adjusted Trial Balance		Income Statement		Balance Sheet	
	DR	CR	DR	CR	DR	CR	DR	CR	DR	CR
Cash	5				5				5	
Accts. Rec.	12				12				12	
Supplies	7			2	5				5	
Ppd. Rent	9				9				9	
Store Eqt.	32				32				32	
Accm. Depr.		18		5		23				23
Accts. Pay.		7				7				7
Carol, Cap.		25				25				25
Carol, Wthdr.	5				5				5	
Fees Rev.		45				45		45		
Wages Exp.	15		3		18		18			
Utlty. Exp.	5				5		5			
Misc. Exp.	5				5		5			
Totals	95	95								
Depn. Exp.			5		5		5			
Supl. Exp.			2		2		2			
Wages Pay.				3		3				3
Totals			10	10	103	103	35	45	68	58
Net Inc.							10			10
							45	45	68	68

PART IV PREPARING FINANCIAL STATEMENTS

Account Title	Income Statement		Balance Sheet	
	DR	CR	DR	CR
Cash			3	
Accounts Rec.			5	
Supplies			1	
Accounts Pay.				4
C. Rodney, Cap.				5
C. Rodney, Wthdr.			1	
Service Rev.		7		
Salaries Exp.	3			
Rent Exp.	2			
Supplies Exp.	1			
Sub Totals	6	7	10	9
Profit (Loss)	1			1
Totals	7	7	10	10

426

Rodney Enterprises
Income Statement
For the Month Ended June 30, 19xx

Revenue:		
Service Revenue		$7
Operating Expense		
Salaries Expense	$3	
Rent Expense	2	
Supplies Expense	1	
Total Operating Expenses		6
Net Income		1

Rodney Enterprises
Statement of Owner's Equity
For the Month Ended June 30, 19xx

C. Rodney, Capital, June 1, 19xx		$5
Add: Net Income for June	$1	
Less: Withdrawals for June	1	
Change in Capital for June		0
C. Rodney, Capital, June 30, 19xx		$5

Rodney Enterprises
Balance Sheet
June 30, 19xx

Assets		Liabilities	
Cash	$3	Accounts Payable	$4
Accounts Receivable	5		
Supplies	1	Owner's Equity	
		C. Rodney, Capital,	
		June 30, 19xx	5
		Total Liabilities and	
Total Assets	$9	Owner's Equity	$9

SOLUTIONS

ACHIEVEMENT TEST 3B
Chapters 5 and 6

PART I MATCHING

1.	c	2.	a
3.	i	4.	d
5.	e	6.	h
7.	g	8.	j
9.	f	10.	b

PART III TABLE COMPLETION

1.	R	2.	N, X
3.	R	4.	R
5.	N,X	6.	R
7.	N,X	8.	N,X

PART II JOURNAL ENTRIES

Decorating Fees	2,000	
Income Summary		2,000
Income Summary	3,900	
Advertising Expense		2,500
Depreciation Expense		900
Insurance Expense		500
P. Kline, Capital	1,900	
Income Summary		1,900
P. Kline, Capital	200	
P. Kline, Withdrawals		200

PART IV BANK RECONCILIATION AND JOURNAL ENTRIES

Checkbook Balance	$470	Bal. per Bank	$380
Add:		Add:	
Note collected	50	Deposit in Transit	180
	$520		$560
Deduct:		Deduct:	
NSF Check	20	Outstanding Checks	75
Service Charge	15		
Balance	$485		$485
	====		====

```
April 30   Cash                     50
              Notes Receivable              50

           Accounts Receivable   20
              Cash                          20

           Miscellaneous Exp.    15
              Cash                          15
```

PART V PETTY CASH JOURNAL ENTRIES

```
Jul 1      Petty Cash           700
              Cash                         700

Jul 9      Petty Cash            50
              Cash                          50

Jul 31     Donation Expense     450
           Postage Expense      100
           Office Supplies Exp.135
           Miscellaneous Exp.    15
              Cash Short and Over         10
              Cash                        690
```

SOLUTIONS

ACHIEVEMENT TEST 4B
Chapters 7 and 8

PART I MATCHING

1.	j	2.	i
3.	f	4.	g
5.	h	6.	b
7.	d	8.	a
9.	e	10.	c

PART II TRUE OR FALSE

1.	F	2.	T
3.	F	4.	T
5.	T	6.	T
7.	T	8.	T
9.	T	10.	T

PART III JOURNAL ENTRIES

Prepaid Workers' Compensation Ins. 1,332
    Cash   1,332

PART IV PROBLEM

Jack Ponds	$356.00
Kate Zimmerman	$350.00
Joy Ford	$427.50

PART V PROBLEM A

Employee A $763.50
Employee B $1,175.05

Salaries Expense	2,500	
FICA-Social Security Pay		130.20
FICA-Medicare Pay		36.25
Federal Income Tax Pay		375.00
Medical Insurance		20.00
Salaries Pay		1,938.55

PART V PROBLEM B

FICA-Social Security	$310.00
FICA-Medicare	72.50
SUTA	250.00
FUTA	40.00

SOLUTIONS

ACHIEVEMENT TEST 5B
Chapters 9 and 10

PART I TRUE OR FALSE

1.	F	2.	F
3.	T	4.	T
5.	T	6.	F
7.	F	8.	T
9.	F	10.	T

PART II PROBLEM

a. $81,500
b. 10,000
c.   700
d. 70,800

PART III PROBLEMS

R. Alexander should pay Joyce $2,625

Net Sales are $16,500

PART IV PROBLEM

a. S   b. GJ
c. P   d. CP
e. CR   f. CP
g. CP

PART V PROBLEM

SALES JOURNAL

Date		Account Debited	Terms	Inv No	PR	Dr A/R Cr Sales
Mar	3	G. Paine	1/10,n/30	10	✓	2,500
	5	B. Edwards	2/10,n/30	11	✓	800
	31					3,300
						======
						(102) (401)

GENERAL JOURNAL

Date		Account Tiles and Description	PR	Debit	Credit
Mar	14	Sales Returns & Allow	403	200	
		Acct. Rec./ Brad Edwards	102/✓		200

CASH RECEIPTS JOURNAL

Date	Cash Dr.	Sales Dis.Dr.	Acct. Rec.Cr.	Sales Cr.	Sundry Acct.	Post Ref.	Amount Cr.
Mar 1	13,000				Trieff, Cap.	301	13,000
13	2,475	25	2,500		G. Paine	✓	
15	588	12	600		B. Edwards	✓	
23	7,000				Equipment	121	7,000
31	23,063	37	3,100				20,000
	======	=======	=====				======
	(101)	(402)	(102)				(x)

GENERAL LEDGER

Cash   101
23,063 |

Sales   401
         | 3,300

J. Trieff Cap 301
         | 13,000

Accounts Rec. 102
3,300 | 3,100

Sales Discount 402
37 |

Sales Ret.and All. 403
200 |

Equipment   121
     | 7,000

Gary Paine
2,500 | 2,500

SUBSIDIARY LEDGER

Brad Edwards
800 | 200
    | 600

432

ACHIEVEMENT TEST 6B
Chapters 11 and 12

PART I WORKSHEET

Account Titles	Bertie Company Partial Worksheet For the Year Ended December 31, 19xx					
	Trial Balance		Adjustments		Adjusted Trial Balance	
	Debit	Credit	Debit	Credit	Debit	Credit
Merchandise Inv.	11		15	11	15	
Store Supplies	10			8	2	
Store Equipment	20				20	
Accumulated Depn. Store Equipment		6		1		7
Salaries Payable				3		3
Income Summary			11	15	11	15
Salary Expense	10		3		13	
Depreciation Expense			1		1	
Store Supplies Exp.			8		8	

PART II PROBLEM

a. $4,146
b. $2,050
c. $2,096
d. $1,696

PART III MATCHING

1.	g	6.	e
2.	c	7.	j
3.	b	8.	h
4.	f	9.	i
5.	d	10.	a

PART IV TABLE COMPLETION

Debit		Credit			
Account	Amount	Account	Amount		
111	*$9*	*411*	*9*	*0.*	*Received cash from customer $9*
520	3	111	3	a.	Paid for mowing supplies $3
525	3	111	3	b.	Paid three months' rental for tractor $3
111	2	520	2	c.	Received a refund for supplies $2
513	10	211	1	d.	Paid the payroll. Gross pay $10, FICA $1, FIT $2
		212	2		
		111	7		
211	1	111	4	e.	Paid the FICA and FIT from d. above. Don't forget the employer's share of FICA
212	2				
514	1				

PART V NORMAL BALANCES

1.	CR	6.	CR
2.	DR	7.	CR
3.	DR	8.	DR
4.	DR	9.	CR
5.	CR		

SOLUTIONS

ACHIEVEMENT TEST 7B
Chapters 13 and 14

PART I PROBLEMS PART A

GENERAL JOURNAL ENTRIES

19X4				
Dec 31	Bad Debts Expense		500	
	Allowance for Doubtful Accounts			500
19X5				
Jan 3	Allowance for Doubtful Accounts		40	
	Accounts Receivable, G. Acres			50
Mar 4	Allowance for Doubtful Accounts		70	
	Accounts Receivable, B. Good			70
Jul 5	Accounts Receivable, B. Good		35	
	Allowance for Doubtful Accounts			35
	Cash		35	
	Accounts Receivable, B. Good			35

PART I PROBLEMS PART B

PATBEN
Balance Sheet
December 31, 19xx
Assets

Current Assets			
Cash		$15,000	
Petty Cash		200	
Accounts. Receivable	$9,000		
Less: Allowance for Doubtful Accounts	200	8,800	
Merchandise Inventory		2,800	
Total Current Assets			$26,800
Plant and Equipment			
Delivery Equipment		$20,000	
Less: Accumulated Depn.		4,000	
Total Plant and Equipment			16,000
Total Assets			$42,800

PART II MATCHING

1.	b		6.	g
2.	j		7.	f
3.	e		8.	i
4.	h		9.	d
5.	c		10.	a

PART III REVERSING ENTRIES
GENERAL JOURNAL ENTRIES

Rent Payable	300	
Rent Expense		300
Fees Income	200	
Accounts Receivable		200

PART IV CLOSING ENTRIES
GENERAL JOURNAL ENTRIES

Sales	50	
Purchases Returns and		
Allowances	4	
Income Summary		54
Income Summary	39	
Sales Salaries Exp.		5
Office Salaries Exp.		2
Purchases		30
Sales Returns and		
Allowances		2
Income Summary	15	
Capital		15

PART V PROBLEM

Time Period	Total Receivables	Estimated % Loss	Amount needed in Allowance Account
Not yet due	4,600	3	138
Days past due			
1-30	3,000	4	120
31-60	970	10	97
61-90	300	20	60
Over 90 days	430	50	215
Total Accts. Receivable	9,300		630

GENERAL JOURNAL ENTRY

Bad Debts Expense	530	
Allowance for Doubtful		
Accounts		530

SOLUTIONS

ACHIEVEMENT TEST 8B
Chapter 15

PART I MATCHING

1.	d	2.	i
3.	h	4.	e
5.	j	6.	b
7.	f	8.	c
9.	g	10.	a

PART II TRUE OR FALSE

1.	F	2.	F
3.	T	4.	T
5.	F	6.	F
7.	F	8.	T
9.	F		

PART III INTEREST AND MATURITY DATE CALCULATIONS

a. $400.00

b. $630.00

c. $150.00

a.   September 3

b.   April 30

c.   March 1, 1997

PART IV JOURNAL ENTRIES

Accounts Receivable/Gray	6,000	
Sales		6,000
Notes Receivable	6,000	
Accounts Receivable/Gray		6,000
Cash	6,120	
Interest Income		120
Notes Receivable		6,000

PART V JOURNAL ENTRIES PART A

Purchases	3,000	
Accounts Payable/Carlsen's		3,000
Accounts Payable/Carlsen's	3,000	
Notes Payable		3,000
Notes Payable	3,000	
Interest Expense	45	
Accounts Payable, Carlsen's		3,045
Accounts Payable, Carlsen's	3,045	
Interest Expense	25	
Cash		3,070

PART V JOURNAL ENTRIES PART B

Nov 1	Cash	9,775	
	Discount on Notes Pay.	225	
	Notes Payable		10,000
16	Notes Payable	10,000	
	Cash		10,000
	Interest Expense	225	
	Discount on Notes Pay.		225

SOLUTIONS

ACHIEVEMENT TEST 9B
Chapters 15 and 16

PART I   TRUE OR FALSE

1.	T	6.	T
2.	T	7.	T
3.	F	8.	T
4.	F	9.	T
5.	T	10.	F

PART III MULTIPLE CHOICE

1.	c	6.	b
2.	a	7.	b
3.	c	8.	d
4.	d	9.	a
5.	c		

PART II   MATCHING

1.	l	6.	a
2.	e	7.	j
3.	m	8.	h
4.	k	9.	i
5.	o	10.	g

PART IV   INTEREST AND MATURITY DATE CALCULATIONS

a. $910
b. $150
c. $600
d. August 22
e. April 30
f. March 1, 1996

PART V   PROBLEM A

a.   6 @ $8 = $48
b.   6 @ $9 = $54
c.   6 @ $8.614 = $51.69

PART V   PROBLEM B

	Cost	Retail
Beg. inventory	$ 1,000	$ 1,500
Purchases	10,000	14,000
Goods available	11,000	15,500
Sales		13,500
		$ 2,000

($11,000/$15,500) * $2,000 = $1,419.35